# YOUR JESUS IS TOO SAFE

## Outgrowing a Drive-Thru, Feel-Good Savior

JARED C. WILSON

*Your Jesus Is Too Safe: Outgrowing a Drive-Thru, Feel-Good Savior*



Published by Kregel Publications, a division of Kregel, Inc., P.O. Box 2607, Grand Rapids, MI 49501.



**Library of Congress Cataloging-in-Publication Data**
Wilson, Jared C.
Your Jesus is too safe : outgrowing a drive-thru, feel-good Savior / Jared C. Wilson.
p. cm.
1. Jesus Christ—Person and offices. 2. Bible. N.T.—Study and teaching. 3. Christian life. I. Title.
BT203.W54 2009 232'.8—dc22 2009015287
CIP

ISBN 978-0-8254-3931-5

Printed in the United States of America

09 10 11 12 13 / 5 4 3 2

# CONTENTS

# FOREWORD

## Ed Stetzer

The pages you are about to read are an antidote.

Those of us in the evangelical church have done remarkably well at practicing, packaging, and marketing our message. We are increasingly creative and innovative. We are relentlessly relevant. And our efforts are paying off in some places: our research shows that the number of large churches is increasing.

Yet, our research also shows that young adults ages 23–30 drop out of the church at a rate of 70 percent,[1] that the number of the unchurched is rising,[2] and that 86 percent of the unchurched do not see anything spiritually necessary about the church.[3]

In one LifeWay Research project, we talked to church-going Protestant Christians and only 70 percent agreed strongly in the doctrine of the Trinity. For that matter, only 72 percent agreed strongly that Jesus

---

1. "LifeWay Research Uncovers Reasons 18 to 22 Year Olds Drop Out of Church," http://www.lifeway.com/lwc/article_main_page/0%2C1703%2CA%25253D165949%252526M%25253D200906%2C00.html.

2. Sally Morgenthaler, "Worship as Evangelism," from May/June 2007 issue of *Rev!* magazine, found at allelon.org, http://archives.allelon.org/articles/article.cfm?id=402.

3. Mark Kelly, "LifeWay Research Unchurched Americans Turned Off by Church, Open to Christians," http://www.lifeway.com/lwc/article_main_page/0%2C1703%2CA%25253D166950%252526M%25253D200906%2C00.html.

died on the cross and was physically resurrected from the dead.[4] Those are not debatable doctrines yet less than three-quarters of Christians could muster the conviction to strongly agree.

Furthermore, in American culture, it has often become hard to distinguish between the body of Christ and the culture of society. Consumerism and sensuality have permeated society, and often those of us who claim to be Christ followers struggle to subvert their effects. Advertising gurus have become the official priesthood of this new and pervasive religion, and we are the congregation.

Levi's jeans premiered a commercial in 2003 called "Born Again." Needless to say, it was not about spiritual rebirth. The commercial portrayed a young lady being baptized into a snug-fitting pair of Levi's. Not only are we battling consumerism, but we are also battling a system that will even use our language and symbols to baptize people into a different kind of community.

We might be offended at their use of our symbols. Culture may take our language and values and twist them to sell something, but we have certainly returned the favor.

If the church is going to be the aroma of Christ in society, the body of Christ is going to have to stand for more than the world is offering. The church must realize that we cannot consume our way into discipleship, nor can we get others to consume their way into being disciples. Retail therapy won't cut it in the church of Jesus Christ. Jesus desires to have followers who find their sense of identity, purpose, mission, and community in him alone.

In *The Prodigal God*, Tim Keller writes:

---

4. See Church Leadership Book Interview with Brad Waggoner, October 29, 2008, at http://blogs.lifeway.com/blog/edstetzer/2008/10/bh-church-leadership-book-inte-1.html.

> The kind of outsiders Jesus attracted are not attracted to contemporary churches, even our most avant-garde ones. . . . That can only mean one thing. If the preaching of our ministers and the practice of our parishioners do not have the same effect on people that Jesus had, then we must not be declaring the same message that Jesus did.[5]

Perhaps we think we are more successful than we really are. Perhaps we've lost our grasp—our understanding and our awe—of the precious message we've been entrusted with.

The gospel of Mark reports the beginning of Jesus' public ministry this way:

> Now after John was arrested, Jesus came into Galilee, proclaiming the gospel of God, and saying, "The time is fulfilled, and the kingdom of God is at hand; repent and believe in the gospel." (Mark 1:14–15)

I am not sure the church has shown it knows what "the kingdom of God" is. And I know we have lost much of our focus on the gospel. Is it any wonder, then, that the kingdom of the church gets bigger and better while the fields closest to home still lay unharvested?

"The gospel of the kingdom" is the essence of Jesus' message, and if we have lost sight of that message, it is unfortunately possible we've lost sight of the Messenger. It's a terrifying thought: the body of Christ, the bride of Christ, the church of Christ is becoming less and less familiar with Christ.

---

5. Tim Keller, *The Prodigal God: Rediscovering the Heart of the Christian Faith* (New York: Dutton, 2008), 15–16.

The irony, however, is that our losing sight of Jesus has not come from neglect. On the contrary, we are continually Jesus-fixated, but as Jared Wilson argues in his introduction, we are fixated on myriad Jesuses. For each and every attempt to "do" the Christian life and the Christian church, there appears to be a different type of Jesus to promote. So on one end of the spectrum, we may find a movement overly fixated on Macho Jesus, while at the other we find Birkenstock Jesus. And there are many other Jesuses at all points in between. We make our Jesus in our own image.

In the same way that we have reduced the gospel to an evangelistic formula, we have reduced the fullness of Jesus Christ to whatever portrait suits our fancy. But as anyone who spends any time with Jesus in the four biblical gospels can rapidly discover, Jesus is not as concerned with our agendas as he is with the Father's.

What we need now, as we have always needed, is a far-ranging recovery of awe over, and trust in, the sheer power of the gospel, beginning with a return to the dangerously full embrace of the God of the universe present in the saving, interceding, exalted person of Jesus Christ. In Ephesians 3, Paul tells us that good servants of the gospel commit to decreasing themselves while preaching the "unsearchable riches of Christ."

The unsearchable riches of Christ. Now that is a treasure worth spending our lives on! That is the treasure worth selling everything for, including our well-intentioned Jesus makeovers.

# ACKNOWLEDGMENTS

This book would not exist without the incalculable inspiration and encouragement I have received over the years from family, friends, and colleagues. I would be remiss in not mentioning:

Larry and Karen Wilson, Jeremy Wilson, Jerry and Bonnie Methvin, Emma Wilson, and Mary Damron.

Eric Guel, David and Sarah McLemore, Mark Miranda, John Northrup, Bill Roberts, Phil Schroeder, and Chris Thomas. They have stirred my heart toward Jesus more than they will ever know.

Michael Asbell, who got the ball rolling by handing me a little book in the mid '90s by N. T. Wright called *The Original Jesus*.

My agent, Steve Laube, and the good folks at Kregel Publications.

Steve Jones and Dr. Thomas Schmidt, both of whom graciously blessed the use of their heart-touching stories in this book.

The two foremost pastoral influences in my life: Dr. Mike Ayers of The Brook Church Community in Houston, Texas, and Dr. Ray Ortlund Jr. of Immanuel Church in Nashville, Tennessee.

Dr. Glenn Lucke, whose support and regard are always way out of proportion with what I actually deserve.

Mentor *in absentia* Michael Spencer.

Dr. Justin Holcomb, Dr. Ed Stetzer, and Phil Wilson, the pullers of strings.

My daughters, Macy and Grace, who have been the most formative influences on my discipleship to Jesus. (Kids'll do that to you.)

Finally, this work is dedicated to:

The Element Church community, past and present. This material was written originally for you, and your relentless worship of Jesus and stubborn fixation on the gospel gave it more life than I could have given it on my own. Thank you for your faithfulness. It is an honor to be your pastor.

Becky, the love of my life. You challenged and you encouraged, but best of all, you believed. It is a blessing of incomprehensible grace to be your husband.

# INTRODUCTION

"Who do you say that I am?"

This is the question Jesus once asked his closest followers.

No question penetrates more deeply or cuts more closely. The answer, like the sword of truth, can unite or divide.

Before Jesus asked this question, he first asked his disciples, "Who do people say that I am?"

The answers to this question are many.

The man known as Jesus of Nazareth—Jesus *the Christ*, or Messiah, to Christians—is undoubtedly the most popular, the most recognizable, the most cited, the most admired, and the most controversial figure in all of history. No other person has been more scrutinized, studied, or cited—*ever.* Entire philosophies and religions have been founded on his teachings. More books have been written about him than about any other person who ever lived. Every day, his name is spoken more than any other name, whether in affectionate admiration by his followers and fans, or in absentminded curses or denouncements by those ambivalent or antagonistic toward his fame.

The figures that loom largest in our cultural history have not been able to avoid him. John Lennon couldn't think of anybody bigger when he said the Beatles were bigger than Jesus.

President George W. Bush cited Jesus as his favorite philosopher.

Friedrich Nietzsche boasted, "Jesus died too early; he himself would have revoked his doctrine, had he reached [my] age!"[1]

The French conqueror Napoleon Bonaparte allegedly said, "Alexander, Caesar, Charlemagne, and myself founded empires; but on what foundation did we rest the creations of our genius? Upon force. Jesus Christ founded an empire upon love; and at this hour millions of men would die for him."[2]

No less a loving soul than Fidel Castro—that big teddy bear—is said to have effused, "I never saw a contradiction between the ideas that sustain me and the ideas of that symbol, of that extraordinary figure [Jesus Christ]."[3]

No message has been more used and exploited and appropriated than Jesus Christ's. It happens whenever a politician co-opts one of Jesus' quotable quotes to promote his own platform. As a result, every careerist soul climbing the ladder of American political engagement—in either major party or neither—and every one of their constituents believe that Jesus is on their side. Every religion in the world, too, Christian or not, has to factor in some appraisal of Jesus himself, whether it's to honor him as one of God's prophets or as an enlightened man, to reject him as a false prophet, or to hail him as king of the universe. Indeed, a handful of religious leaders today cannot even avoid claiming actually to *be* him.

With all this talk over all these years, it's no wonder that no man is probably more misunderstood than Jesus. The great irony is that, despite being the most discussed and confessed figure in all of history, no historical figure has been more marginalized and commoditized

1. Alexander Tille, trans., *Thus Spoke Zarathustra* (New York: Macmillan, 1896), 100.

2. F. N. and M. A. Peloubet, *Select Notes on the International Sunday School Lessons: The Gospel According to Mark* (Boston: W. A. Wilde, 1882), 153.

3. Anthony Boadle, "Factbox: Quotes from Fidel Castro," *Reuters*, February 20, 2008, http://www.reuters.com/article/newsOne/idUSN1922656120080220.

than Jesus. For many today he is a generic brand, a logo, a catchphrase, a pick-me-up. He's been fictionalized by *The Last Temptation of Christ*, humanized by *The Passion of the Christ*, and satirized by *South Park*. He's been romanticized by countless admirers, and sanitized by the Christian consumer culture.

Yes, even the church itself is guilty when it comes to the marketing of Jesus. We've put our own gloss on him, our own spin. It's no wonder the world doesn't *get* Jesus, because we've spent decades selling a Jesus cast in our own image. Even our religious ancestors feared the stern taskmaster Jesus. This quasi-Puritan Jesus liked to smack you on the knuckles with a ruler when you got out of line. Later, we received Postcard Jesus—the Coppertoned, blond-haired, blank-stare Jesus of the gold-framed portrait, a bland, two-dimensional figure occupying moral tales that help us to be better people. This flat portrait evolved into the Get-Out-of-Hell-Free Jesus, and this Jesus has inspired millions to say a prayer to get his forgiveness—and then go on living lives devoid of his presence.

In the 1970s, when pop culture merged with fundamentalism in phenomena like the Jesus Movement, we promoted Hippie Jesus. The Doobie Brothers sang "Jesus is just all right," our parents all said "groovy," and Jesus became a good buddy who was cool like us and hung out in a van down by the river and would never harsh our vibe, because he liked rock music and wore blue jeans. In the 1980s, we welcomed ATM Jesus. This Jesus is still quite popular today. You can go home and turn on your TV and learn that Jesus just wants you to be happy and successful, but most of all, rich.

One of the more amusing caricatures today is Grammy Award Speech Jesus. Have you seen him? Tune in next time the film or music industry is patting itself on the back for the stuff it produces and passes off as art these days. It's inevitable—an artist who wins an award for a work celebrating promiscuous sex or wanton violence, and filled with obscenity and profanity, will then grace the stage and thank his or her "Lord and Savior Jesus Christ." One night Bono, the musical artist and prophetic provocateur, came to the podium after a few of these artists had thanked Jesus for their incongruent efforts, and said something to the effect, "I bet God is looking down and saying, 'Don't thank me for that.'"

Today we have an amalgamation of all—and more—of these Jesuses running rampant in the world and in the church. These versions of Jesus confuse the former and misrepresent the latter. In much of the church today we worship a convenient Jesus. We designate him our "Lord and Savior," but this phrase tends to serve as merely a label that, in our superficially spiritual lives, belies his real function—our Great Example. He's there when we need to lean on him, but a bit out of mind when we feel more self-confident. He's Role Model Jesus. He's Therapeutic Jesus. We know a bit about what he said and did in these gospels of ours, but not enough to be dangerous with it. And the stuff we do know, we frequently misunderstand or take out of context to suit our agendas. How often do you hear "Judge not lest ye be judged," or "Let he who is without sin cast the first stone"? These are probably the two most often quoted of Jesus' many sayings, but not because we face a constant threat of legalistic judgment. Instead, it's because we want to justify how we live, without the pesky burden of what Jesus requires of us.

You'd think if anyone's got a handle on Jesus, it would be the Christian church. But we've settled for the glossy portrait. We've used him and abused him, made him into types and stereotypes, taken his message out of context and made it about being a better person or being cool or helping us to help ourselves. Consequently, what we have today—in a world where Jesus is most cited, most recognized, and most admired—is a generation of people who don't know the Gospels very well—which means we don't know Jesus very well.

In the world of biblical academia, the "Jesus of history" and the "Jesus of faith" are set against each other, as if never the two shall meet.

The two shall meet here—in this book. The purpose of *Your Jesus Is Too Safe* is to remind us, for the glory of God and the hope of the world, of the original message of the historical person Jesus Christ, who was, in fact, God in the flesh. We're going to remove the gloss. We're going to venture beyond the hype and beneath the misconceptions to see the real, historical figure of Jesus Christ in his biblical and cultural context—and in this way to know God more fully, to see what God wants us to know about the revelation of himself in his son.[4]

To really know God, one must really know Jesus. There are no two ways about it. So throughout the next twelve chapters, we'll examine (and perhaps reexamine) Jesus and the Gospels together. We'll view twelve portraits of Jesus of Nazareth, each one meant to help us see the man as he really was and to hear his words as they would have been heard by his original audience. Brace yourself. Turning over tables is a messy business.

But first things first. We have to start at the beginning . . .

---

4. The theologically savvy reader will at this point be wary of the author's theological matrix in exploring perspectives on Jesus. I can't blame you; the "quest for the historical Jesus" deserves reasoned skepticism and sound biblical evaluation. For the sake of those curious about my working assumptions, I will state them briefly: I affirm the historic orthodox view of the incarnation, believing that Jesus Christ is both fully man and fully God, born of a virgin into a life fully lived, tempted as we are yet without sin. I believe the four gospels are, as the rest of Scripture is, historically accurate and reliable; and moreover, that all of Scripture is inspired by God, infallible and authoritative for the knowledge and practice of the Christian faith. Though I favor a symphonic view of the array of biblical perspectives of the atoning work of Christ, I affirm the doctrine of penal substitutionary atonement. I'm aware that the latter is rather important in these days of the debate over the so-called New Perspective. So I'll explain my view in greater detail in chapter 6, "Jesus the Judge." My theology is evangelical (with a Reformed flavor), and my scholarly and spiritual influences, measured against Scripture and the tradition of biblical orthodoxy, come from various streams in the church universal.

# 1

# JESUS THE PROMISE

The Jordan River Valley is the lowest point on the face of the earth. As scholar N. T. Wright says, "If you want to get any lower than that, you'd have to dig."[1] This is the place, remember, where Moses led the wayward children of Israel. The book of Exodus tells us the story of the long, wandering discipleship of the Israelites, who had been enslaved for 430 years in Egypt, before God sent a stuttering prophet to lead them out in a dramatic escape . . . across the Red Sea and into the wilderness. That Red Sea crossing became, for the nation of Israel, the historical moment of salvation. The Jews of Jesus' day looked back to the exodus in much the same way that Christians today look back to the crucifixion. It was the watershed moment of redemption, the moment of God's faithful intervention into time, the milestone in the Israelites' long memory of salvation history. The Israelites would always look back to the exodus as the moment when God's covenantal faithfulness invaded human history.

Furthermore, the children of Israel viewed the exodus event as a promise of salvation *yet to be completed*. It was a dramatic redemption,

1. Tom Wright, *The Original Jesus: The Life and Vision of a Revolutionary* (Grand Rapids: Eerdmans, 1996), 23.

to be sure, but also a down payment of sorts on a redemption yet to come. After the escape into the wilderness, the nation wandered for forty years. Moses was able to lead them right up to the cusp of the Promised Land before he died. And then, if you paid attention in Sunday school, you know that the mantle of leadership passed to Joshua, Moses' trusted lieutenant. Joshua took over command and led the nation of Israel across the Jordan River into Canaan.

It was not all cheese and crackers, however, after that deliverance. After entering the Promised Land, the nation of Israel began a long, multigenerational history of spiritual adultery, cheating on God at every turn. Their lack of faithfulness is a recurring theme in the TV-MA Lifetime movie that is the Old Testament. The nation that God favored, the people he called *his* people, compromised themselves and became lovers of the world. They became idolaters, going after pagan gods or grafting the cultures of false gods into their own culture. Thus began an epic push-and-pull romance between God's love for his children and their wandering eyes, God's allowing them to enter captivity and their stumbling toward repentance. God's faithfulness was met with stubbornness, and God's judgment was met with desperation.

By the end of the Old Testament, the nation of Israel, living in the land of their alleged deliverance, is once again waiting to be delivered. They are living in occupied territory, where the land of promise has become a land of persecution. As the New Testament opens, the Promised Land is under the dominion of the Roman Empire. There is no longer an autonomous nation of Israel. The Jews are living under Roman rule and occupation, and are pining for God to intervene in human history and deliver them once again.

They always expected this deliverance would occur in the wilderness—in the Jordan River Valley, to be exact, the same place to where God had brought them ages before, in the days of Moses and Joshua. For this reason, during the time of the Roman occupation, bands of

Jews would go out to the wilderness, away from the prying eyes of the city, and form armies or communes.

The Essenes, for example, were a sort of gnostic Jewish sect expecting the Messiah to bring the end of the world. So they removed themselves into a proto-monastic existence in the wilderness, where they lived on psychedelic mushrooms and listened to lots of Ravi Shankar.[2] These are the same dudes who kept the Dead Sea Scrolls, secreting them away in caves where they weren't discovered until the twentieth century. Eventually, the Romans came after the Essenes . . . well, put yourself in the sandals of the Romans: your king is Caesar and your empire is founded on his rule, so you can't have a band of radicals on the outskirts of society who might be conspiring to enthrone a new king and declare a new empire. So the Essenes got snuffed out.

That's usually how it worked if you'd lived back then. If you still hoped for God to intervene in history and send the Messiah to overthrow the ruling authorities, if you expected him to demolish the oppressive Roman empire, and reestablish the nation of Israel as the ruler and occupier of the Promised Land, you'd go out into the wilderness and attract followers, and you'd plot and scheme and wait for the right moment. Eventually, there'd be a skirmish, and every would-be messiah—or military leader hoping to pave the way for the Messiah—would wind up dead, usually dead on a cross, which was the preferred mode of execution for insurrectionists, real and imagined.

But the followers of YHWH God kept trying. And the wilderness is where it all went down. Take in this breathless proclamation from the prophet Isaiah:

---

2. This is all true. Well, all except for the part about the 'shrooms and Ravi Shankar. Nobody listens to Ravi Shankar.

> A voice cries:
> "In the wilderness prepare the way of the Lord;
> make straight in the desert a highway for our God.
> Every valley shall be lifted up,
> and every mountain and hill be made low;
> the uneven ground shall become level,
> and the rough places a plain.
> And the glory of the Lord shall be revealed,
> and all flesh shall see it together,
> for the mouth of the Lord has spoken." . . .
> Get you up to a high mountain,
> O Zion, herald of good news;
> lift up your voice with strength,
> O Jerusalem, herald of good news;
> lift it up, fear not;
> say to the cities of Judah,
> "Behold your God!"
>
> (Isa. 40:3–5, 9)

Conventional thinking of the time went like this: The way of the Lord is prepared. His inauguration began in the wilderness, so the expectations begin there as well. If you want and need God to make the world right, to "fix it," to rescue you, to turn things upside down, you'd better get out into the wilderness.

By the time Jesus was in his late twenties or early thirties, his eccentric cousin, John, had gone into the wilderness with the expectation that the Messiah would come in from the wilderness. Cousin John ventured into the Jordan River Valley, but instead of starting a commune, instead of seeking out angry dudes with swords, who wanted to conspire and bust some Roman heads, he put on his camel-fur galoshes, stood in the river, and began receiving people who shared his expectation. Cousin John was the perfect man for this perfect time, because he was a guy who really *got* the wilderness. This is a guy wearing animal skins and eating crickets and wild honey, who made the Crocodile Hunter look like Mister Rogers. I don't know if you realize what it took to eat wild honey in those days, but wild honey presupposes there are wild bees in the vicinity. I seriously doubt John had one of those cool white suits and a can of smoke to make the process of extraction safe. The next time you're picking up some honey in the cute little plastic bear at your grocery store, think about that.

People referred to Cousin John as "the Baptizer," from the Greek word *baptizo*, which means "to immerse," or "to plunge," or even "to drown," because John was dunking people in the Jordan River. He was clearly a citizen and a product of the wilderness, and he went out as a prophet does, expecting and hailing once again the arrival of God's intervention in human history, to redeem and rescue his people. He did it by going to the place of entrance into the Promised Land and getting people wet. There is, of course, an echo here of religious ritual cleansing. The Bible says that John was baptizing them for the repentance of sins. We have our own Christian spin on baptism, obviously, because we think of having our sins "washed away." And in John's baptism there was definitely an element of that in play. But the main thrust of Christian baptism is an outward sign of repentance, the *turning away* from something, the turning from one thing to another, the moving from one *place* to another.

John, however, was in essence re-creating the exodus. He performed a highly symbolic act that evoked memories of a sacred historical event—crossing the water to freedom. More than that, he did it in the same river that divided the wilderness of wandering from the land of promise. He was saying, "God is about to do his new thing; God is about to bring his deliverance. Turn away from every other way you are seeking for God's kingdom, turn away from every other kingdom, and do *this*. Because God is coming again—*right now*." What, after all, do the Gospels tell us? That John and Jesus were preaching, "The kingdom of heaven is *at hand*" (Matt. 3:2; 4:17; emphasis added). Not that it was coming eventually or someday, but that it was breaking into history *right then*.

One day, as John was going about his prophetic business, Cousin Jesus came to visit. Recalling Isaiah's grand expectation, Mark's gospel sets the scene:

> The beginning of the gospel of Jesus Christ, the Son of God.
>
> As it is written in Isaiah the prophet,
>
> "Behold, I send my messenger before your face,
> who will prepare your way,
> the voice of one crying in the wilderness:
> 'Prepare the way of the Lord,
> make his paths straight,'"
>
> John appeared, baptizing in the wilderness and proclaiming a baptism of repentance for the forgiveness of sins. And all the country of Judea and all Jerusalem were going out to him and were being baptized by him in the river Jordan, confessing their sins. Now John was clothed with camel's hair and wore a leather belt around his waist and ate locusts and wild honey. And he preached, saying, "After me comes he who is mightier than I, the strap of whose sandals I am not worthy to stoop down and untie. I have baptized you with water, but he will baptize you with the Holy Spirit."
>
> In those days Jesus came from Nazareth of Galilee and was baptized by John in the Jordan. And when he came up out of the water, immediately he saw the

> heavens being torn open and the Spirit descending on him like a dove. And a voice came from heaven, "You are my beloved Son; with you I am well pleased." (Mark 1:1–11)

What happened next? Jesus went into the wilderness!

> The Spirit immediately drove him out into the wilderness. And he was in the wilderness forty days, being tempted by Satan. And he was with the wild animals, and the angels were ministering to him.
>
> Now after John was arrested, Jesus came into Galilee, proclaiming the gospel of God. (Mark 1:12–14)

Notice, too, that Jesus went into the wilderness for *forty days* to be tempted by the Devil. This is his first fulfillment of the promise of exodus history: the forty days of Christ's withdrawal correspond to the forty years of desert wandering by the Israelites. During their ordeal, the children of Israel complained and succumbed to temptations, they compromised the covenant and were unfaithful to God, and they lusted after food and power. Jesus was presented with these same temptations, in much the same way, but this time in order to redeem Israel's historic unfaithfulness, God's chosen one remained faithful to God's will.

So here we have, in a cricket-eating prophet and his carpenter cousin, the apparent fulfillment of God's hundreds of years of promise to his children. "One day," YHWH said to them way back when, "I will deliver you. I will once again infiltrate your existence and be wild in the wilderness" (see Hosea 2:14–23). The deliverance wasn't happening the way that so many people expected, as neither John nor Jesus had a sword, and neither advocated actually overthrowing the government. Instead, they wielded something far more dangerous: the radical message of a new kingdom. They said with clarity and forcefulness, "God's kingdom is now arriving."

Talk about confusing. Imagine that you're an adult Jew in Jesus' day, praying daily for the Messiah to come and wipe out the pagans, who basically own the land you think is yours. They pretty much own *you*. Your religious leaders are corrupt; your political leaders are in cahoots with the oppressors. You believe in God, and you try to stay faithful to the law of Moses, but you keep wondering, *If God loves us so much, why is there a pagan emperor in charge of the world God has promised to us?*

And then along comes some guy from around the block, who has his kooky cousin dunk him in the river, and then he says, "Good news! The kingdom is coming." Wouldn't you be inclined to say, "Dude, where's your sword? Where's your army? If you're the king, or if you're bringing the kingdom, how exactly do you expect to do that—like *this*?"

There is a crucial truth at work here, though—something we must remember at every point of our long journey of spiritual expectation and groaned-for deliverance. That truth is this: *God keeps his promises in unexpected ways.*

## GOD KEEPS HIS PROMISES IN UNEXPECTED WAYS

Does God keep his promises? Yes, always. He is a faithful God, which is a testament to his enduring love, which is in turn a testament to his *grace*, given how unfaithful we are. But does God always keep his promises in the way we expect him to? No. Sometimes he does. Quite frequently he doesn't.

The Jews of Jesus' day were looking for the promise of political and national freedom, a freedom that would allow them to make more money, own more land, and maintain power over the Romans and other nations.[3] They desired for God to once again give them influence and

---

3. Before we come down too hard on the people of Jesus' day for their mistaken

dominion over the civilized world, which is, of course, exactly the position they'd messed up before. If they couldn't handle all that privilege throughout their history, why would God give it to them again?

No, the real good news of the kingdom of God arriving to reign over the world is that the promise is not in *stuff*, but in God himself, manifest in the person of Jesus Christ. The promise is not a monetary or political inheritance. The promise is the king himself. The promise is Jesus.

Jesus of Nazareth was the messianic promise kept, despite his not being the Messiah that everyone expected. This is how Luke records the reaction of the people in Jesus' hometown:

> And he came to Nazareth, where he had been brought up. And as was his custom, he went to the synagogue on the Sabbath day, and he stood up to read. And the scroll of the prophet Isaiah was given to him. He unrolled the scroll and found the place where it was written,
>
> "The Spirit of the Lord is upon me,
> because he has anointed me
> to proclaim good news to the poor.
> He has sent me to proclaim liberty to the captives
> and recovering of sight to the blind,
> to set at liberty those who are oppressed,
> to proclaim the year of the Lord's favor."
>
> And he rolled up the scroll and gave it back to the attendant and sat down. And the eyes of all in

---

expectations, let's remind ourselves that way too many of us today still expect following Jesus to result in more money, more stuff, and more prestige. And these promises aren't just the currency of televangelists anymore either. The prosperity gospel has infiltrated many evangelical churches.

> the synagogue were fixed on him. And he began to say to them, "Today this Scripture has been fulfilled in your hearing." And all spoke well of him and marveled at the gracious words that were coming from his mouth. And they said, "Is not this Joseph's son?" (Luke 4:16–22)

Oh, how quickly an audience can turn! Jesus, in the synagogue on the holy day, read one of God's ancient promises, one that all of God's people had been clinging to and hoping on for generations, and when he finished he basically said, "This is about me."

Now, at first, this story tells us, they were taken aback. They sort of admired him. They liked the cut of his jib. "That Jesus, he's all right! He knows his stuff." But after a while, as you can see in the larger context of Luke 4, they turned on him. After a while, the admiration started to fade, and the real implications of what he said began to dawn on them. By verse 28, the previously admiring crowd was "filled with wrath" at Jesus' self-regard. "Wait a minute. Isn't this Joseph's kid? I know him. He grew up with my son. He missed that game-winning basket in the JV championship. I knew him when he was a runny-nosed kid. No way is he the fulfillment of liberty to the captives!"

Yet he was. (And is!)

There was no way, of course, they could see Jesus as the fulfillment of the promise, so long as they were thinking of liberty in one way and God was thinking of it in another. But if they had followed the trajectory of Christ's life and ministry, what would they have seen? He helped the poor. He set people free from demon possession and lifelong illnesses. He raised the dead. He gave sight to the blind. And though he may not have broken the yoke of Roman oppression on national Israel, he did give them a new way to live under a new, lighter yoke. He gave them a way to break the spirit of oppression by living in a new kingdom, no matter what earthly ruler reigned over the physical space they were occupying.

Jesus showed up and said that the kingdom of God was here *now*, coming and breaking into history. And he said the kingdom was coming by, in, and through *him*. This was a hard pill to swallow—then and now. Let's be frank: if you find the message of Jesus easy to digest, you'd better check the label on the box. You may be consuming a diluted version of Christianity. The message of Jesus—that he himself is life and you can't get it anywhere else, least of all in yourself—is the hardest message we could ever hear, because it goes completely against our perceptions and conceptions, our prejudices and our opinions. It goes radically against the bent of our souls.

Our hearts are crooked. Our hearts are turned in on themselves, and we are full of ourselves. But Jesus Christ says we must be filled with *him*, that we must make all of life about *him*. He commands us to change direction, to get inside of *him*. He calls each of us to take up our individual cross and die to our worldly selves.

That is the unexpected path to life in the kingdom of heaven.

Who will deny that real faith in Jesus Christ is hard? We believe that the work of salvation has been done by Jesus himself, and that we can't get into the kingdom by our own efforts. Jesus earned our way in for us. But what a difficult thing it is to actually *live* as if that's the case. *Belief* and *faith* (which is belief put into *action*) are two separate things.[4] This is why Jesus will at one point tell a rich young man, "If you've got a lot of stuff, it'll be hard for you to get into the kingdom, because the principle of kingdom entrance is that you're ready to give up everything."

The bitter pill for the Jews of Jesus' day was not just the disappointed hope of a physical liberation from the Roman kingdom. What

---

4. To clarify, I am affirming with Jesus' brother James that faith without works isn't really faith. I am not saying our works save us. I am saying, like a good Martin Luther fanboy, that we are justified by faith alone but not faith that is alone.

was even harder to swallow was that some wannabe Messiah could come in and claim authority over the Law, which they'd been studying for centuries—*and claim to be the fulfillment of that law.*

## JESUS KEEPS THE PROMISE MADE BY THE LAW

Here's the way the New Testament speaks of the Mosaic law: it's good, but it can't save you. It's from God, and so it's good, just as all of God's gifts are good. And following the Law was the way God's people could demonstrate that they were God's people. But a person didn't get saved by following the Law, even in the Old Testament. A lot of Christians don't understand this. We like easy dichotomies: in the Old Testament, people were saved by following the Law; in the New Testament, they are now saved by Jesus. But that's a false dichotomy—and bad theology. No . . . the Law provided the sign and the boundaries of kingdom life. We don't follow the Law to *get* saved, we follow the Law because we *are* saved—just as under the covenant of Christ, we don't do good works to get salvation; we do good works because we have salvation. Works, then and now, are the result of kingdom citizenship, not the keys into the kingdom.

With this in mind, the New Testament calls the Old Testament laws and rituals "shadows," the foreshadows of the new covenant.[5] Walking in the way of the Law is the way we trust that we are walking *somewhere.* The temple rituals, the sacrifices, the ceremonial cleansings—these were all symbols of God's real presence to come, God's sacrifice to come, God's cleansing to come. The Mosaic law and the culture instituted around it was a promise of God's salvation.

This was not an easy point to grasp for the Pharisees and Sadducees. For them, the Law was not a means to an end, the *pointer to* salvation; it was the end itself, the *point of* salvation. They didn't take kindly

---

5. Colossians 2:16–18; Hebrews 10:1.

to a carpenter's son who, despite his apparent lack of professional training, had more knowledge than they about the Scriptures, and who was saying at every turn, "Actually, fellas, the point is *me*." Jesus was, in fact, so confident in this regard that the powers that be wondered—for instance, in response to his famous Sermon on the Mount—if he were abolishing the Law.[6] But no, Jesus didn't come to abolish the Law, but to put it in its rightful context—which is to say he put the Law in the context of himself.

This is how Jesus responded to the charge:

> Do not think that I have come to abolish the Law or the Prophets; I have not come to abolish them but to fulfill them. For truly, I say to you, until heaven and earth pass away, not an iota, not a dot, will pass from the Law until all is accomplished. Therefore whoever relaxes one of the least of these commandments and teaches others to do the same will be called least in the kingdom of heaven, but whoever does them and teaches them will be called great in the kingdom of heaven. For I tell you, unless your righteousness exceeds that of the scribes and Pharisees, you will never enter the kingdom of heaven. (Matt. 5:17–20)

The Law and the Prophets, then, are not some plan A, and Jesus is now plan B. God didn't scrap the Law as if it were a mistake. Jesus

---

6. That's another point Christians sometimes miss. We think, "Ah, Jesus showed up to give us grace, so we don't need the Law anymore." The New Testament writers and the early church considered this the heresy of antinomianism, which basically means "against the law." The truth, however, is that while "by the law will no man be justified" (see Rom. 3:28), we should not "sin all the more so that grace may abound" (see Rom. 6:1). Paul also writes in Romans 3:31, "Do we then overthrow the law by this faith? By no means! On the contrary, we uphold the law."

isn't a do-over. Jesus is the culmination of the hopes cultivated by the Law and the Prophets. He didn't come to cover their mistakes but to answer their calls to righteousness and deliverance. The Law tells us, "We're messed up and we need fixing," and Jesus says, "I know—and I'll do that." The Prophets tell us, "All we like sheep have gone astray. We are unfaithful. We deserve fiery judgment for all of our sins." And Jesus says, "I know—and I will save you from that."

The Law and the Prophets are God's promise to save his people, to enter into history once again and redeem his people. And although the way the promise was kept didn't look like what was expected, and although his kingdom and his plan were not what many of them would have preferred, Jesus' message is, "I am the promised one. I am the promise kept."

This "promise kept" issues a deeper call, of course, one in which demands are made upon us. These demands are something else the contemporary church has conveniently eroded from our teaching on Jesus. We like the whole "forgiveness for sin" thing, and we love the whole "grace" thing. But we don't really cotton to the idea of self-crucifixion. We don't like the idea of dying to ourselves because, frankly, we think we're pretty good people. (I am awesome, this I know, for Tony Robbins tells me so.) We like to think of ourselves as having "issues" or problems. Or we have personality quirks. But we don't tend to think of ourselves as sinners who need salvation. We reckon ourselves unsuccessful people who need some practical tips from Jesus on how to succeed in life. So because that whole "take up your cross" thing doesn't sell very well, we leave it off. And we forget that forgiveness of sin calls for blood.[7]

Do you recall the story of Abraham and Isaac? Talk about a hard faith! In Genesis 22, we get this little story that may be the most chilling narrative in all of Scripture.

---

7. Hebrews 9:22.

One day, Abraham was out minding his own business and God gave him an order: "Hey man, I want you to go up this mountain with your son Isaac, and kill him. I want you to take him up there and present him as a burnt offering to me."

Most scriptural narratives are written without much literary nuance. No extra details are included other than those necessary to advance the plot. If I were writing this scene, it wouldn't go by so quickly, with such apparent lack of drama. But in Genesis, we have God saying, "Go do this crazy thing," and Abraham apparently saying, "Yeah, okay."

Abraham took his kid and a few of his men, and they began the dutiful trudge up the mountain. At one point, Abraham told the helpers, "You guys wait here, and Isaac and I will go up the rest of the way." What's really interesting, though, is that he said to them, "And then we'll come back down to meet you." I don't want to think Abraham is lying to them here. It's obvious he wouldn't want to tell the hired hands, "I'm going to kill my son up there." But I want to read the plural "*we* will come back" another way—as Abraham's trusting God that there'll be a way out. Somehow. Eventually. Even as he and Isaac are closing the distance to the mountain top, Isaac was looking around, and wondering, "Hey, Dad, I see we've got rope and a knife and some kindling. But where's the offering?" And Abraham told him, "The Lord will provide the sacrifice."

No matter which guy we're talking about in this story, his heart's gotta be pounding. The scene gets so far as to have Isaac bound upon the altar—I don't know if he went willingly or with resistance, but he's tied up on the altar—and Abraham had his knife raised high to kill his only son.

I just don't get this. When I was a little kid, this story completely freaked me out. I was probably six years old or so, but I came home and chewed on this story that had been told with such straightforward simplicity in "children's church." There might have even been flannelgraphs involved. But this is not a story to be told with the use of felt. This is a story sharp as a knife and heavy as an altar. You don't tell it and then serve crackers and apple juice.[8]

The very idea that God would say, "Take your son and kill him for me," and that Abraham would trust God enough to do it, seriously shook me up. I could only think of my father and myself. For a six-year-old, the crisis of faith this story provoked was heavy.

I'll go on record here and now: I wouldn't do that. I want to love Jesus more than I love my family, because that's something Jesus calls us to do, but I'll say that if he ever shows up and says, "Kill your kid," I'm not doing it.

But of course I don't have to. The truth of the matter is that the sacrifice has already been made.

## JESUS KEEPS THE PROMISE OF A SACRIFICE

What Abraham was trusting in, even to the last second, when his own son's life hung in the balance, was this radical promise from God: "If you are willing to sacrifice your own life, you will gain the promise of provision of the real sacrifice" (see Hebrews 11:17–19).

What happened next? Abraham is standing with his knife in the air, poised to strike, and God intervened. He told Abraham to stop. And he told him, "You've proven you trust me, because you haven't withheld your only son from me." He directed Abraham to a ram trapped in the thistles. Isaac had probably never been happier to see a ram in all his life. I bet he kissed that ram on the lips.[9] God provided this offering for them, and they killed the ram as a burnt offering back to God.

---

8. Which is not to say we shouldn't be telling our kids the stories of the patriarchs. Lord knows our kids could use something more substantial than the spiritual syrup we're raising them on now.

9. Which, for the ram, had to have been the strangest thing ever to happen to him. And as they were slitting his throat a few minutes later, I bet he looked at Isaac and was like, "What the heck?"

That is the promise God makes to us as well. "Trust me for the provision of a sacrifice," he says. "Take up your cross to follow me, sacrificing your selfishness and self-worth, up until the moment of death to yourself, and you will find real life."

God has not withheld his only son from us. The sacrifices we make, big and little, perfect and imperfect, are indicators of the promise of Jesus Christ and the sacrifice he has made for us.[10]

Jesus, in fulfilling this sacrificial promise—from Abraham's trust regarding Isaac all the way to the apostle Paul's call to us to crucify our flesh—erects a kingdom that infiltrates our hearts and minds and changes the course of history. Through this emptying of ourselves, the crooked ways are made straight, the rough places are made plain, and the high places are made low, just as Isaiah promised. Everything gets straightened out, and will get straightened out for good when the Lord returns. Here are some promises to those on the low side of the upside-down world:

> Blessed are the poor in spirit, for theirs is the kingdom
> of heaven.
> Blessed are those who mourn, for they shall be comforted.
> Blessed are the meek, for they shall inherit the earth.
> Blessed are those who hunger and thirst for
> righteousness, for they shall be satisfied.
> Blessed are the merciful, for they shall receive mercy.
> Blessed are the pure in heart, for they shall see God.
> (Matt. 5:3–8)

This again is from the Sermon on the Mount. Here's the important thing to remember about the Sermon on the Mount: it's not some long prescription for behavior modification. Now, there are some obvious

10. A fuller treatment of Jesus as final and fulfilling sacrifice awaits in chapter 9.

calls to "do stuff," some clear commands to live a certain way. There's no denying that. But focusing on these words purely as law is the same pharisaical disorientation that prompted Jesus to say, "Don't think I've come to abolish the Law with this stuff."

"No," he said. "This stuff fulfills the Law."[11]

So the Sermon on the Mount, more than being stuff to do, is stuff to *be*. The Sermon on the Mount is a description of kingdom life. It is what the kingdom of God looks like. So for those on the hoping side of hope, it's a *promise*. It's reassurance to those at the bottom of the barrel that they will be redeemed. It's a pledge to those who are low that they will be raised up. Jesus' kingdom blueprint is the announcement that God has kept his promise to all who hope for deliverance in him.

## JESUS' KINGDOM KEEPS THE PROMISE OF HOPE

In Christ, the spiritually impoverished may not be made monetarily rich, but they will inherit God's kingdom! In Christ, the spiritually empty are fulfilled, and filled up, in God's kingdom. In Christ, those who mourn death will be comforted in seeing that Christ has conquered it. In Christ's kingdom, the meek will rule the new earth, because it isn't ruled by military might or political power. All of our hopes for God's redemption are here now, in Jesus Christ and the kingdom he brings.

He is the promise of salvation, both in his death and in his resurrection. It's by his death we get to avoid hell, but it's in his resurrection that we will one day see a glorious redemption from the pains of this world to the wonders of the next. The New Testament calls Christ's resurrection the firstfruits of more to come.[12] This means that Christ's resurrection is a promise of our future resurrection. One day, you and I will get to slip out of these physical bodies, but God has promised, through

11. Matthew 5:17.
12. 1 Corinthians 15:20.

the resurrection of the real person of Jesus Christ, to raise us up, and to fulfill our hopes for a new world where there's no pain or trouble or grieving or mourning or addictions or abuse or adultery or global warming or carsickness or morning breath. Amen? Isn't that a hope worth exulting over? Isn't that a promise worth desperately clinging to in the face of all life may bring us?

Christ's life is a promise to you—and me—of new life. Christ's death is a promise to us that death is not in vain. Christ's resurrection is a promise to us that we will rise up out of the grave one day, and the kingdom we live in spiritually now will one day drown out the kingdoms of this world for all eternity.

This world may be in the proverbial handbasket. It may be circling the drain. Our bodies are indeed winding down (and more than a few of us have bodies widening downward). But our help comes from the Lord, the maker of heaven and earth, *the keeper of promises.* Our Redeemer lives. And one day, he will descend with a shout, and this old earth will get an extreme makeover in an eternal splash of glory, the likes of which will make the aurora borealis look like a Lite-Brite. Our sagging flesh and aching bones and slowing hearts and diseased cells will be taken from us, and we'll get fresh legs, a freshly purified heart, and fresh lungs to breathe the fresh air of the new heaven and the new earth. We'll get fresh eyes to finally see Jesus face-to-face.

Children of God, we've been rescued once. And that rescue was a promise kept and a promise of glory to come. Someday, we'll be rescued again in such a way that we may laugh at all the things that make us cry today. Our anguish over this world and our hurt from the experience of living in it will become joy in the new world and the worshipful pleasure it brings.

None of this is possible, or even preferable, without the promise of Jesus the Christ.

2

# JESUS THE PROPHET

The Old Testament prophet Malachi rocks some hard-core prophecy in this exquisite bit of warning and admonition:

> For behold, the day is coming, burning like an oven, when all the arrogant and all evildoers will be stubble. The day that is coming shall set them ablaze, says the Lord of hosts, so that it will leave them neither root nor branch. But for you who fear my name, the sun of righteousness shall rise with healing in its wings. You shall go out leaping like calves from the stall. And you shall tread down the wicked, for they will be ashes under the soles of your feet, on the day when I act, says the Lord of hosts.
>
> Remember the law of my servant Moses, the statutes and rules that I commanded him at Horeb for all Israel.
>
> Behold, I will send you Elijah the prophet before the great and awesome day of the Lord comes. And he will turn the hearts of fathers to their children and the hearts of children to their fathers, lest I come and strike the land with a decree of utter destruction. (Mal. 4:1–6)

Coming as it does at the close of the Old Testament, this fantastic slice of hellfire and brimstone serves as a great big "To Be Continued."

True to form, the Israelites have been complaining. This is true to their name, as well, because the word *Israel* itself means "struggles with God." Talk about your self-fulfilling prophecy. This reminds me of Jerry Seinfeld's bit about parents who name their kid Jeeves. They're pretty much determining right then and there that he's gonna grow up to be a butler.[1] Inspired by their individual namesake, Jacob, God called the nation "Struggles with God." And true to their name, they gave him grief from the get-go.

That's how the Old Testament ends, with this passage from Malachi. It's a warning and a promise from the last of Israel's prophets. He tells them, "Remember to obey," because Elijah's going to come and usher in the "great and awesome day of the Lord." The day of the Lord will bring reconciliation for some but destruction for others.

That's some heavy-metal prophecy right there. Malachi isn't messing around. This is real prophecy, not some limp-wristed televangelist appeal: "Ooh, I feel there is someone out there in TV land with a headache; come put your hand on the screen." No. Malachi's message is cataclysmic stuff: "God is coming—be prepared. He's going to bring restoration to his people. He's going to bring judgment. Which outcome are you preparing for?"

After Malachi draws the curtain on the Old Testament canon, roughly four hundred years pass before the events that open the New Testament. Four hundred years trickle by slowly, and in this time the nation of Israel manages to wriggle out of Babylonian captivity, but they don't exactly enjoy freedom. They fall prey to a succession of invaders and oppressors. The temple that Solomon built is defiled—this actually

---

1. Proving there's an exception to every rule, though, is my good friend Bozo, who runs a not unsuccessful funeral home.

happens during the time of the Old Testament—but in the interim, it is rebuilt and refurbished by Herod the Great. The very place where Israel is said to experience the literal presence of God has been ruined and then restored by a non-Jew.

These four hundred years chronicle a dwindling of Jewish covenantal faithfulness. Heavily influenced by infiltrating cultures, the nation of Israel succumbs to new customs. Traditional Jewish distinctions get their edges smoothed off. Without a king, without a real nation, they divide into factions. The Pharisaical tradition, the conservative stream of Hebrew theology, attempts to maintain some continuity between the old age and the new. The Pharisees were sort of the evangelical pastors of their day. They tried to remain faithful to the law of Moses, just as Malachi instructed, and they tried to think of ways to make this faithfulness practical to everyday life. The Pharisees were not happy about the Roman occupation, but they generally committed to living at peace with the foreign oppressors, even while they practiced a sort of civil disobedience.

At the same time, a group we call the Zealots advocated violent overthrow of the Roman government and the forceful reestablishment of the nation of Israel. Come hell or high water, the Zealots wanted revolution.

You may also have heard of the Sadducees. These guys were sell-outs, essentially making their living on the Roman payroll. The Sadducees were theologically bankrupt, having given up all belief in the supernatural. They were "cultural Jews," which basically means they were traitors, exploiting their own people for political and monetary gain. They profited from the sacrifices purchased at the temple. I'd compare the Sadducees to our modern politicians who are "Christians in name only," the ones who don't really adhere to Christian beliefs but talk the talk when convenient just to gain support or campaign contributions.

During that four-hundred-year interlude, the Jews gradually abandoned the Hebrew language. By the time of Jesus' day, the Jews of Palestine mostly spoke Aramaic. And the Old Testament Scriptures were not usually cited in the original Hebrew, but in Greek, from the popular translation called the Septuagint.[2]

The priestly tradition had deteriorated so much that none of the Jewish priests were able to trace his ancestry back to Aaron, as previously prescribed. A king was on the throne, who reigned over Israel, but he wasn't a descendant of Jacob. His name was Herod, and he was a descendant of Esau.[3]

The entire Israelite enterprise was corrupt. Divided. Wayward. Despite a few pockets of hard-core faithfulness to YHWH, Israel was essentially a nation estranged from God. Again. The place was a mess. And this is why it is not a coincidence that Jesus came into this time and this place.

Imagine you're watching this whole story like in a Spielberg movie. The black-and-white footage of Malachi ends with "To Be Continued" and fades out. The next scene opens . . . and the music swells . . . and the long awaited sequel shines in blazing colors onto the screen.[4]

The prophetic ministry in Israel had ceased with Malachi, who went into retirement as apparently the last of his kind. On his way out, he hung his "Repent for the End Is Near" sandwich board on a nail by the door and closed the shop for four long centuries. And then John the Baptist came in, wiped off the dust, and put the sign back on.

John is "Elijah," by the way. Malachi said that Elijah would appear again and herald the day of the Lord. Well the Jews may have forgotten how

---

2. Which is where we get the popular phrase "It's all Septuagint to me."

3. Esau . . . you know, the guy God *hated* (see Rom. 9:13).

4. If you're like me, when you start reading the New Testament, you hear and feel that stirring John Williams score from the opening of every Star Wars movie. I remember the anticipation of *Episode 1: The Phantom Menace* when it came out in 1999. I'd been waiting nearly twenty years for the continuation of a movie series that had really captivated and characterized the childhoods of my generation. Sitting in the theater, waiting for the opening, and then having that familiar LucasFilm logo pop up with Williams's majestic theme heralding the moment . . . well, it gave me goose bumps. The movie reeked, of course, but I couldn't have anticipated that at the time. In any event, that emotional, expectant thrill is just a taste of what we should feel when we move from the Old Testament to the New.

to follow God, but they hadn't forgotten everything. And this prophecy about Elijah is one of the things they ask Jesus about in the Gospels. As the implications of Jesus' being the promised Messiah began to settle in, they wondered, "Hey, isn't Elijah supposed to come first? Where's Elijah?"

Do you know what Jesus told them? "Hey, you had Elijah and you killed him." He was referring to his cousin John.[5]

John the Baptist came as a prophet, as the prophet Elijah, preaching that the kingdom of God was at hand—meaning, it had arrived—and that it was time to be ready. To repent. Repentance is the bottom-line call of any real prophet. It's not all about predicting the future or just being a religious rabble-rouser. It's about calling people to turn around, because the prophet wants them to have a heads-up for when God arrives. We'll see a bit later why this is important, but first people needed to buy the idea that John and Jesus were picking up the prophetic ministry of Israel four hundred years after it had ceased. Folks would have to make sure that Jesus was really a prophet, that he adhered to what it means to be a Jewish prophet.

Even during the four hundred years of silence, various people came forward from time to time and declared themselves as prophets of God. Some were even able to attract followers. But how would people know, "Yeah, this person is God's spokesperson to his people," or "No, this guy's a wacko"? Sometimes it's hard to tell the difference. But there are some general criteria that anyone can gather from the collective ministry of the Old Testament prophets, and use them to test prospective prophets.

## REAL PROPHETS HAD A SPECIFIC ENCOUNTER WITH GOD HIMSELF

The prophetic mantle was recognized when a would-be prophet authenticated a special recognition from, and commissioning by, YHWH.

5. See Matthew 17:10–13.

So in the case of Moses, God disrupted his shepherding with a burning bush. Amos was a fig farmer when God told him to go preach to Israel. Jonah was basically harassed by God because of his reluctance to go and harass the Ninevites on God's behalf. So a prophet isn't just someone who has a special spiritual sense, or who, in our feel-good vernacular, "feels led." Rather, a prophet is someone who's called out unequivocally by God to speak on God's behalf.

Was Jesus commissioned this way? Surely his baptismal and dove experience with John counts as a calling out. His self-authentication should count, as well—when he unrolled the scroll in the synagogue and attributed the words of the prophet Isaiah to himself, and then went out and fulfilled the prophecy point by point. And although the transfiguration occurred well into Jesus' ministry, it also should count as a direct, God-dispensed, revelatory anointing.

## REAL PROPHETS ADMONISHED THE NATION

The Old Testament prophets spoke judgment and declared God's ultimatums to the people of Israel. In our day, we have a constricted view of prophecy in relation to Jesus, focusing mostly on his prescience. That is to say, we've narrowed our definition of prophecy to the ability to foretell the future. Certainly, prescience is part of prophecy. As just one example among many, when Jesus says to Peter, "You will deny me three times before the rooster crows," that's a pretty specific prophecy! And it comes true. Undeniably, acts of prescience tend to accompany God's real prophets.[6]

---

6. By the way, the penalty for false prophecy in the days of antiquity was death. If someone claimed to speak for God and was found to be a liar, they could be killed. Contrast this prophecy insurance policy with today's lax standards under which any enterprising lunatic with airwave access can make all kinds of predictions about things that don't come true, and even though he's lying, we reward him with television networks and private jets and millions of dollars. These false prophets are fortunate to live in the days of tolerance of blasphemers. As prophets, they wouldn't have profited in the olden days.

Jesus certainly foretold the future with startling accuracy. The real put-yourself-out-there risk of claiming to speak for God, though, was in his claim to be speaking for God in dealing with God's people. All the Old Testament prophets acted as God's go-between with Israel: "If you don't stop being stupid, something really bad is going to happen to you. But if you humble yourself and do what I say, I will bless you."

Now you'd think it would go without saying that if we disobey God, we'll be punished, and if we obey God he will bless us. We have a sort of commonsense approach to faith like that. And this quasi-karma is somewhat satisfying to believe, given our innate sense of justice. But the whole cause-and-effect thing gets extremely complicated when expanded to a national scale, particularly when one person stands up to an entire culture and nation and political system, announcing with authority, "You are corrupt. You are not following God. And bad things are going to happen to you."

Suddenly, Hippie Jesus is out of his van and taking everyone on one bummer of a trip, man. Nobody wants to hear it. Think of what it would be like if some guy walked up to Capitol Hill and proclaimed, "If you don't repent of all your corruption, you'll be destroyed." What would happen? Would anyone listen to him? If you believe what Scripture teaches about sowing to corruption, such prophecy wouldn't be a lie. It would even make sense if you believed in the lie of karma. But not only would such a prophet not be listened to, he would be considered crazy. He'd be locked up for spouting threats.

Ultimately, such prophecy wouldn't fly because it requires people to acknowledge they are wrong on a collective, cultural level. We have a hard enough time admitting our faults and confessing our sins as individuals. Try getting an entire nation to agree to an admission of guilt.

Now, as a test of Jesus' standing as a prophet, did he admonish the whole nation? Yes, absolutely. He pronounced woes over Jerusalem. "You stone the prophets," he lamented over his homeland. "How I would love to gather you under my wings like a loving mother hen, but you won't have any of it."[7]

Another example. He occasionally spoke of the temple with a vague foreboding. Remember the parable of the man who builds his house on the sand?[8] Jesus likely had the temple in mind there. This is part of what hacked off so many of the Jewish religious leaders about Jesus. He basically said, "Your faith right now, which is centered on a stone temple, is really like a man building on sand. But if you listen to *my* words, *then* you're really building on a firm foundation."

In Mark 11:23, likely while standing within sight of the temple mount, Jesus says, "Whoever says to this mountain, 'Be taken up and thrown into the sea,' and does not doubt in his heart, but believes that what he says will come to pass, it will be done for him."

Jesus curses a fig tree, a symbol of national Israel, and it withers (see Mark 11:12–14, 20).

Those are threats, folks—threats on a nation, religion, and culture. "Follow me, or things will go badly for you as a people." These are the kinds of threats made only by a terrorist, a kook, or a prophet of God.

We don't suffer fools gladly. And people who claim to speak for God, who use that alleged commissioning to go around warning people and telling people what to do, we find irritating and inconvenient. We like the "you're gonna be rich!" prophets. We don't like the "you're gonna be destroyed!" prophets. But Jesus, who promised blessings to those hungering for righteousness, also promised eternal punishment to those who didn't follow him.

Not so tolerant now, is he? He is definitely a Harsh-Your-Vibe Jesus now.

---

7. See Luke 13:34.
8. Matthew 7:24–29.

## REAL PROPHETS PREACH REPENTANCE

The call to repent—to change our ways—is a third major sign to identify real prophets of God. Repentance is not just about changing our minds; it's about really changing the way we think, in such a way that our bodies follow. "Repent!" is the call to make a complete turnaround in our lives.

Did Jesus call people to repentance? All the time. In fact, he began his ministry carrying on the torch from John the Baptist: "Repent, for the kingdom of heaven is at hand!"

"Stop what you're doing; drop everything!"

Jesus came into this divided and corrupted earthly world, into a culture that had been infiltrated and diluted by paganism and pluralism, into an oppressed nation ruled by a foreign king, and told everyone he encountered, "God's kingdom is now coming in, and I am the king in charge. If you want to be a part of God's re-forming nation, you will turn away from trusting the kingdom you can see and start following me into this invisible kingdom."

Talk about audacity! That's why it was easy for some to reject Jesus. In one incident recorded in the Gospels, Jesus remarked that prophets are not, in fact, acknowledged even in their own hometowns.[9] What would happen if someone in your family or your small town came out and said, "Hey, I speak for God now"? And what would happen if that same person also insinuated that he was actually God himself?

You think Joseph's brothers hated him for his uppity dreams? Think of Jesus' brothers. What would it be like having an older brother casting a God-sized shadow? We know, for instance, that Jesus' brother James did not believe in him—until after the Resurrection. This is the guy who wrote the epistle of James in the Bible. So Jesus lived his whole earthly life and died on the cross without the affirmation and support

---

9. In all four gospels, but see especially Luke 4:24 and John 4:44.

of at least one of his brothers. His mother was there at the cross, but James was not.

Jesus called for repentance and thereby provided grounds for people to reject him. Their submitting to this "ordinary" person's authority required a humility that was outweighed by their pride. Still, in his commissioning, in his mode of prophesying, and in his calls of repentance that eventually led to his rejection, Jesus Christ authenticated himself as a prophet of God.

## A PROPHET WARNS US TO BE PREPARED

In Matthew 24, we find one of Jesus' epic prophecies.[10] In this lengthy passage, as Jesus preaches from the Mount of Olives, we see all facets of Jesus' authentication as a prophet, as well as some major prophecies, including prophecies about the end of the world.

Matthew 24 is a complicated chapter. As such, our aim here is not really to cover the so-called end times—although I'll offer a personal interpretation about one particularly famous section of the chapter. I can't do justice to the full scope of the Olivet discourse in this book. Entire books have been written on this one passage and subject, so I won't pretend that a few paragraphs can even begin to do the intensive work of real exegetical illumination.[11] Instead, we'll hop through the passage and look at some of the highlights. We'll start with the opening verses and then jump to verse 34 to look at the conversational bookends of the prophecy:

> Jesus left the temple and was going away, when his disciples came to point out to him the buildings of the

---

10. Parallels are found in Mark 13 and Luke 21.

11. To mention just two, I would recommend R. C. Sproul, *The Last Days According to Jesus* (Grand Rapids: Baker, 2000); and George R. Beasley-Murray, *Jesus and the Last Days: The Interpretation of the Olivet Discourse* (Vancouver, BC: Regent College, 2005).

> temple. But he answered them, "You see all these, do you not? Truly, I say to you, there will not be left here one stone upon another that will not be thrown down."
>
> As he sat on the Mount of Olives, the disciples came to him privately, saying, "Tell us, when will these things be, and what will be the sign of your coming and of the close of the age?" And Jesus answered them, . . .
>
> "Truly, I say to you, this generation will not pass away until all these things take place." (Matt. 24:1–4, 34)

This is a very startling prediction. When Jesus says, "This building will be destroyed," he is referring to the center of Jewish religion and life, the place where God himself is supposed to dwell. So this is life-changing, earthquake-type news to his followers. No wonder Isaiah, and then Matthew, referred to the arrival of Jesus as the mountains being smashed, and the rough places being smoothed, and the valleys being raised. Think about the fall of the Berlin Wall. Or September 11, 2001. What sort of language was used to describe these events? Earthshaking? Earth-shattering? How much more earthshaking would be the coming of God himself in the flesh?

Jesus said to people whose entire relationship with God revolved around the temple and the sacrifices made there, "This place is going away." That would be distressing, to say the least. So they say to him, "When? When will this unthinkable event happen?"

Jesus replies, "A generation." Now in that day a generation was roughly forty years. We may surmise that this conversation took place somewhere around A.D. 30, knowing Jesus began his ministry around the age of thirty. The temple was destroyed in A.D. 70. That's forty years later, give or take. His prediction came true.

But it wasn't just a neat trick. Jesus isn't the ancient Kreskin. This dire warning was a promise of judgment on a corrupt nation. But it was also a promise we can be thankful for—of God's presence *outside* the temple courts. Remember what Jesus says at another time to his followers: "The kingdom of God is *within you*."[12] Paul later tells us that our bodies are temples of the Holy Spirit.[13]

The Spirit of God isn't bound to the temple in Jerusalem. The temple's physical destruction, then, symbolizes the very real freedom we have in the Holy Spirit, who is the presence of God with us now. The Ark of the Covenant, which resided in the Holy of Holies in the temple in Jerusalem, once represented the presence of God among his people. But now the Spirit of God resides in his followers, not in a building.

Is that not a glorious truth? Isn't it a God-glorifying wonder, worthy of praise and joyful submission? The God of the universe—the God of the wilderness—is not and cannot be contained, but roams free like the wind, moving and inhabiting whomever he will. Isn't it amazing that the gift of Jesus Christ brings us to God, whoever we are, and wherever we may be found, regardless of borders and buildings, irrespective of nationalities and cultures?

We have such a great Savior and God! He alone has made us truly free by his incomprehensible grace. What a shame, then, that we are so easily led astray, that we so often settle for cheap imitations, putting our trust in false idols.

Looking at another set of "bookend" verses in Matthew 24, consider this prophetic warning from Jesus:

> Jesus answered them, "See that no one leads you astray. For many will come in my name, saying, 'I am the Christ,' and they will lead many astray. . . .

12. Luke 17:20–21 NIV.
13. 1 Corinthians 6:19.

> Then if anyone says to you, 'Look, here is the Christ!' or 'There he is!' do not believe it. For false christs and false prophets will arise and perform great signs and wonders, so as to lead astray, if possible, even the elect. See, I have told you beforehand. So, if they say to you, 'Look, he is in the wilderness,' do not go out. If they say, 'Look, he is in the inner rooms,' do not believe it." (Matt. 24:4–5, 23–26)

In these verses, Jesus warns his followers not to accept any impostors. The temptation, as we have seen, is to reject the prophet because he's just that guy you knew from around the block, or he's telling you there's something wrong with you. (And good grief, doesn't everyone know you're awesome?)

Beware of the false prophets who will tell us what our itching ears want to hear, as Paul warns Timothy.[14] They will redirect our unceasing worship toward more appetite-satisfying idols. In the days when we are down and downtrodden, it will be very tempting to opt for feel-good prophets. When we are corrupt, dead in sin, oppressed, and depressed, it doesn't feel very nice to have someone telling us that something is wrong with us, that we have to change our ways. We want to believe that it's everyone else who needs to change, that our problems are the fault of everyone else.

We're easily pleased, easily wowed, easily impressed. You'd think we wouldn't be so easily fooled. Even as I write this, there's some moron in Miami saying he's Jesus Christ, and he has allegedly attracted thousands of followers.[15] Perhaps you've seen him on the news recently.

---

14. 2 Timothy 4:3.

15. His name is Jose Luis de Jesus Miranda, and he's an ex-con who claims to be the second coming of Jesus. He "preaches" from a "church" called Creciendo en Gracia (which means "Growing in Grace," even though I think they're growing in something

In the Olivet discourse, Jesus warns his followers—then and for generations to come—that as tempting as it may be to discard the real deal for someone more showy or flashy or persuasive, there will be dire consequences for us if we do. Nevertheless, and unfortunately, we have a generation of alleged Christians today who are not satisfied with Christ.

Jesus has some scary words for those who would abandon him for the promise of something or someone else:

> As were the days of Noah, so will be the coming of the Son of Man. For as in those days before the flood they were eating and drinking, marrying and giving in marriage, until the day when Noah entered the ark, and they were unaware until the flood came and swept them all away, so will be the coming of the Son of Man. Then two men will be in the field; one will be taken and one left. Two women will be grinding at the mill; one will be taken and one left. Therefore, stay awake, for you do not know on what day your Lord is coming. But know this, that if the master of the house had known in what part of the night the thief was coming, he would have stayed awake and would not have let his house be broken into. Therefore you also must be ready, for the Son of Man is coming at an hour you do not expect. (Matt. 24:37–44)

Now we're getting into some end-times type stuff. This is the infamous passage that inspired the *Left Behind* phenomenon. If you

---

I can't print here because my grandma will read this book). He doesn't even pretend to hide his claim to antichrist status, proudly bearing a tattoo on his arm that reads 666, and his followers sport the same on caps and T-shirts. What do we make of an antichrist claiming to be Jesus who proudly flaunts his anti-Christianity?

believe in a pretribulation rapture of the church, like the authors of the novels that started the merchandising blitz, you read in this passage an account of how Jesus will come back and take his followers away to heaven.

In the interest of full disclosure, I must confess that I am not a pretribulationist.[16] Without getting too much into the various views of eschatology, I will say that when I read this passage, I don't see being taken away as a good thing.

Let me explain.

Notice Jesus compares his coming to the flood that came in Noah's day. At that time, people were minding their own business, eating and drinking, going about their daily lives, unprepared and unaware of the imminent danger. Suddenly God came and wiped them away. In the same way, Jesus says, he is coming, and people who are minding their own business and are not prepared for the invasion of the physical kingdom of God will be taken away. I believe this means they are taken away to judgment. Can we agree that a thief coming into your house is not a good thing?

Further, if you keep reading into the subsequent verses, Jesus tells a story about a master finding an unfaithful servant and having him chopped into pieces. I don't know about you, but that doesn't sound too rapturous to me. I mean, it's a no-brainer for me. I think I'd prefer to get left behind with Kirk Cameron than to go get vivisected.[17]

Whatever you think of this passage, however you interpret it eschatologically, Jesus is clearly saying, "You don't know when I am coming; be prepared."

---

16. I used to be, however, and still have the membership card.

17. I'm referring, of course, to Kirk Cameron's character in the *Left Behind* film adaptations. However the Lord's return occurs, I trust that Kirk Cameron—the talented actor, ambushing evangelist, and all-around good guy—will be raptured safe and sound. *Growing Pains* was a pretty good show. It's not like he was on *Alf* or anything.

## A PROPHET INTRUDES ON OUR SPACE

Prophets have an annoying habit of interrupting us. Jesus has this incredible habit of harassing us when we're least expecting him, or least wanting him. He has no respect for our personal space.

In a great story from John's gospel, Jesus presumes upon a woman's sense of privacy, as only Jesus can.[18] He had come to a town in Samaria called Sychar, which was near the historic location of Jacob's well. I guess the disciples couldn't afford the note on their VW bus anymore, so they were hoofing it everywhere. Jesus, worn and weary, went to the well to rest and find refreshment.

Around noon, a Samaritan woman approached. I don't know if Jesus forgot his bucket or if the disciples had inadvertently taken it with them when they dropped him off (they had gone into town to buy food), but he asks the woman for a drink.

Let me set this scene for you, if you haven't already read between the lines. This is a Samaritan woman coming to the Jews' home turf at the hottest part of the day. Back then, if you wanted to draw water, you'd head out in the cool of the morning or evening, not at noon. This woman, though, goes out of her way to be alone, goes out of her way to be where she won't be recognized. As we soon find out, she has her reasons for wanting privacy.

She sees a man sitting by the well as she approaches. What does she do? She's already come a long way; she doesn't feel like going somewhere else. And the whole time she's walking, as she gets closer and closer, she's muttering to herself, "Please don't talk to me, please don't talk to me, please don't talk to me . . ."

And then he talks to her. This Jewish *man*, asks her, a Samaritan woman, for a drink. Doesn't he know this isn't kosher? Samaritans are lower than dogs to the Jewish people, and Samaritan women rank even

---

18. John 4:5–26.

lower. If this man only knew the layers of scarlet letters she's wearing at this moment . . .

So she decides to be up-front about the situation. She asks, "How is it that you, a Jew, ask for a drink from me, a woman of Samaria?"

Jesus responds in a cryptic way, but also in a nonthreatening way in order to engage her in conversation: "If you knew the gift of God, and who it is that is saying to you, 'Give me a drink,' you would have asked him, and he would have given you living water."

This was before Facebook was invented, so she was probably not used to people referring to themselves in the third person. Who knows? In any event, she's still furlongs from understanding what he's getting at. She says, "Sir, you have nothing to draw water with, and the well is deep. Where do you get that living water?" Then she goes on to bring up the history of the well, perhaps in a bit of subterfuge. She is keen on keeping the conversation in the realm of small talk.

Jesus is not big on small talk.

He says to her, "Everyone who drinks of this water will be thirsty again, but whoever drinks of the water that I will give him will never be thirsty again. The water that I will give him will become in him a spring of water welling up to eternal life."

Now we're talkin'! The woman—let's call her Barbara—replies, "Sir, give me this water, so that I will not be thirsty or have to come here to draw water."

You have to love Barbara's eagerness. Jesus loves it too—I am sure of it. But first things first. Eagerness does not healing bring or repentance make.

Now Jesus gets really, really personal. "Go, call your husband, and come here," he commands.

Barbara blushes. She doesn't have a husband and says so, not yet realizing this man knows how many hairs she has on her head.

Jesus just comes right out with it: "You are right in saying, 'I have no husband'; for you have had five husbands, and the one you now have is not your husband."

Then comes the understatement of the millennium. Barbara says, "Sir, I perceive that you are a prophet."

No duh.

Jesus has reached right into her heart here, seen right through her desire for solitude and her conversational ploys for theoretical chit-chat, and told her the hard, uncomfortable truth of her life. He has done, one-on-one, the job of a prophet. And he is not done proclaiming. Neither is Barbara done defending.

"Our fathers worshiped on this mountain," she says, "but you say that in Jerusalem is the place where people ought to worship."

Do you see what she's doing now? Jesus got a little too close for comfort, and rather than spill her guts about her personal life, she's deflecting the conversation once again. So she brings up an ages-old religious dispute. Like many of us spiritual types who prefer our spirituality nice and hypothetical—as opposed to dangerous and personal—she wants to debate theology.

Jesus may be a carpenter's son from the wrong side of the tracks, a wilderness prophet who spends all his time with blue-collar nitwits, but he is no rube. He takes her aimless theological musings and redirects them right back onto himself. Just like he freaked out the disciples when he talked about "no more temple," he's about to rock this woman's world: "location, location, location" is no longer on God's eschatological radar.

"Look," he tells her, "pretty soon it won't matter if you're on this mountain or in Jerusalem. If you don't know the truth about the Father, it won't matter who you are or where you are. If you really want to worship, if you really want to know God, then you'll have to worship God in spirit and in truth. That's the kind of people God is seeking to worship him, not people hung up on buildings and borders."

Barbara is taken aback, naturally. Any theological conversationalist in those days would realize something right off the bat. Someone who talked like this, with such know-it-all authority, who so completely disregarded the long cherished traditions of religion and culture, would have to be either a liar, a lunatic, or the Lord.[19]

"I know that Messiah is coming," she says. She's dangerously close to the revelation of an explosive truth. "When he comes, he will tell us all things."

"Lady," he tells her (and you can almost see him grin), "you're looking at him."

This is what a prophet does. This is what Jesus the Prophet does. He inserts himself into our workaday lives, he invades our space and exposes our hearts. He tells us the ugly truth about ourselves, but not to shame or punish us, but to open us up, to provoke us and prompt us, to disarm our defenses and turn us—all of us, our *whole* selves—toward him. He dismantles our bland religion and hypothetical spirituality, he tears down our heartless theology and our faithless works. He infiltrates the very core of our existence and proclaims not our betterment or our improvement or our worthiness, but his own glory and power.

Jesus the Prophet calls us to stop messing around, to stop living our own private lives in our own private kingdoms—and he makes us reckon with his challenge. He makes us reckon with *him*.

Through failed relationships, through the seeking of solace in sex and surface spirituality, Barbara, this person of despised race and marginalized gender, finds redemption—not from a message of self-improvement or empowering spiritual enlightenment, but in the Giver giving himself as the gift. She came for a drink and got swept away by the living water.

Do you know about Sundar Singh? He was born to a wealthy Indian

19. C. S. Lewis, *Mere Christianity* (New York: Macmillan, 1952), 55.

family in 1889 and enjoyed a relatively carefree childhood with loving parents and a comfortable home. Although Singh came from a prominent Sikh family and received regular training from a Sadhu (a Sikh ascetic holy man), his mother sent him to a Christian mission school so he could learn English.

When Singh was fourteen years old, his mother died, and the grief and pain thrust him into a horrible despair and a terrible rage. He lashed out at the Christian missionaries, ridiculing them and persecuting their converts. So focused was his hatred for the Christian faith, he once burnt a Bible one page at a time in the presence of his friends.

The satisfaction of burning the Bible, however, did not fulfill him. That same night, he lay down on the railroad tracks, hoping to end his pain forever. The train never came. But Jesus did.

By dawn, Sundar Singh was a changed man. He confidently told his father that he'd seen a vision of Jesus Christ, and that he now aimed to follow the Christian God all of his days. His father begged him to renounce his conversion, but Singh was unmoved. Eventually, his family disowned him and he was left essentially homeless.

He got baptized on his sixteenth birthday and went to live in a Christian mission for lepers, serving and ministering to the leprosy patients. Eventually, Singh made a full commitment to a life of homelessness, renouncing all possessions, in the hopes of truly walking and living as Jesus had walked and lived. He wanted to bring the gospel to his fellow Indians, in the guise of their own culture, so he modeled himself after a Sadhu, becoming a Jesus-worshiping, Jesus-following, Jesus-preaching Indian ascetic mystic.

Sundar Singh basically wandered the earth, like a Bible-toting Kwai Chang Caine from *Kung Fu*.[20] Here was a guy who, like Paul, had hated

---

20. Please tell me you remember the television show *Kung Fu*. If not, repent and find it on DVD.

Jesus and hated Jesus' church, yet found his life invaded by Jesus when he least expected it. Now, Sundar Singh renounced everything that prevented him from becoming more like Jesus. One fateful day, Singh began an annual trek up the mountains to Tibet, never to be seen again. He simply disappeared.

That was one radical dude. Imagine actually giving up everything you've ever known, and leaving everyone you've ever loved, for absolute devotion to Jesus Christ. Jesus did say, after all, "If anyone comes to me and does not hate his own father and mother and wife and children and brothers and sisters, yes, and even his own life, he cannot be my disciple."[21]

The Christian community I pastor was meeting one night for Bible study. In the sharing time, several of us spoke of difficulties at work or relatives undergoing surgery. Then one new attendee, an Iranian immigrant who had been a Christian for only a few months, said, "If I go back home, they will kill me." Long, awestruck silence followed. And then she added, "But it's okay."

That was perhaps the best and deepest thing ever said in the history of our Bible study.

Sundar Singh was once asked by a Hindu professor, "What have you found in Christianity that you had not found in your former religion?"

"I have found Christ," Sundar Singh said.

"Oh yes, I know," said the confused professor. "But what particular doctrine or principle have you found that you did not have before?"

"The particular thing I have found," Sundar Singh replied, "is Christ."

That, friends, is full, complete, ultimate, singular devotion to Jesus Christ. That simple statement is the fruit of a life that has been interrupted, redeemed, and transformed by the power of Jesus Christ. That

21. Luke 14:26.

is the testimony of a life that has found Jesus Christ all-satisfying, all-nourishing, all-completing.

That is what irritates about Jesus the Prophet. That is what disturbs about Jesus the Prophet. That is what offends about Jesus the Prophet. He has no interest in our self-interest, no concern for our personal space, no enablement for our self-satisfaction. He proclaims and prophesies himself, and he makes no bones about it.

"I am the way, the truth, and the life, and if you want to get to God, you have to go through me."[22]

Nothing else gets us to God. *Nobody* else gets us to God. God in the flesh dwells among us, and in the flesh we get to see God.[23]

And that is the fundamental question Jesus asks us, the question that ends with a question mark shaped like a cross: Will you be satisfied in Christ alone?

---

22. John 14:6, author's paraphrase.
23. See Job 19:26.

# 3

# JESUS THE FORGIVER

We have so sanitized forgiveness it's all out of focus. We idealize it as nice and virtuous, the dominion of children and their insignificant squabbles. We forget, though, just how messy, how difficult, how scandalous forgiveness really is until we're faced with the opportunity to experience it ourselves. If you've ever cried out for a forgiveness withheld from you, or if you've ever had to face the sometimes excruciating process of forgiving someone who has sinned greatly against you, then you know what I'm talking about. If you haven't experienced either opportunity, just wait.

The Scriptures give us perhaps the most vivid, most scandalous depiction of radical forgiveness in action in the story of the prophet Hosea. God—as a way of creating a live portrait of his own relentless grace for his relentlessly unfaithful people—orders Hosea to take a prostitute for a wife.

Hosea obeys God in good faith, but Gomer—yes, her name was Gomer, adding insult to injury—despite bearing Hosea three children, continues to "play the whore" (old habits die hard).[1] Hosea, like

1. Hosea 2:5.

YHWH with the nation of Israel, finds himself in a covenant relationship with an adulterous bride.

Amazingly, as Gomer persists in prostituting herself with reckless abandon, Hosea persistently forgives her with the relentlessly steadfast love of a faithful covenant keeper. This, friends, is grace. This is the starkest picture of grace as it really is: a hurt, broken, angry husband refusing to meet his cheating wife's every sin with anything less than forgiveness. Think of how often most of us deny others forgiveness for sins much less vile.

People are messy, so forgiveness is messy. People are radically broken, so grace is radically healing.

By the time we get to the end of Hosea's sordid ballad of messy romance, the prophet's poetry has clearly connected his own stern love to God's disposition toward us, and Gomer's wanton immorality to our predilection for idolatry. This is the gospel: the human commitment to sin is overcome by a divine commitment to forgiveness and grace. And the reputation we're pursuing with our spiritual prostitution is not the reputation God is preparing for us.

Our sin makes a cuckold of God.[2] But our great God, and his great love, continues to woo us. Look at this beautiful passage from the concluding love song in Hosea's book:

> O Israel, come back! Return to your God!
>     You're down but you're not out.
> Prepare your confession
>     and come back to God.
> Pray to him, "Take away our sin,
>     accept our confession.
> Receive as restitution our repentant prayers.

2. Look it up; it's really a word.

Assyria won't save us;
horses won't get us where we want to go.
We'll never again say 'our god'
to something we've made or made up.
You're our last hope. Is it not true
that in you the orphan finds mercy?"

"I will heal their waywardness.
I will love them lavishly. My anger is played out.
I will make a fresh start with Israel.
He'll burst into bloom like a crocus in the spring.
He'll put down deep oak tree roots,
he'll become a forest of oaks!
He'll become splendid—like a giant sequoia,
his fragrance like a grove of cedars!
Those who live near him will be blessed by him,
be blessed and prosper like golden grain.
Everyone will be talking about them,
spreading their fame as the vintage children of God.
Ephraim is finished with gods that are no-gods.
From now on I'm the one who answers and satisfies him.
I am like a luxuriant fruit tree.
Everything you need is to be found in me."
If you want to live well,
make sure you understand all of this.
If you know what's good for you,
you'll learn this inside and out.

(Hosea 14:1–9 MSG)

If you're a follower of Christ, you'll learn this lesson inside and out. Perhaps the hard way. Anyone who takes the risk to redeem a sinful experience will discover that God will provide "everything we need." An incomprehensible healing awaits in the incredibly disturbing experience of either receiving a great forgiveness or granting it. This is the life of grace—the radical grace—that God calls us into when we turn to follow his son in discipleship. This grace is not a feeling, or a sentiment, or a grand ideological philosophy; it's a quality of the heart overflowing in faith and forgiveness—forgiveness received, leading to forgiveness given.

And this is one of the most incredible, scandalous demands that Jesus makes on us: love our neighbors—who happen to be everyone we encounter. And even more—love them the way Jesus loves us. So much that we forgive them over and over and over again, with an endless forgiveness born of an eternal grace.

It was a scandal when Jesus went around forgiving people of their sins. In the theological culture of that time, only God had the authority to forgive sins. So it was considered blasphemy that Jesus would act as God would. And the scandal only deepened in the way Jesus commanded everyone else to forgive each other the same way.

A story in Mark's gospel illustrates the power of God's forgiveness:

> And when he returned to Capernaum after some days, it was reported that he was at home. And many were gathered together, so that there was no more room, not even at the door. And he was preaching the word to them. And they came, bringing to him a paralytic carried by four men. And when they could not get near him because of the crowd, they removed the roof above him, and when they had made an opening, they let down the bed on which the paralytic lay. And when Jesus saw their faith, he said to the paralytic, "My son, your sins are forgiven." Now some of the scribes were sitting there, questioning in their hearts, "Why

> does this man speak like that? He is blaspheming! Who can forgive sins but God alone?" And immediately Jesus, perceiving in his spirit that they thus questioned within themselves, said to them, "Why do you question these things in your hearts? Which is easier, to say to the paralytic, 'Your sins are forgiven,' or to say, 'Rise, take up your bed and walk'? But that you may know that the Son of Man has authority on earth to forgive sins"—he said to the paralytic—"I say to you, rise, pick up your bed, and go home." And he rose and immediately picked up his bed and went out before them all, so that they were all amazed and glorified God, saying, "We never saw anything like this!" (Mark 2:1–12)

What an incredible scene! This is one of my favorite gospel stories. Imagine the audacity of the paralytic's friends in tearing a hole in the roof to get him to Jesus. Their zeal is, in fact, a wonderful, dramatic picture of the lengths Jesus goes to bring healing to us; tearing the roof off the house reminds me very much of the tearing of the veil in the Holy of Holies.[3]

Notice also the close connection between the forgiveness and the healing. Recall how the prophet Hosea vividly connected forgiveness to restoration: the forgiven will have "a fresh start." That's the true power of real forgiveness: healing. Forgiveness is not about going our separate ways; it's not just about clearing the air or letting bygones be bygones. Forgiveness is about the restoration of something—someone!—that is by all indications irreparably broken.

Now, we're very keen on acknowledging our brokenness. We're pretty clear on the idea that we may be messed up. But generally speaking,

3. Matthew 27:51.

we're influenced by a therapeutic culture that maintains, "You're really okay deep down, but you get to this innate wellness by acknowledging that you're dysfunctional." Except the therapeutic process tends to insist that we blame our dysfunction on anyone and everyone but ourselves. Are you screwed up? Well, blame it on your parents or your background or a childhood bully or a learning disability or an addiction. We can't discount these powerful influences on the way we manifest our brokenness. Clearly, powerful forces are at work in how we act out and how we receive affliction from our problems. It's true we grow up with baggage. But that baggage is ours to carry around or leave behind.

That's the difference between the culture's acknowledgment of our "issues" and Christianity's acknowledgment of our brokenness. The culture says, "It's not your fault." Christianity says, "You are a sinner in need of a Savior." That's an offensive claim—even to many Christians.

But we've tried to dodge responsibility from the beginning, haven't we? My religion professor in college, the late, great M. B. Jackson, called this dodge Blame Transference Syndrome, which he said is in our DNA from the time of Adam and Eve.[4] What did Adam say when God called him on his sin? "This woman you gave me! It's her fault!" And what did Eve say when she was called on her sin? "It's the snake's fault! He made me do it."[5]

We're always passing the buck. And this condition of denying our fallenness is part of our fallenness too. We're broken, messed-up people. And we're broken and messed up not simply because of psychosis or "issues" or formative experiences in our childhood—although all those things compound and aggravate our real problem into myriad expressions of brokenness. No—we're broken, messed-up people *pri-*

4. For a theology nerd like me, who missed out on seminary and wasted away in a state university, M. B. Jackson was a dream come true. Princeton trained. White hair. Tweed jacket. Smoked a pipe. Dr. J was the bomb diggity.

5. Genesis 3:11–13.

*marily* because we are sinners. We're sinners not because we live in a sinful world; we live in a sinful world because we're sinners. We have received the sin nature of Adam, and that's why we're messed up. Sin is a cancer in us, a condition of the heart that needs eradication.

But it's not merely that our behavior needs augmentation. It's our hearts. That's why forgiveness brings healing! Forgiveness is not just about inspiration or encouragement, any more than sin is just about behavior. God's forgiveness of us is not just a way of making us feel good, or making us happy, or teaching us some sort of altruistic affection for our fellow man, although his forgiveness can do and, indeed, does all those things. God's forgiveness is about reforming us, mending our brokenness.

If you've experienced a huge forgiveness—either as the receiver or the giver—you know how liberating it can be—for the person giving and the person receiving. Freedom is the glorious aftermath of the radical grace of forgiveness. Grace, though, has built into it an acknowledgement that the sin committed does not deserve forgiveness, but we're getting it anyway.

We're bombarded with a continuous daily onslaught of sensational news stories about violence and mayhem. You likely remember that in October 2006, Charles Carl Roberts IV, gun in hand, walked into a little Amish schoolhouse in Quarryville, Pennsylvania, and murdered five little girls before taking his own life. If you followed the story, your horror over this incomprehensible tragedy was likely complicated by the Amish community's response.

Media outlets strained to play up the religious angle of the story, knowing that even mainstream religious folks in America find the Amish "unique." But what they found in the collective response of the afflicted families was something that both religious and irreligious observers remain puzzled over: forgiveness. As MSNBC reported, "Rita Rhoads, a local nurse and midwife who delivered several children in the Amish community, told NBC's Ann Curry that the mother of a thirteen-year-old girl who died has forgiven Roberts. 'She holds no ill will toward the shooter. She's very forgiving. Christ forgave us, and we in turn forgive, and they honestly have forgiven,' she said. 'Even last night, there was no anger toward the shooter.'"[6]

In 2007, film director Spike Lee's HBO documentary on the Hurricane Katrina disaster garnered a lot of attention. But one of Lee's best movies is another documentary that came out ten years earlier. *Four Little Girls* recalls the 1963 Birmingham church bombing by white supremacists that left four little African American girls dead. Lee revisits the scene, interviews witnesses, including the families of the victims, uses archival footage and old news broadcasts, tries to recapture the cultural climate of the times—the forefront of the civil rights movement. At one point, some of the families speak of having forgiven the murderers. This surprises and confounds Lee, who for the most part does not intrude upon the footage he is shooting. But the idea that these families could forgive the murderers of these little girls just blows him away.

Forgiveness can do that. That's the scandal of grace. The same week of the Amish schoolhouse murders, one of our church's pastors told the story of a mother who'd forgiven the drunk driver who killed her teenage son. Not only had she found her way past the anger and bitterness to forgive the driver, but she and her husband had also pursued the messy work of reconciling a relationship with the man, even though they had no prior relationship with him. Her husband, who was a pastor, even presided over the man's marriage.

Can you imagine that? Essentially adopting the guy responsible for the death of your child? Performing his marriage ceremony? It's outrageous!

---

6. "Pa. school shooter said he'd molested relatives," MSNBC Online, October 3, 2006, http://www.msnbc.msn.com/id/15113706/.

## FORGIVENESS IS JUST PLAIN WEIRD

The world finds Christianity and Christians very weird. They think we're weird for all sorts of reasons, some of them justifiable and some of them not. But may they always find us weird for what was most weird about Jesus—being radical about the incredible, scandalous gift of the grace of God. May we always be found weird for our ability to forgive those considered unforgivable. To do that is irrational, inconceivable, countercultural. And it glorifies God.

Back to Rita Rhoads, the nurse involved with the grief-stricken Amish community. "There's two things that happen to your faith," she said. "Either you let it go and get bitter, or you grow stronger—and we'll grow stronger."

See, not only is forgiveness healing to the forgiven, it's healing to the forgiver. Whenever we embrace grace rather than judgment, whenever we free someone of their debts, we enjoy the same grace and freedom ourselves.

Grace and forgiveness are countercultural because they run counter to the values and ethics of a culture that is as yet untransformed by the kingdom of God. Forgiveness is also unnatural because it runs counter to our sinful nature, which demands that others live up to personal standards that we can't even meet ourselves. Our sinful nature is self-righteous and cannot fathom unmerited favor. Grace can be confusing, bewildering. Even infuriating.

Ben and Ann Wilson (no relation to me) are a married couple who are marriage counselors. They maintain a blog called *Marriages Restored*, which is how I first heard of their incredible story of forgiveness, healing, and restoration.[7]

Ann had an affair, cheating on Ben for a while with another man. Ben had what they call an emotional affair, cheating on Ann with another woman. Today they live and minister as a great witness to the scandal of

7. http://marriages.typepad.com/marriages/.

grace. The following is from Ben and Ann's blog, quoting from an e-mail they received from a reader:

> Ben, Your marriage is not restored. Once your wife cheated on you, you have no marriage. It's over. It is a terrible thing to continue the charade. Turn her ou[t] and get a decent woman who will be faithful. You are just fooling yourself and playing a dishonest game. She is no good and deserves the worst. You are acting like a fool. The Almighty has a decent woman out there for you. Just have the courage to look.[8]

My own initial response to this message is, "Why is it your business, angry man, what these folks choose to do in glorifying God in their marriage?" How ridiculous it is—and how weird—that God's powerful work of forgiveness and healing in the Wilson's marriage would spark such a hateful response.

This is from Ben's reply:

> I had not received an e-mail like this before. It just makes me shake my head and wonder what gospel he knows. . . . This Kingdom Journey is not all about me. I do not claim to have the perseverance of Hosea. But I know something of his walk. If I thought only of what brought me the least pain in the moment, I would have sent [Ann] out. I would have missed out on what God really means for marriage. I would not know the joy that he has set for us in this life between husband and wife. Suffering really

---

8. Ben Wilson, "My Response to an Ugly Email or My Wife Is a Beautiful Glorious Woman," blog, August 13, 2004; www.marriages.typepad.com/marriages/ 2004/08/ grafted_in_to_t.html.

> does produce perseverance, and perseverance really does produce character, and character really does produce hope. Hope in Him. I walked with the bride of my youth through The Valley and we both entered into His Hope.
>
> My Lord and Savior did not send women out. He castigated the men who thought themselves worthy of doing so. He chastised the ones who said, "Thank God I am not like the sinner." He treated the hearts of women like treasures of great value instead of viewing women as a mere possession.
>
> Jesus encountered the adulterous woman. . . . And then he offered her great words of hope. He conveyed to her that she was not her worst behavior. She was more than a woman who slept around. She could leave that life of sin and be more.
>
> My Ann is more. . . . The pain of her sin has been used by God to make her even more beautiful and glorious. It is Father's great gift to me that I am permitted to be her husband.

Ben Wilson is a guy who gets the scandal of grace, the outright *offense* that the life of grace is. Where the angry, ignorant e-mailer sees only the sin, Ben sees a gift. "It is Father's great gift to me that I am permitted to be her husband." That is such an inconceivable reversal of perspective.

Please notice how that perspective began. It was informed to a great extent by Ben's copping to his own sins. He writes earlier in the blog,

> I, too, deserved to be turned out. I was let into this party undeserved myself. I was a drunk. I missed my son's first birthday getting drunk at a golf course. I blasphemed. I didn't provide for my family. I lived a

> coward's life *then*. I could fill up an entire blog of why I do not deserve this gracious love of Father.

The spirit of Christian forgiveness is not "I forgive you because I'm a nice person," but, "I forgive you because I know I desperately need forgiveness myself." We forgive *as* we have been forgiven.[9] I forgive your sin because God has forgiven mine.

Look . . . there may be big and little sins when it comes to the pain they inflict on people in our lives, or in the consequences they bring, but we're all in the same boat when it comes to sin. There are no big and little sins in the scope of eternity. We all pop out of our mommies on equal footing when it comes to sin, and we all shuffle off this earth deserving the exact same thing, regardless of what we've done or not done.

The spirit of forgiveness is proclaimed in the Lord's Prayer itself: It doesn't say, "Forgive us because we have forgiven," as if God forgives us based on our works. No—it says "Forgive us our debts, as we also have forgiven our debtors." It suggests a dynamic relationship between the two forgivenesses, a connection just like the link between "love the Lord your God" and "love your neighbor as yourself" in the Great Commandment. This flow of forgiveness is a quality of the heart. A heart that has experienced the forgiveness of God ought to be overflowing with forgiveness for others.

How arrogant would it be not to forgive others? How sinful would it be to be stingy with grace, to selfishly hoard God's grace? Withholding grace from others certainly wouldn't demonstrate that we've been changed by it ourselves.

God became incarnate in the man Jesus Christ, who is the embodiment of forgiveness. God, in his great love for us, wanted to forgive our irreparable offense to his holiness, so he came himself in the person of Jesus to work this miracle of forgiveness. Have you heard the phrase "grace has

9. Matthew 6:12.

a face"? That's the active work of the incarnation of Christ, and the task of incarnational ministry for those who follow Christ: to put a face on grace.

Let's define grace again—love and forgiveness given by God to those who don't deserve it—and then let's talk about how grace should play out in the lives of those who claim to follow Jesus.

## WE ARE TO FORGIVE BECAUSE WE HAVE BEEN FORGIVEN

No other reason is necessary. We must forgive because God has forgiven us and because God commands it. It shouldn't depend on how we expect the other person to respond or whether or not he or she is repentant. From time to time you'll hear someone teach that you can't forgive an unrepentant person. That's just not true.

There's a difference between forgiveness and reconciliation. Reconciliation is a two-way street that requires the person who has sinned to be repentant and the person who was sinned against to be forgiving. When these two parties come together, work out their differences, and restore their relationship, that's reconciliation. But a sinner can be repentant without being forgiven by the other person. This happens all the time. And we can always forgive someone who has sinned against us, even if that person isn't sorry or repentant for what they've done. And we can forgive someone, even if he or she doesn't know about it. Certainly the Amish families who forgave Charles Roberts couldn't expect repentance from him, because he'd already taken his own life.

Please note the differences between these two states—forgiveness and reconciliation—because the confusion of them has been cause for some to justify their unwillingness to forgive or repent. Forgiveness and repentance are attitudes and actions done by individuals; reconciliation requires two willing hearts. But one willing heart can forgive, and if you're a Christian, your heart should forgive, whether the other person has repented or not.

Just to hammer this point in more strongly, the moment you make your granting of forgiveness contingent on another person's attitude or worthiness, you're slapping God in the face. Again, this is why: *you yourself are not* worthy *of God's forgiveness.* You can never deserve it. You aren't good enough or smart enough—and doggone it, God didn't grant you forgiveness because you're likeable. He did it because he loves you and because grace is the way he shows it.

So forgive others because you've been forgiven, regardless of the condition or attitude of the person you're forgiving. We love, not because everyone's so lovable, but because God first loved us.[10]

## WE ARE TO FORGIVE *AS* WE HAVE BEEN FORGIVEN

When the Bible says that we are to forgive *as* we have been forgiven, it means we are to forgive endlessly, relentlessly, and patiently.

Remember when Peter came to Jesus and wondered, "Hey, when can I stop forgiving? After seven times?"[11]

Jesus said, "No, after seventy times seven," which doesn't mean 490 so much as it means we don't stop. The grace we've been given by the sacrifice of Jesus Christ is a payment that covers an infinite debt. It's good for sins past, present, and future. And this is why forgiveness is not just a specific act, granted at specific times. It's a quality of the heart, a condition and attitude and way of life. When do we stop forgiving? We don't. We keep forgiving—as often as needed. We just keep doing it.

Does this mean we let abusive people continue to abuse us? No. Does this mean we make ourselves doormats? No. But it does mean we give up the option for vengeance, that we relinquish the spiritual power that unforgiveness can have over us. We don't have to always maintain a sinful relationship *as is*, but we're to bring a radical forgiveness to our

10. 1 John 4:19.
11. Matthew 18:21–22.

relationships, in the trust and hope that God will work healing and restoration through our efforts.

We are to keep forgiving, and keep persevering in grace, because that is God's commitment to us.

This is what Paul says about relentless forgiveness:

> Put on then, as God's chosen ones, holy and beloved, compassionate hearts, kindness, humility, meekness, and patience, bearing with one another and, if one has a complaint against another, forgiving each other; as the Lord has forgiven you, so you also must forgive. And above all these put on love, which binds everything together in perfect harmony. And let the peace of Christ rule in your hearts, to which indeed you were called in one body. And be thankful. (Col. 3:12–15)

Look at all that's tied up in how we are to live with one another: compassion, kindness, humility, meekness, and patience. This is the peace of Christ *ruling* in our hearts. This is the call of the gospel to life in Christ—bearing with each other, forgiving each other, granting grace to everyone. And thanking God through everything. This is how Jesus the Forgiver continues to reign in the body of Christ, his church: by our being the face of grace to each other and to an unbelieving world.

Maybe you're having trouble with this. You wonder why you can't forgive, why it's been so hard to let something go. It may be that you have yet to really contemplate and embrace how Jesus has forgiven you. Jesus the Forgiver stands before you, having died to cover your sins, and he offers you forgiveness. You can't earn it—but that's not why he's offering. You can be restored, reconciled to God, by turning (repenting) to embrace this forgiveness. Remember that reconciliation is a two-way street. Christ has done the work; embrace it.

Maybe you're having trouble with forgiveness because you're in desperate need of it from someone, and though you're truly repentant, the person has not forgiven you. Don't lose hope. Don't give up. God honors repentance, even when other people do not.

Maybe you're having trouble with forgiveness because you've been badly burned by someone. Someone has abused you, offended you, cheated on you, or wronged you in some way. Maybe there's a huge chasm between you and someone you love (or want to love). You understand intellectually that you ought to forgive, but the idea is so painful because of what this person has done to you. Your spirit is willing but your flesh is weak. You may have thought at some point while reading this chapter, *That's easy for you to say. You don't know what I've been through.*

You're right; I probably don't know what you've been through. But that emotion you're feeling right now, that weight, that discomfort you feel when you ponder the gravity of forgiving such huge wrongs against you, is a taste of the scandal of grace.

I'm not sure I can even express this strongly enough: grace is scandalous. It's unbelievable. It's weird. It's nonsensical. It disturbs us and confuses us. It burns.

But it heals.

It's difficult. It's messy. The scandal of grace is that it took the death of Christ to flesh out forgiveness for us. And that's why it takes our dying to ourselves to flesh out our forgiveness for others.

Jesus the Forgiver came into this world to bring the kingdom of God—an upside-down, backward counterculture that blew people's minds as it reformed their souls and revolutionized their spirits. It scandalized them—and that's how we are to live and experience and proclaim the presence today of the kingdom of God in our lives and in our world: by forgiving and forgiving and forgiving, and thereby creating a shocking scandal in a world predicated on and committed to "an eye for an eye."

# 4

# JESUS THE MAN

If you've ever been through a time of deep despair or depression, ever wrestled with doubt or sin or abuse, grieved or mourned a loss, pondered life's deepest mysteries and complexities—and happen to be a reader of the Bible—chances are you've found yourself in the book of Psalms. This big book of songs contains not just an endless tribute to the glory of God, and an exhaustive catalogue of heartfelt praise, it also reflects the warp and woof of the human condition. In poetic form, David and the other psalmists reflect on and illuminate what it means to be alive. They capture vividly the nature and the travails of humanity in the darkness of the world's corruption and in the light of God's wisdom.[1]

David had a lot to lament. He was the king of Israel, but this was not a title he could maintain with clean hands. You probably know his backstory. He was a liar, an adulterer, a murderer.[2] He failed to execute justice when his son Amnon raped his daughter Tamar.[3] And aside from the burden of his own sins, he was frequently on the run for his

1. This means that the psalmists were sort of like the first bloggers, and David was the first emo kid.

2. 2 Samuel 11.

3. 2 Samuel 13:1–21.

life. Many times, when he didn't feel like a man wanted dead, he felt like a man who was dead already. Check out Psalm 38, for instance, and get ready to call the waaaaambulance.

David, without question, was a man with unclean hands and an impure heart. With this in mind, let's read a portion of one of his songs:

> The earth is the LORD's and the fullness thereof,
> the world and those who dwell therein,
> for he has founded it upon the seas
> and established it upon the rivers.
>
> Who shall ascend the hill of the LORD?
> And who shall stand in his holy place?
> He who has clean hands and a pure heart,
> who does not lift up his soul to what is false
> and does not swear deceitfully.
> He will receive blessing from the LORD
> and righteousness from the God of his salvation.
> Such is the generation of those who seek him,
> who seek the face of the God of Jacob.
>
> (Ps. 24:1–6)

In this passage, we find a summary of what it means to be a godly man. This is what godly humanity looks like. This is David—corrupted, afflicted, persecuted David—encapsulating the human ideal. Who will go to the place where God is? Those with clean hands and a pure heart.

Do you fit that description? How about this: Have you ever lived according to a falsehood or made promises you didn't keep? Are you innocent of these things? If you said yes, you're automatically guilty, because anyone who says they've never lived according to a falsehood is a liar. Gotcha.

David is saying, "The one who will receive God's favor is the one who is perfect." David himself was far from perfect. Yet God called him a man after his own heart.[4] How is this possible? How is it possible that we—who, like David, fail every day to live up to this ideal of holiness and perfection—can still be considered within God's realm of bestowed perfection and holiness?

The answer is the one human being who fulfilled the ideal of holiness perfectly. Only one man in the history of mankind ever had clean hands and a pure heart and never lifted up his soul to falsehood and never lied and perfectly sought the Lord. That man is Jesus. And in this portion of our survey, we'll consider Jesus the Man.

It's important to talk about Jesus the Man, to talk about Jesus *as* man these days, because we who believe in the tenets of the Christian faith live in a tension of competing cultural ideologies about Jesus' humanity. On the one hand, the world would have us believe that Jesus was *just* a man. They would deny his deity and yet have us believe that Jesus was a good teacher, perhaps enlightened in some sense, certainly an idealist and revolutionary, and a *good* man, but still just a man. So, on the one hand, we're trying to counter the rationalists and the skeptics, arguing that Jesus was more than just a good man, and on the other hand, we're trying to maintain his humanity.[5]

In the culture of the fundamentalist/evangelical church, though, we're frequently uncomfortable with the notion of Jesus as man. We like the bit about his loving women and children. And we like the whole carpenter thing—"salt of the earth" and all that. But we try not to wade too deeply into his human condition. Watch any seriously religious person's face if you ever want to bring up the fact that on occasion Jesus used the restroom. Or

4. Acts 13:22.

5. Arguing that Jesus was a "good man" is odd, considering that anyone who went around suggesting that he was God and that people ought to die for him would probably not be considered all that good by those who disbelieved him.

had hormones that might have caused acne, back hair, the changes in the onset of puberty. As a real man, Jesus was attracted to women sexually.

Maybe you're feeling a skosh angry right now. If so, why? These things are part of being human, a part of man's biological being.

What we tend to see in some institutional church circles these days is actually a reflection of something the young church had to fight very early on. At one time, the early Christians had to battle the notion that Jesus wasn't really human. An insidious strain of early heresy, birthed from the Gnostics, is a belief called Docetism, which holds that Jesus only *appeared* to be a man. Docetists believe Jesus' humanity was merely an illusion because, logically speaking and seemingly quite obvious to the Docetists, God cannot be a human. They reasoned that because physical flesh is temporary and inherently frail and sinful, as the Gnostics believed, God could not inhabit it literally. The doctrine of the incarnation was a colossal bummer to these guys, and they consequently rejected the notion that Jesus Christ was both fully God and fully (really) man. Of course, the early church had to tell the Docetists not to let the door hit 'em in their frail and sinful keisters on the way out.

Look at John's strong words about this movement's burgeoning theological infiltration of the church's thinking:

> By this you know the Spirit of God: every spirit that confesses that Jesus Christ has come in the flesh is from God, and every spirit that does not confess Jesus is not from God. This is the spirit of the antichrist, which you heard was coming and now is in the world already. (1 John 4:2–3)

John says that denying that Jesus Christ was really, literally man is "of the antichrist." To be *pro*-Christ, then, is to accept and admit that God really did incarnate himself in actual flesh and bone.

Still, the discomfort remains. When pastor Mark Driscoll of Mars Hill Church in Seattle preached on the humanity of Jesus in his 2006 sermon series "Vintage Jesus," his efforts at illuminating the earthier aspects of what it meant for Jesus to be human got him kicked around in some corners of the Christian press for being "irreverent."[6] It's all well and good to admit that Jesus was really a man, but in the church you must hover at the surface of that admission or wind up making people angry.

I don't enjoy making people angry,[7] so I'm not going to cover Jesus' sexuality or anything, but I am unapologetically going to cover the biblical implications of what it means to know Jesus as Man. What was his story, and what sort of man was he?

## JESUS: A BRIEF BIOGRAPHY

We'll begin with a brief overview of the man known as Jesus of Nazareth—brief because you probably already know the story. We get our information from the four biblical gospels, but mainly the so-called Synoptic Gospels—Matthew, Mark, and Luke.[8] John's gospel, which is historically true, defies precise classification, and its surreal style reads like you should be playing the Grateful Dead or Strawberry Alarm Clock while reading it. In any event, the three synoptic gospels give us a more direct narrative of the scope of Jesus' life. Matthew and Luke give us glimpses of the beginning of it, while Mark's story skips

---

6. Well, kinda. To be accurate, Driscoll mostly got kicked around by the Pajamahadeen in the blogosphere. The "Vintage Jesus" series has now been adapted into a book: Mark Driscoll and Gerry Breshears, *Vintage Jesus: Timeless Answers to Timely Questions* (Wheaton, IL: Crossway, 2007).

7. Okay, sometimes I do enjoy making people angry. I admit I get a cheap thrill out of asking telemarketers for their home phone numbers so I can call them back at my convenience.

8. The prefix *syn*, as in the word *synonymous*, basically means "same" or "similar." *Optic* refers, of course, to the eye. So *synoptic* basically means "to see from the same or a similar perspective."

right ahead, begins with the action, and just sort of plows through more action at breakneck speed. Mark's story is like the *Die Hard* of the Gospels.[9]

A synthesis of Matthew's account with Luke's tells us that a woman named Mary was engaged to a man named Joseph when she became pregnant. The Gospels tell us (and orthodox Christians believe) that this pregnancy was miraculous, that the baby was conceived in Mary's womb by the Holy Spirit. Joseph, knowing that "It's a miracle!" doesn't really fly—then or now—considered "dismissing" Mary for the sake of her reputation. He obviously changed his mind because, we're told, he was visited by an angel, who told him that Mary wasn't cheating on him.

The Gospels call Mary a virgin, and primarily from this information we get the doctrine of the virgin birth. This miraculous phenomenon is in fulfillment of a prophecy in Isaiah 7. Many scholars today will (correctly) point out that the Hebrew word for *virgin* in Isaiah 7, *'almah*, may simply mean "young woman" or "young girl of marriageable age." But Matthew's gospel makes it a point to say flat out that Joseph and Mary did not have marital relations—that's sex, for all who are playing at home—until after she gave birth to Jesus, which was after they were married.[10] So regardless of what the word *virgin* usually means in the original language, Matthew, at least, expands it to say that Mary was a virgin in the sense that she had not had sexual intercourse.[11]

So Joseph married Mary, and Luke's gospel tells us that they had to go to Bethlehem to register for a census. While they were there, Jesus was born in the stables—which might have actually been more like a

---

9. Angry yet?

10. Matthew 1:25.

11. See Craig L. Blomberg, *Jesus and the Gospels* (Nashville: Broadman and Holman, 1997), 200. Also, C. Stephen Evans, *The Historical Christ and the Jesus of Faith* (Oxford: Clarendon, 1996), 152. Evans even helpfully and persuasively connects the "rationale" of the Spirit's conception of Jesus in the virgin womb to the pretext of God's creation of the world *ex nihilo*.

cave or a courtyard, depending on which history scholar you listen to. I like the stable story because it keeps me from having to buy a new nativity scene, and it also allows me to tell the following joke: From then on, after Jesus grew up and left doors open, smart-alecky relatives asked, "Hey, were you born in a barn?" He answered, "Why, yes I was, thanks for asking." (Even if Jesus did leave doors open, he probably always remembered to say "please" and "thank you.")

Jesus was born in Bethlehem, and though we don't really know how long the family stayed there, it might have been a couple of years by the time the Magi show up. The head honcho of the region, Herod, was paranoid because the riffraff were saying a new king had been born, so he sent out the goon squad to kill kids two years old and under in the Bethlehem area. Before this happened, however, Joseph took his family into Egypt for a brief time to escape the danger.

Eventually, Herod died, the danger passed, and Joseph brought Mary and Jesus back into Israel. They settled in the land of Galilee, in a town called Nazareth. Depending on how you interpret the composite history of Matthew and Luke, Nazareth may have been where Joseph and Mary were originally from.

After the family returned from Egypt, we're told practically nothing about Jesus' childhood. Luke does give us one story about Joseph taking his family to Jerusalem for the Passover, when Jesus was about twelve years old. Jesus wandered off (like any sixth grader, he had his reasons), leaving Joseph and Mary to have one of those panicky parent moments when they quite naturally freaked out at suddenly realizing their kid had disappeared.

If you're a parent, you can really identify with this. It's the worst feeling in the world, isn't it? It happened to me once when I was with my two little girls at a crowded public pool. I looked down for what felt like merely a second, looked back up, and my youngest was nowhere to be seen. It's a horrible sensation, especially at a place like a public pool.

When I was a kid, I wandered off from my mom at a flea market just a short walk from the Mexican border. She found me hiding under a clothes rack. I didn't register her panic then, but I totally sympathize with her now.

For most of us, when we finally locate our kids, they're in the toy aisle of the store eating their boogers or something. Jesus turned up (four days later, by the way!) in the temple, where he was talking to the religious teachers and asking questions. When his parents found him, they were all like, "We've been worried sick!" And Jesus was like, "Didn't you know I'd be in my Father's house?" And we're all like, "Whoa. Did Jesus just tell his parents to step off?" Oh no he didn't!

Kids, do not try this at home. It worked for Jesus, because he's Jesus. The old, "Didn't you know I'd be looking at the Hot Wheels and eating my boogers?" doesn't work quite as well.

After this, Luke tells us that Jesus grew in wisdom and stature. Basically, he grew up. And then we don't get much until he's about thirty years old and begins his public ministry.

This biographical gap, by the way, should not inspire skepticism about the Gospels' historical accuracy or reliability. Though it's beyond the scope of this book to defend the historicity of the Gospels, I will just mention that, *as a genre*, the Gospels are unique in that they are unabashedly biased propaganda that nonetheless purports to honestly reflect historical events. I do not mean "propaganda" in a pejorative sense. I just mean that they are stories told from singular perspectives, with some facts left out and some facts included for various reasons—like the intended audience, the personalities of the authors or compilers, or the theological or referential points the authors are trying to highlight in specific scenes. One thing all four gospels have in common with other ancient biographies of the time is the virtual ignoring of a subject's childhood. In other ancient biographies of significant persons, we get a birth story and then—boom!—The Adventures of Grown-up

So-and-So.[12] In this respect, the Gospels are not unique in their exclusion of their protagonist's childhood. In his book *Four Gospels, One Jesus?* Richard Burridge writes,

> While Mark's Jesus bounds on to the stage fully grown, Matthew makes his account more like ancient biographies by providing some information about Jesus' ancestry, origin, and birth. Ancient lives often included these topics, before jumping ahead to the subject's arrival on the public scene, although this was usually done briefly, rather than the full treatment we expect in modern biography.[13]

And though we'd love to know more about Jesus as a child, the gospel writers were more interested in telling us about the powerful and redemptive work of his adult ministry than in satisfying our curiosity about his childhood. The modern imaginative insistence—that the church excised from the Gospels and then concealed whatever happened in Jesus' adolescence—is not only fanciful, it is also anachronistic—it assumes the Gospels must adhere to the forms and conventions of modern biographies.

What did Jesus do in his twenties? It's hard to say—again, because the Gospels don't tell us. Many readers infer that he was a carpenter, although the two texts that refer to this occupation could be interpreted

---

12. See, for instance, the discussion in *Four Gospels, One Jesus?* by Richard Burridge (Grand Rapids: Eerdmans, 1994). On the similarities between the Gospels and the content of Greco-Roman biographies, Burridge writes that both "begin with a brief mention of the hero's ancestry, family, or city, followed by his birth and an occasional anecdote about his upbringing; usually we move rapidly on to his public debut later in life" (7).

13. Ibid., 67.

to mean merely that he was a carpenter's son.[14] Only Mark's gospel, in fact, appears to identify Jesus as a carpenter, but in the context of quoting remarks made by people who'd heard Jesus teach in the synagogue. They could have been mistaken, having made an assumption based on knowing Joseph's trade.

So we can't state with certainty that Jesus was a carpenter, though it could be likely, given that it was common for boys to follow in their father's trade. It's also likely, however, that Jesus trained as a rabbi. There's actually more inferential evidence for this in the texts, given that Jesus is constantly addressed as "Teacher," even early in his ministry and by people he doesn't know. But whether carpenter or rabbi—or some kind of super-awesome carpenter-rabbi—he was a hometown son of Nazareth.

Jesus likely lost his father at a young age, because even as Mary reappears throughout his later ministry, we don't hear about Joseph again. As the eldest of the children—and the Gospels do indicate at various points that Jesus had siblings[15] (one of whom, James, later became a church leader in Jerusalem and wrote the New Testament epistle bearing his name)—Jesus would have been charged with taking care of his mother. At his death on the cross, he even passed the baton of caring for his mother to John the apostle.[16] There would have been no need to do this if Joseph were still living, and indeed, John takes Mary into his home to live thereafter. Mary's widowhood would partially explain Jesus' close relationship with her throughout the gospel stories. The other explanation for maintaining such a close, sweet relationship with his mother is just that he was a perfect son.

There is not much else we know about Jesus' private life. There has been some speculation throughout history—which has enjoyed

14. Matthew 13:55 and Mark 6:3.
15. See Mark 6:3.
16. John 19:26–27.

a return to fashion today thanks to speculative fictions such as Dan Brown's runaway hit *The DaVinci Code*—that Jesus might have married during this time and perhaps even had kids.[17] I don't say that it would be wrong or irreverent to suggest that Jesus had been married, because if I did say that, it would reflect that sort of Docetist tendency to deny the reality of Jesus' humanity. I don't see any theological problems with Jesus the Man marrying and raising a family, and if he had, he would have been prepared both emotionally and spiritually to be the greatest husband and father in the history of the world. There would be, in fact, some value in this being true, as it would provide a great example and inspiration for Christian marriages and families from the very life of Christ himself.

Historically and logically speaking, though, Jesus' being married is highly unlikely. Historical orthodoxy believes it didn't happen because the Gospels don't record a marriage and family. No references to either are made anywhere else in the New Testament. This is not an insignificant point. The Gospels don't shy away from Jesus' saying uncomfortable things and doing provocative things. Marriage and family, however, would not have been provocative, and as a significant part of Jesus' life, certainly worthy of mention. Don't believe for a minute, then, the modern claims that the church would want to cover up this information. That doesn't make sense; it doesn't hold up. And even if, for some odd reason, they had wanted to, the early church was not nearly organized or powerful enough to conceal something like this. No evidence has yet appeared to say that Jesus was married. It's just a fashionable speculation.

Affirmers of biblical orthodoxy don't think Jesus was married

---

17. Dear readers, in addition to being historically and theologically bankrupt, *The DaVinci Code* is just terribly written. How can you read that stuff? Honestly, has there ever been a work of literature less deserving of best-seller status? (Well, some Christian apocalyptic novels come to mind . . . Angry yet?)

because he knew from early on that he needed to take care of his mother, and he knew he was on a mission from God that would end his earthly tenure at a relatively young age. So, we say Jesus wasn't married because, wow, what an awful husband and father he would have been to have abandoned his family to go off traveling with twelve guys, heading into his own death, later ascending into heaven.[18] Perfect men don't abandon their families. Being responsible would mean not willingly and knowingly leaving a widow and orphans behind. It just wouldn't make sense.

Additionally, most of the proponents of the conspiracy theory about Jesus' family, when they do refer to historical sources, derive their conclusions from highly questionable artifacts, documents both extrabiblical and *un*biblical. What is odd, ironic even, is that the persons making these claims mean to establish a more earthy Jesus, a Jesus more "like us," yet the historical sources they most often draw from (like the so-called Gospel of Judas or the popular Gospel of Thomas) are Gnostic in origin, featuring the disembodied dialogue of an ethereal, mystic, un-earthy Jesus.[19] While the incarnation is the very truth of God inhabiting the "like us," those who want to make Jesus merely "like us," marrying him off and having him die of old age, draw their evidence from books starring no more than a Fortune Cookie Jesus.[20]

The canonical gospels of Matthew, Mark, Luke, and John are still the most reliable sources for how Jesus lived his life and how his earthly life ended up. That these documents—which have served the church

---

18. I do not think it's theologically insignificant that those most intent on denying Jesus' lifelong bachelorhood also seem most intent on denying his resurrection and ascension. Both views reveal a distrust of Scripture.

19. The Gospel of Judas, which was not newly discovered, has enjoyed a renewed interest of late. See N. T. Wright, *Judas and the Gospel of Jesus: Have We Missed the Truth About Christianity?* (Grand Rapids: Baker, 2006).

20. On the reliance of alternative histories of Jesus on unreliable texts, see Ben Witherington III, *The Gospel Code* (Downers Grove, IL: InterVarsity, 2004).

and the world quite well for centuries and have held up to relentless scrutiny—continually suffer relegation to the backseat of popular historical inquiry prompts N. T. Wright to cheekily charge, "One sometimes gets the impression that anything will do, in this strangely mixed set of bedfellows, as long as it is nothing like orthodoxy."[21]

To sum up, it's not necessarily that Jesus *couldn't* have been married and had kids; it's that he *didn't*, because it doesn't make historical and logical sense.

When Jesus hit thirty, he began his public ministry. Mary sort of outed him at a party with that whole water-to-wine thing, and then he went into the wilderness and took over his cousin John's ministry. After that, he spent roughly three years preaching about the kingdom of God, with himself at the center as the finally arrived Messiah-King. This ended, as all attempted messianic revolutions did back then, with the self-proclaimed Messiah's execution. And then, if you believe the Gospels and if you call yourself a Christian, you believe Jesus literally rose from the dead three days later, spent some more time with his followers, and then went back home to be with his real Daddy.

As far as a Jesus biography, then, we have, really, only three years to work with. These three years, though, take up a lot of pages in the Gospels—pages of sayings and scenes by which we are able to answer the pressing question, "What sort of man was Jesus?"

Answering that pressing question is what we now turn our attention to. We know his story, sort of. We acknowledge, as good pro-Christs (not antichrists), that Jesus really did come in the flesh. Now let's ask ourselves, *Given that Jesus was a man, what sort of man was he?*

Despite the limited sources, our answers could be quite lengthy, but I'll focus on four characteristics of Jesus' humanity that are as important as they are misunderstood or ignored.

---

21. N. T. Wright, *Jesus and the Victory of God* (Minneapolis: Fortress, 1996), 74.

## JESUS WAS A HUMBLE MAN

Most of us know that Jesus was humble. This is not a characteristic of his that gets left out of the discussion. But the unique quality of Jesus' humility is, I think, frequently unexplored, and I wish to touch on it here.

Humility in the "Jesus sense" does not necessarily mean, as it does typically for us, modesty or lack of self-interest. Certainly, Jesus said some pretty provocative things about himself:

- "I am the way, the truth, and the life."
- "If I give you water, you won't thirst ever again."
- "Come to me everyone who is weary, and I will give you rest."
- "Knock me down, I dare you, and I will rebuild again in three days."

In any other mouth, these would not be modest words.

Jesus wasn't humble in the sense that he never put himself at the center of the world or claimed special status. No . . . Jesus' teaching, in fact, demanded that everyone arrange their orbits around him. He constantly reinterpreted Israel's dearly held beliefs and rigorously followed traditions in light of himself. So Jesus' humility wasn't about removing himself from the salvation equation. It was about *emptying.* About giving. About relentlessly serving. About the power of radical grace.

> Christ Jesus . . . being in very nature God,
> did not consider equality with God something to be grasped,
> but made himself nothing,
> taking the very nature of a servant,
> being made in human likeness.
> And being found in appearance as a man,

> he humbled himself
> and became obedient to death—
> even death on a cross!
> Therefore God exalted him to the highest place
> and gave him the name that is above every name,
> that at the name of Jesus every knee should bow,
> in heaven and on earth and under the earth,
> and every tongue confess that Jesus Christ is Lord,
> to the glory of God the Father.
>
> (Phil. 2:5–11 NIV)[22]

We know from this beautiful poem in Philippians 2 that, for Jesus, humility meant not exploiting his God-ness. He relinquished the rights and honors of his deity to experience and redeem what it means to be human. In Matthew 21:5, he says, "Behold, your king is coming to you, humble, and mounted on a donkey." We see him washing his disciples' feet. We see him suffering the betrayal of friends and submitting to the religious and political authorities.

Jesus was a humble man in the sense that humility meant giving up fleshly controls. He was an endless giver of himself.

## JESUS WAS A BRILLIANT MAN

Here is something we tend to overlook or fail to invest in—if we even consider it: Jesus, being God in the flesh, was the smartest man who ever lived. Does Jesus ever show up on anybody's list of the greatest thinkers of history? Greatest gurus, perhaps. Sages, maybe. The world may think him wise in some Confucian sense. We think of him as an idealist, as an enlightened man, as a revolutionary. But generally speaking, we also tend to regard him as naive or simple. We tend to

22. This chorus was possibly a hymn sung by the early church.

think, as Friedrich Nietzsche once said, "If he had lived to my age he would have repudiated his doctrine."[23]

The world does not regard Jesus as savvy or practical and, if we're honest with ourselves, neither do we in the church. I think that our frequent failure to obey his commands stems essentially from a practical disbelief that he could really be right about how we ought to think and act. But if we really believe that Jesus is who he said he is, we know we have recorded in Scripture—and available at our convenience—the greatest human mind of all time.

How vast is the wisdom of Jesus? As vast as the resources of almighty God. Revisit this extended passage from Luke's gospel and remind yourself how all-encompassing Jesus' knowledge is—and how all-illuminating our knowledge of Jesus can be:

> That very day two of them were going to a village named Emmaus, about seven miles from Jerusalem, and they were talking with each other about all these things that had happened. While they were talking and discussing together, Jesus himself drew near and went with them. But their eyes were kept from recognizing him. And he said to them, "What is this conversation that you are holding with each other as you walk?" And they stood still, looking sad. Then one of them, named Cleopas, answered him, "Are you the only visitor to Jerusalem who does not know the things that have happened there in these days?" And he said to them, "What things?" And they said to him, "Concerning

23. Nietzsche considered the ethic (i.e., set of moral principles) of the Sermon on the Mount wholly impractical, which of course it is; but let's not forget that it is an ethic (i.e., guiding philosophy) of earthly kingdoms that are in opposition to the kingdom of God that they equate *practical* with "useful" or "right."

Jesus of Nazareth, a man who was a prophet mighty in deed and word before God and all the people, and how our chief priests and rulers delivered him up to be condemned to death, and crucified him. But we had hoped that he was the one to redeem Israel. Yes, and besides all this, it is now the third day since these things happened. Moreover, some women of our company amazed us. They were at the tomb early in the morning, and when they did not find his body, they came back saying that they had even seen a vision of angels, who said that he was alive. Some of those who were with us went to the tomb and found it just as the women had said, but him they did not see." And he said to them, "O foolish ones, and slow of heart to believe all that the prophets have spoken! Was it not necessary that the Christ should suffer these things and enter into his glory?" And beginning with Moses and all the Prophets, he interpreted to them in all the Scriptures the things concerning himself.

So they drew near to the village to which they were going. He acted as if he were going farther, but they urged him strongly, saying, "Stay with us, for it is toward evening and the day is now far spent." So he went in to stay with them. When he was at table with them, he took the bread and blessed and broke it and gave it to them. And their eyes were opened, and they recognized him. And he vanished from their sight. They said to each other, "Did not our hearts burn within us while he talked to us on the road, while he opened to us the Scriptures?" And they rose that same hour and returned to Jerusalem. And they found the

> eleven and those who were with them gathered together, saying, "The Lord has risen indeed, and has appeared to Simon!" Then they told what had happened on the road, and how he was known to them in the breaking of the bread. (Luke 24:13–35)

Jesus sidled up to these guys and basically revealed himself to them in the Bible. He illuminated Scripture to them. He answered their questions in such a fulfilling way that their hearts *burned* within them.

When Jesus imparts his knowledge to us, it's not just head knowledge; rather, it's a godly wisdom of the sort that should be our constant resource and inspiration and guide through all of life. In the Sermon on the Mount, Jesus is giving us not just a list of things to do, but an invitation to real life as Holy Spirit–enlightened people. His commands are not simply calls to right behavior, but calls to embrace a quality of the heart that leads to a pattern of life that burns with real knowledge from God. We call this real knowledge *truth.*

Jesus was absolutely brilliant, and yet we don't refer to or access that brilliance with much regularity, do we? We tend to make our own decisions, utilize our own reason, and then ask God to okay it, confirm it, bless it.

Dallas Willard, a philosophy professor at the University of Southern California, spends much of his time writing and teaching about Jesus the Thinker. Willard himself is a phenomenal Christian writer and thinker, having written two of the best books on the Christian life in the last twenty years, *Renovation of the Heart* and *The Divine Conspiracy.*[24] In *The Divine Conspiracy*, winner of *Christianity Today*'s Book of the Year Award in 1999, Willard writes,

24. You can read more about and from Dallas Willard at www.dwillard.org. Seriously, this dude has mad brain skills, yo.

> The world has succeeded in opposing intelligence to goodness. . . . And today any attempt to combine spirituality or moral purity with great intelligence causes widespread pangs of "cognitive dissonance." Mother Teresa, no more than Jesus, is [not] thought of as smart—nice, of course, but not really *smart*. "Smart" means good at managing how life "really" is.[25]

We Christians are great at compartmentalizing our lives. We believe that Jesus' knowledge is for our "spiritual lives," but that our everyday lives require a more modern knowledge, a more *realistic* knowledge. Street smarts, perhaps.

The same error is committed whenever Christians deny the importance of the intellectual life altogether, as quite a few do. Some in the church today believe and teach as modern subscribers to Tertullian's famous query: "What has Jerusalem to do with Athens, the Church with the Academy, the Christian with the heretic?"[26] In Tertullian's view, the Christian life is over here, and the intellectual life is over there, and never the twain shall meet. I would argue that anytime a Christian denies the importance of reading, learning, and studying—anytime one denigrates the importance of intellectual pursuit—one is, practically speaking, denying the incarnation. This is not to say that every Christian should be involved in academia, or that everyone should be reading big, heavy works of theology and philosophy—although doing that probably couldn't hurt some people. I only say that we recognize that Jesus the Man had a brain, and that we put our own brains to very good use when we attempt to grow in wisdom and

---

25. Dallas Willard, *The Divine Conspiracy: Rediscovering Our Hidden Life in God* (San Francisco: HarperCollins, 1998), 135.

26. "The Prescriptions Against the Heretics," *Early Latin Theology*, The Library of Christian Classics, ed. S. L. Greenslade (Philadelphia: Westminster, 1956), 5:36.

stature as he did, not compartmentalizing the "intellectual" and the "spiritual."

A holistic approach to Christian intellect is part and parcel of our having "the mind of Christ,"[27] or our loving God with all of our minds.[28] Too many Christians, though, seem to think that this merely means that we interrupt our "regular" thoughts of earthly things with "better" thoughts of heavenly things, that we remind ourselves, "Someday we'll be in heaven," but in a sense that mitigates the reality that Jesus is Lord *now*, and that our taking on the mind of Christ has real bearing on our lives and our thoughts about our lives now.

Our faith cannot and must not be disembodied.

"Our commitment to Jesus," writes Dallas Willard, "can stand on no other foundation than a recognition that he is the one who knows the truth about our lives and our universe. It is not possible to trust Jesus, or anyone else, in matters where we do not believe him to be competent."[29]

Most of us today have to get into the habit of thinking of Jesus as competent in certain areas of life, but it isn't enough that we settle for Jesus' mere competence. We must embrace his all-surpassing brilliance. He's not just a storehouse of facts or data; he is the wellspring of all truth. Jesus the Man didn't just teach and live the truth; he was, as he said himself, the truth itself.[30]

We have to get past an anxiety-prone existence in which we acknowledge Jesus' moral perfection and good teaching and miraculous power but, perversely, not to the extent that we think him "in touch" with what we're really going through. In one of the great ironies of our modern evangelical subculture, we are very big on "making" the Christian faith practical and "relevant," yet by and large we go on

---

27. 1 Corinthians 2:16.
28. Matthew 22:37.
29. Willard, *Divine Conspiracy*, 94.
30. John 14:6.

living our lives as if Jesus had nothing relevant to say about what we do and say, who we date or marry, what sort of jobs we take, what sort of families we raise, where we spend our time, and who we spend it with.

We're cool with Jesus being good and nice, but we're hesitant to live as if he is omniscient as well.

## JESUS WAS A WHOLE MAN

Jesus was an "integrated man," the most integrated man who ever lived—which is to say he was the only man ever to be perfectly integrated with the will of God. He lived an earthly life, with most earthly limitations, and subject to most earthly imperfections, but he also walked consciously and purposefully within the realm of heaven. This integration is definitely a reflection of Jesus' dual nature. The doctrine of the incarnation tells us that Jesus was both fully God and fully man, so it makes sense that he would walk both perfectly in the kingdom of the world into which he was born and perfectly conformed to the heavenly reality from which he came.

Spiritually and practically speaking, this meant for Jesus that he was perfectly aligned as a man with the will of God. Look at how John's gospel illustrates the absolute interconnection between Jesus the Man and God the Father, from the words of Jesus himself:

> So Jesus said to them, "Truly, truly, I say to you, the Son can do nothing of his own accord, but only what he sees the Father doing. For whatever the Father does, that the Son does likewise. For the Father loves the Son and shows him all that he himself is doing. And greater works than these will he show him, so that you may marvel. For as the Father raises the dead and gives them life, so also the Son gives life to whom he will. The Father judges no one, but has given all

> judgment to the Son, that all may honor the Son, just as they honor the Father. Whoever does not honor the Son does not honor the Father who sent him. . . .
>
> "I can do nothing on my own. As I hear, I judge, and my judgment is just, because I seek not my own will but the will of him who sent me. If I alone bear witness about myself, my testimony is not deemed true. There is another who bears witness about me, and I know that the testimony that he bears about me is true. You sent to John, and he has borne witness to the truth. Not that the testimony that I receive is from man, but I say these things so that you may be saved. He was a burning and shining lamp, and you were willing to rejoice for a while in his light. But the testimony that I have is greater than that of John. For the works that the Father has given me to accomplish, the very works that I am doing, bear witness about me that the Father has sent me." (John 5:19–23, 30–36)

Jesus the Man acknowledged his reliance on, and submission to, God the Father. He derived his authority and commissioning from the Father. He knew that his Father's will being done on earth as it is in heaven meant seeking not the will of his humanity but the will of the Father.

He was an integrated man, a whole man, which means he was an *unfallen* man. Jesus, as one unstained by the mark of Adam's sin, perfectly reflected the holiness of God. He was whole, so when we look at Jesus and hear what he said and see what he was doing, we are looking at and hearing no one less than the one true God himself.

In Hebrews 4:15, the author tells us that Jesus suffered the same temptations of all humanity, uniting him to us in sympathy. Yet unlike the rest of humanity, he was without sin, uniting us to him in sacrificial atonement. Here's how Paul explains the wonderful implications of Christ's perfect integration with God's will:

> For if, because of one man's trespass, death reigned through that one man, much more will those who receive the abundance of grace and the free gift of righteousness reign in life through the one man Jesus Christ.
>
> Therefore, as one trespass led to condemnation for all men, so one act of righteousness leads to justification and life for all men. For as by the one man's disobedience the many were made sinners, so by the one man's obedience the many will be made righteous. Now the law came in to increase the trespass, but where sin increased, grace abounded all the more, so that, as sin reigned in death, grace also might reign through righteousness leading to eternal life through Jesus Christ our Lord. (Rom. 5:17–21)

You may be asking at this point, "What's so special about the idea of Jesus being a whole man?" If we believe Jesus is God in the flesh, wouldn't we automatically believe he is an integrated man in this sense? Perhaps. But as in the divorce between our explicit understanding of Jesus as omniscient and our implicit attitude that the facts of life come from anywhere but him, we can often be guilty of affirming that Jesus knew and lived the will of God perfectly, but yet living and acting ourselves as if Jesus is somehow incidental to our own integration with God's perfect will.

We affirm this misunderstanding every time we treat our Christian faith as if it meant merely our behaving in a moral way. Jesus even provocatively drew the inference between himself and God's holiness when the rich young ruler asked him what good things must be done to earn eternal life.[31] Jesus' response—"Why do you ask me about what is good? There is only one who is good."—directs the man not to mere "good deeds" but to the very source—God—and very embodiment—Jesus—of goodness itself.

Reflecting on Jesus as a whole man, a man fully integrated with the perfect will of God, is important whenever we begin to worry about our own works being good enough (they aren't), or whenever we begin to actually trust that our own works *are* good enough. The gospel proclaims to us that we are only made perfect by the perfection of Jesus Christ, by having his wholeness imputed to us.

Believing in Jesus as a whole man is integral to our understanding of, and rejoicing in, the glorious gospel of salvation by grace.

## JESUS WAS A WEATHERED MAN

No, not a weather man.[32] A *weathered* man. Jesus was a man who experienced all the highs and lows and rejections and disappointments any man or woman ever could. Jesus was a man who weathered the storms of life.

Hebrews 2:14 tells us, "Since therefore the children share in flesh and blood, he himself likewise partook of the same things."

If you've been through it, Jesus has been through it.

"Ah," you say, "there's no way. Jesus hasn't been through drug addiction; he was never sexually molested or raped; he never had a spouse abuse him or cheat on him." No, perhaps Jesus hasn't been through your specific trial, but *he has been through the pain of it.*

Have you ever agonized in grief over losing a parent or a close

---

31. Matthew 19:16–17.

32. Although being able to control the weather would have made him the most awesome weatherman ever.

friend? Having lost his earthly father, Jesus has. The shortest verse in the Bible, John 11:35, tells us simply that "Jesus wept," and his tears came from mourning his dear friend Lazarus.

Have you ever been rejected by family members or betrayed by close friends? Jesus has. His brothers didn't believe he was who he said he was until after his resurrection. His closest friends slept while he anguished in the garden of Gethsemane, and then bailed on him after his arrest and before his crucifixion, the moments of his greatest fear and vulnerability.

Have you ever been through so much stress and anxiety it severely affected your health? Jesus has. In Gethsemane, he was so overcome by fear and anxiety, he sweated blood.[33]

Have you ever been gossiped about, falsely accused of something, or had your reputation ruined? Jesus has.

Have you ever been humiliated and ridiculed? Jesus has.

Have you ever been assaulted, beaten, or tortured? Jesus has.

Have you ever been killed? Well, if you're reading this, of course not. But Jesus has.

Jesus has been through what you've been through. The Bible even says he's been tempted as you've been tempted:

> Since then we have a great high priest who has passed through the heavens, Jesus, the Son of God, let us hold fast our confession. For we do not have a high priest who is unable to sympathize with our weaknesses, but one who in every respect has been tempted as we are, yet without sin. Let us then with confidence draw near to the throne of grace, that we may receive mercy and find grace to help in time of need. (Heb. 4:14–16)

---

33. Luke 22:44.

Here's the thing, though, about this notion that Jesus was tempted in every respect as we are, and it's the great theological conundrum of the ages. Could Jesus have sinned? *Could* he? The author of Hebrews says he was tempted as we are. The prevailing theological consensus, which has the added benefit of being correct, is that Jesus did not have a sinful nature. Although he was really human and had in general the limitations of an aging, flawed flesh, he did not have sin in him. So does that mean he couldn't have sinned?

This is where it's important to keep in mind that even though our physical flesh bears the marks of the fall—we get saggy and wrinkled and chubby and marked with age spots and, in some of our cases, have hair growing out of our ears—our flesh in and of itself is not bad or sinful. That's one of those Gnostic beliefs still influencing the church. Our flesh in its deterioration is *affected* by the fall, but physical flesh is not inherently bad or sinful. So Jesus had a flawed body in that it was flesh, but he did not have a flawed nature.

The New Testament calls Jesus "the last Adam."[34] We take this to mean that he was like Adam before the fall. He had a nature unstained by sin, unmarred by the fall, and he also had the freedom—again, just like Adam—to sin or not to sin. Both Adam and Jesus had free will.

I believe Jesus could have chosen to sin. Otherwise the "tempted as we are" in this verse is not much comfort. If Jesus was *unable* to have given in to temptation, then he would also be unable to "sympathize with our weaknesses," and it wouldn't make much sense for the author of Hebrews to mention it.[35] So Jesus was capable of sinning . . . *but*! This provocative potential must be held in tension with the absolute truth that Jesus did not sin, for which we have plenty of biblical evidence.

At this point, you may be asking, "What good does that do me

---

34. 1 Corinthians 15:45.

35. This is just my personal, unprofessional opinion, mind you. Your mileage may vary. Put your fightin' hat on and get angry, why don'tcha?

then? If he doesn't know what it's like to have given in to temptation, how does that help me?"[36]

A better question is this: How could he help us at all if he *had* given in? If the New Adam hadn't redeemed what the Old Adam had screwed up, we'd be in big, big trouble. We have the incomparable comfort of knowing that our Savior has been through our same temptations, he knows the lures and the agony, but we also have the phenomenal reassurance of knowing he consistently withstood temptation when we consistently do not.

That he did withstand it is the great wonder and beauty of the incarnation. That is the great benefit and redemptive power of Jesus' humanity, the fullness and depth and purpose of his being flesh and blood. It's not something that easily lends itself to "personal application," at least not in the way thousands of Sunday school classes and small groups exercise personal application in their Bible discussion time. We may ask, "What does the incarnation mean *to me*?" but the answer has little to do with "Six Keys to Powerful Living" or "Seven Steps to Successful Whatever."

I'm going to tell you the shocking truth: we can't implement this. Furthermore, that's pretty much the point. Jesus is perfect because we are not.

When Jesus says, "You therefore must be perfect, as your heavenly Father is perfect,"[37] he doesn't mean, "Try really, really hard to be as good as God." That doesn't work, and Jesus—who was brilliant—knows it. When he says, "You therefore must be perfect," he means, "You will be *made* perfect," and he means, "You will have my perfection imputed

---

36. I keep assuming that you're someone who speaks aloud to books. If I were you, I wouldn't do this if you're seated next to someone in a waiting room or on an airplane. Unless you really want to freak people out and give them a good story to tell their friends. In that case, go ahead, weirdo.

37. Matthew 5:48.

to you." That's a big theological word there—*imputed*—but it basically means "transferred," "assigned to," "imparted to," or "imbued."

The idea of Jesus' perfection shouldn't distance us from God. The very motive for it was to bridge that distance. They called him Immanuel, which means "God with us," but Jesus went above and beyond the calling of his name to also be God *for* us. That is glorious gospel truth.

Jesus was perfect—turn your sarcastic "Oh great" into a joyous "Thank God!"—so that we might be made perfect also. That is why we can draw near to his throne with confidence. Not because we've done great things and have achieved perfect humanness, but because he has done that for us!

If you feel distant from God, unworthy, or unloved, I have good news for you. And it comes in the form of a command: draw near to his throne of mercy with the boldness of one who believes that Jesus the Man has achieved all that God the Father sent him to do for you, with the confidence of one who desperately needs the grace that Jesus the Christ wants to keep giving, on and on, forever and ever, without end.

Remember King David's idealism in Psalm 24? He asks, Who can stand where God is? and he basically answers, The one who is perfect. We have now answered "How can we be perfect?" We answer it with "We can't, but Jesus has been perfect on our behalf." Now let's look at the second part of that psalm. This is how David follows up his intimidating declaration that only someone perfectly holy can enter God's presence:

> Lift up your heads, O gates!
>     And be lifted up, O ancient doors,
>     that the King of glory may come in.
> Who is this King of glory?
>     The LORD, strong and mighty,
>     the LORD, mighty in battle!

Lift up your heads, O gates!
And lift them up, O ancient doors,
that the King of glory may come in.
Who is this King of glory?
The Lord of hosts,
he is the King of glory! *Selah*
(Ps. 24:7–10)

Do you know what this word *Selah* means? You'll see it a lot in the Psalms. It's actually sort of a literary mystery, and speculation abounds, but a general consensus is that it's a sort of pause, a sort of musical version of saying "Amen," a denotation of time to reflect on what's just been sung, a call to stop silent and worship. *Selah* is like a holy sigh, a release of breath. It's a prayerful sigh of relief.

Who can ascend God's holy mountain? Who can abide in his presence? Only the blameless and perfect and holy.

But look up! Lift up your chin! Draw near to the throne of mercy with confidence! Here comes the King of glory, bringing grace into our presence and making us perfect so that we can stand before God. Jesus has intruded into this world, tearing the veil of separation from top to bottom to redeem our lives and sweep us away from our despair and bring us into the very presence of the Almighty God, who loves us with an unfailing love.

Lift up your heads, the King of glory has come for you.

Take a deep breath!

*Selah*

# 5

# JESUS THE SHEPHERD

One night about two thousand years ago, a few working stiffs were lazing about in a pasture. They had the overnight shift in the boss' sheep-watching company. I'm a child of the 1980s, raised on a healthy diet of Cap'n Crunch, Kool-Aid, and Saturday morning cartoons. When I think about this sheep-watching gig, I can't help but think of the Looney Tunes shorts with Sam, the big white sheepdog, dutifully, if casually, watching the sheep and ending up having to thwart the devious plans of Ralph the wolf to kidnap (sheepnap?) them.[1] In one episode, they both clock in, like it's their job to handle short-fused dynamite and gigantic catapults and Acme rocket-powered roller skates for eight hours. The reality of sheep-watching is far more mundane, I'm guessing. You'd have to keep your eyes open for wolves or other predators, and to make sure none of your flock wanders off too far, but aside from that, watching over sheep is probably pretty boring—the night watch especially.

The shepherds in the story of Jesus' birth are just hanging around, watching their sheep, when suddenly an angel appears, and the "glory

1. Ironically, and in a feat of pre-postmodern metafictional characterization, Ralph the wolf was played by Wile E. Coyote.

of the Lord" shone all about them.[2] They were, naturally, terrified, but the angel tells them not to be afraid. And then, as if to test their obedience, the sky fills up with a host of angels. I don't know about you, but I think I'd be more than a little scared. Today these guys would be on the news talking about UFOs and nobody would believe them. But the angels were heralds of God, filling the skies with the glorious announcement that the long-awaited Messiah had been born.

If you were a lowly shepherd and a host of angels showed up to tell you the king had been born, you'd probably want to go pay your respects. You'd probably think you should begin looking for him at some palace or mansion. You'd scrub your hands and your face, put on your nicest sandals, slick down your cowlick, take your best shepherd's staff, and walk up the steps to knock on the door. But these guys go from the fields with the animals . . . to a barn with the animals. And they find the Savior of the universe in a feeding trough.

Such are the inglorious lengths God has gone through to identify with mankind. He didn't swoop down on a flaming chariot "burninating" the peasants (although that'd be kinda cool).[3] He was born with the livestock. And throughout Jesus' ministry, he continued to identify and commingle with the common folk, the working stiffs, the—as we might say—"salt of the earth" people. When he told stories and offered illustrations, he related to his working-class, agrarian cultural communities. He didn't tell exciting tales of palace life or far-flung adventure; he talked about fishing and gardening and owing money to somebody. And one of the recurring themes that Jesus used for illustration—recurring because it carried with it a wealth of meaning and history in the lives of the nation of Israel—was that of shepherding. He called himself the Good Shepherd and made frequent use of references to sheep and shepherding.

---

2. Luke 2:9.
3. Watch www.homestarrunner.com/sbemail58.html. You're welcome.

In contemplating Jesus as Shepherd, I'm most tempted to make a short list of things shepherds do—the shepherd's responsibilities chart—and cram Jesus into it and see how he fits. Some books actually take this tack.[4] I believe this is a backward way to go about things—sort of getting the cart before the horse . . . or the sheep, I guess. Rather than come up with stuff about shepherds and then thrust it back onto Jesus, I think we should just start with the Shepherd himself. In what ways did Jesus envision himself as a shepherd? If Jesus was a shepherd, what sort of shepherd was he? How did he explain his shepherding?

In Matthew 9, we see a lengthy chronicle of some of Jesus' healings and teachings and ministry to people. We see that he and his followers attract large crowds. As they make their way through the towns, Jesus confronts the Pharisees one minute and casts out demons the next. He teaches on the kingdom of God one minute and heals sickness and paralysis the next.

Anyone who's traveled extensively and ministered continuously knows how utterly exhausting it can be. It's taxing of energy and spirit. At the end of a long day with all this stuff packed into every second, you or I would feel like kicking up our feet on the ol' La-Z-Boy, cold one in hand,[5] and sighing, "If I see one more demoniac today, I'm going to explode."

But Jesus doesn't do that. What does he do? At the end of this long and exhausting day of activities, "When he saw the crowds," says Matthew 9:36, "he had compassion for them, because they were harassed and helpless, like sheep without a shepherd."

Jesus looks out on all the people—the ones he's been able to minister to and the huge number of people he hasn't even had the time to make eye contact with. He sees perhaps acres of hurt and disease and sadness and brokenness, and he realizes he's barely scratched the

4. If I felt it were important, this is where I'd mention the nicely written and entirely pleasant book I have in mind.

5. By "cold one" I mean, of course, "glass of milk."

surface of bringing the good news of himself to them. Yet instead of despair or frustration, he feels *compassion*.

What kind of shepherd is Jesus?

## A COMPASSIONATE SHEPHERD

*Compassionate* doesn't mean merely nice or sympathetic. The compassion that Jesus feels is compassion in its deepest sense. It is an identifying love, a shared hurt. The Greek word used in Matthew for "had compassion" is *splagchnizomai*,[6] which connotes a yearning *from the bowels*. This isn't just an emotion; it's a visceral reaction. Jesus, who would know harassment and helplessness himself, looks out on a dirty, stinky, needy mess of people—remember, Matthew tells us they were "harassed and helpless"—and is moved to a deeply felt compassion.

The crowds are "like sheep without a shepherd." This means they're both without guidance and without protection. They're out in the open, going about life, just minding their own business, eating grass and generally being sheep, and they're unaware that any minute a wolf could come sneaking in. They don't even know that when the grass is gone, they won't know how to get to the next pasture. And this ignorance is a burden that Jesus feels in his insidest inside. His reaction is crucial for us to realize, so I'll risk redundancy to emphasize the point one more time: this reaction is no mere intellectual acknowledgment for Jesus. He sees this crowd and is moved to compassion—immediate, natural, deep compassion.

This kind of response is a hard, if not impossible, switch for you or me to flip on. We can see or hear people hurting and feel compassion for them. But it's hard for us to look out at people doing the routine things that people do and immediately feel compassion for them. I confess that I'm generally unmoved by the crowds I encounter every

---

6. *Gesundheit*.

day, and if I'm naturally inclined toward any emotion at all, it's usually frustration, followed by disdain. But when I'm deliberate about how I view others, I'm able, by the grace of God, to view them through Jesus' eyes, even if only in momentary glimpses.

I've sensed my own shift in outlook when being confronted head-on with ignorant people acting desperately. When I was a teenager, I made the dumb mistake of going with some friends to a particular Houston pool hall. I lasted all of five minutes. I was scared to death. The second we walked in, some dude standing by the door blew a cloud of cigarette smoke into my face. Through the haze, I saw a smattering of ZZ Top rejects slouched around the tables and wearing black leather jackets. They fondled pool cues, but it appeared they'd rather use them for beating our brains in than for shooting pool. This was a bar, for goodness' sake, and we were Baptists! Not wanting to die so young, I turned to my friends and said, "Let's leave." And we did.

A few years later, I went with some friends to see our favorite band at a downtown Houston rock club. This rock club wasn't the same as a nightclub. I've never been inside a nightclub, but I imagine it has flashing lights, and super-tanned dudes in suits, and super-plastic chicks with go-go boots dancing inside cages hanging from the ceiling. Is that right?[7]

This place, though, had a huge concrete floor that might've doubled for a slaughterhouse kill floor, with a bar on one end and a stage on the other. We'd come for what was on the stage, whereas most everybody else had come, it seemed, for what was at the bar.

As the place filled up, and we were all packed in like sardines, I saw and heard some stupid stuff. I saw the increasing drunkenness, heard the intoxicated laughter, avoided assorted intoxicated shenanigans,

---

7. I asked my friend Ashley, who's visited nightclubs now and again, if this was an accurate description, but instead of answering me, she just laughed and laughed and laughed. I suppose that was an answer in itself.

and then smelled the tangy scent of "funny" cigarettes. Above all, I remember getting angry. I felt, as any good hellfire holiness Christian would, a heapin' helpin' of righteous indignation. I was irritated (praise God). I was offended (praise Jesus). I was an incredibly sensitive jerk for Jesus. As I looked at all those lost people doing—gasp!—lost people things, my sense of moral turpitude kicked in, and I just wanted them gone. I didn't want to brush shoulders with such people.

To sum up the story thus far: pool hall, scared; rock club, angry.

Fast forward about ten years. I'd done some growing up, let me tell you. One spring evening, I went with a few of the guys from church to the only place we could find that would let us smoke cigars inside, which in froufrou, artsy-fartsy Nashville happens to be a place just a skosh more sophisticated than a biker bar. It was a weird scene, man. A couple of guys with a guitar and a harmonica played gravel-voiced renditions of The Allman Brothers and Bob Seger. The audience was a weirdly diverse crowd—a good mix of college kids and middle-aged couples, and, as if to justify the armada of Harleys in the gravel parking lot, a fair number of those ZZ Top reject dudes.[8]

The kids were getting drunk. A few of the girls had that goofy-eyed "come hither" countenance that says to less-than-genteel boyfriends, "Come hither and take advantage of me." One girl stumbled outside and her male companion pulled her tube top down. I happened to miss the grand unveiling, thank goodness.

Someone in our group spotted a lady he knew, who happened to be married but was having drinks with a succession of men who happened not to be her husband.

The ZZ Top dudes were sitting around looking angry.

In my former life, I would have been scared to death in such a place. Or I would have been angry at all the sin packed into such close

---

8. You know, guys who would beat me up for using the word *froufrou*.

quarters. But this night—as I looked around and saw people doing desperate, deadly things, all in the guise of having fun—I felt, above all things, sad. I don't know if it was the growing up I've done, or the desperate, deadly things I've been through in my own life. I'd hesitate to skirt pride and say it was because I'm closer to God now. A few days later, I was discussing the scene with one of the ministers who'd accompanied us, and I told him that the only thing I could think of that night was Matthew 9:36. I thought of when Jesus looked at the crowd and had compassion, because they were like sheep without a shepherd.

I somehow glimpsed, beneath stony exteriors, years of hardship and bitterness; beneath desperate flirtation, years of emotional neglect and insensitivity; beneath drunken behavior, years of spiritual emptiness. And seeing these people—not just their behavior—I was moved.

It was only a glimpse, and it was certainly colored by my own attitudes and limitations and sins, but that—multiplied by infinity—is how Jesus looks at us. And it's not just those crazy drunks and freaky fornicators who need compassion. It's us prideful, self-centered, grace-withholding sinners who need it too. And Jesus isn't just a clock-punching shepherd who tends to us only out of obligation. He's a Shepherd who cares for us with everlasting kindness, with a deep concern for us and how things will end up for us. He is a compassionate shepherd.

## A SACRIFICIAL SHEPHERD

> So Jesus again said to them, "Truly, truly, I say to you, I am the door of the sheep. All who came before me are thieves and robbers, but the sheep did not listen to them. I am the door. If anyone enters by me, he will be saved and will go in and out and find pasture. The thief comes only to steal and kill and destroy. I came that they may have life and have it abundantly. I am the good shepherd.

> The good shepherd lays down his life for the sheep. He who is a hired hand and not a shepherd, who does not own the sheep, sees the wolf coming and leaves the sheep and flees, and the wolf snatches them and scatters them. He flees because he is a hired hand and cares nothing for the sheep. I am the good shepherd. I know my own and my own know me, just as the Father knows me and I know the Father; and I lay down my life for the sheep. And I have other sheep that are not of this fold. I must bring them also, and they will listen to my voice. So there will be one flock, one shepherd." (John 10:7–16)

Jesus is so intent on shepherding us the way we need to be shepherded, that he is willing to put his own life on the line to protect us. He lays down his life for the sheep. That's not just a good shepherd—that's a great shepherd! That's a crazy shepherd. See how he contrasts this sort of shepherding with that of a hired hand? A hired hand doesn't really care about the sheep. He only cares about his paycheck. So when the wolf comes, the hired hand is thinking, *I don't want to get hurt*, and he bails. But the good shepherd risks his own life. The good shepherd lays down his life for the sheep.

The connection between sacrifice and sheep is not lost on the people Jesus is talking to in John 10. When Jesus tells sheep stories, he calls to mind not only the agrarian lifestyle of the people, where tending sheep and raising livestock would resonate, but also the centuries of sacrifices conducted by the Jewish people, in which a spotless lamb was required.[9]

Jesus goes a full leap further, though. Not only does he identify himself as the Good Shepherd who sacrifices himself for the sheep, he

9. Leviticus 4:32, among others.

also places himself in the role of sacrificial lamb. In John 10, he may call himself the Good Shepherd, but in John 1, John the Baptist calls him the Lamb of God.[10] He is both the shepherd and the sheep.

That's how far Jesus was willing to go to save us. That's how far he's willing to go to identify with us. That is the inglorious scandal of the incarnation. God becoming a man is like a man becoming a sheep. Imagine, if you like, that you and I are so in love with ants, extremely desirous of a relationship with ants, incredibly eager for ants to know us, that the only way we could achieve this connection is to become an ant. The analogy breaks down, as all analogies do, but to go from the God of the universe, with all powers at his disposal, to a crying, burping, pooping baby in a feeding trough in a barn . . . that's a sacrifice on par with man becoming an ant.

That's the kind of shepherd we have. We have a sacrificial Shepherd.

Let's not forget, however, that the "hired hands" analogy isn't just an illustration. Jesus was referring to some of his contemporaries, to the people charged with spiritually shepherding Israel. The religious leaders, the ones in charge of watching over God's people, had dropped the ball. They weren't sacrificial shepherds. They weren't even good shepherds. They were self-interested, money grubbing, uncompassionate shepherds.

All the way back in the Old Testament, God had already offered some harsh words for them—and, at the same time, some words of hope for the sheep in their care. During a time of national tumult and cultural crisis, God told the prophet Ezekiel to make this announcement:

> The word of the Lord came to me: "Son of man, prophesy against the shepherds of Israel; prophesy, and say to them, even to the shepherds, Thus says the Lord

10. John 1:29–36.

> GOD: Ah, shepherds of Israel who have been feeding yourselves! Should not shepherds feed the sheep? You eat the fat, you clothe yourselves with the wool, you slaughter the fat ones, but you do not feed the sheep. The weak you have not strengthened, the sick you have not healed, the injured you have not bound up, the strayed you have not brought back, the lost you have not sought, and with force and harshness you have ruled them. So they were scattered, because there was no shepherd, and they became food for all the wild beasts. My sheep were scattered; they wandered over all the mountains and on every high hill. My sheep were scattered over all the face of the earth, with none to search or seek for them." (Ezek. 34:1–6)

That's the bad news. Let's skip to verse 11 and get the good news:

> For thus says the Lord GOD: Behold, I, I myself will search for my sheep and will seek them out. As a shepherd seeks out his flock when he is among his sheep that have been scattered, so will I seek out my sheep, and I will rescue them from all places where they have been scattered on a day of clouds and thick darkness. And I will bring them out from the peoples and gather them from the countries, and will bring them into their own land. And I will feed them on the mountains of Israel, by the ravines, and in all the inhabited places of the country. I will feed them with good pasture, and on the mountain heights of Israel shall be their grazing land. There they shall lie down in good grazing land, and on rich pasture they shall feed on the mountains

> of Israel. I myself will be the shepherd of my sheep, and I myself will make them lie down, declares the Lord God. I will seek the lost, and I will bring back the strayed, and I will bind up the injured, and I will strengthen the weak, and the fat and the strong I will destroy. I will feed them in justice. (Ezek. 34:11–16)

The "lost sheep" imagery, then, is not original to the Gospels. It goes back to the Old Testament, setting the scene and the precedent for Jesus and his message. What was true in Ezekiel's day was true in Jesus' day. The spiritual shepherds in place—the Pharisees, the Sadducees, the scribes—had no real regard for the sheep. The Pharisees turned inward, caring more about appearing righteous, more about keeping up appearances and worrying about who God's kingdom must exclude. The Pharisees maintained a very small sheep pen. The Sadducees were greedy. They'd turned the temple system—the system by which God's people were supposed to encounter God and get made right with God—into a profitable marketplace.

Spiritually speaking, the place was in shambles. And each successive generation of faithful Jewish believers, submitting to the yoke of each successive generation of corrupt authorities, was confronted with the same message: Meet the new boss, same as the old boss. Until Jesus of Nazareth. The ongoing spiritual failure of Israel's designated shepherds culminates with God's keeping the promise he made in Ezekiel 34:16: "I will seek the lost, and I will bring back the strayed."

I imagine the religious leaders of Jesus' day got their panties in a wad over that one. His saying that he was going to assume this role would, after all, be an unambiguous allusion to God's promise to personally shepherd us. I imagine their confusion and consternation upon confronting in the flesh the God who, unlike them, does not shepherd the sheep by exploiting them. The Good Shepherd's sacrifice of his life included sacrificing his rights to power and authority and freedom.[11] Unlike the self-appointed shepherds of Israel's culture, the self-sufficient Shepherd of all creation exuded humility and exhibited servanthood. His motives were pure. Thank God we don't have a Shepherd who ignores us or despises us or manipulates us.

This embraced selflessness flows directly from Jesus' natural sinlessness. For the sacrificial shepherd to be the sacrificial lamb, sinlessness is required. And because death is required to forgive our sinfulness, our sacrificial Shepherd puts his money where his mouth is and actually takes the place of the spotless lamb of the sacrifice.

Recalling the regulations for sacrificial atonement under the old covenant, Peter, writing under the new covenant, compares Christ to "a lamb without blemish or spot."[12] Paul proclaims that "Christ, our Passover lamb, has been sacrificed."[13] So where the previous hired hands shepherded us by using fear and constraint, Jesus places on us a yoke that is easy, and a burden that is light.[14] It is for freedom that we have been set free.[15] Here's how Paul celebrates the sacrificial Shepherd's becoming the sacrificial sheep to secure our liberty:

> All have sinned and fall short of the glory of God, and are justified by his grace as a gift, through the redemption that is in Christ Jesus, whom God put forward as a propitiation by his blood, to be received by faith. This was to show God's righteousness, because in his divine forbearance he had passed over former sins. (Rom. 3:23–25)

---

11. Philippians 2:5–8.
12. 1 Peter 1:19.
13. 1 Corinthians 5:7.
14. Matthew 11:30.
15. Galatians 5:1.

How awesome is that? A hired hand wants to be paid to protect the sheep, but the Good Shepherd does it for free. Not only that, but when payment comes due, he pays for the protection of the sheep himself with his very own blood.

## A SHEPHERD WHO SEEKS AND SAVES

> Now the tax collectors and sinners were all drawing near to hear him. And the Pharisees and the scribes grumbled, saying, "This man receives sinners and eats with them."
>
> So he told them this parable: "What man of you, having a hundred sheep, if he has lost one of them, does not leave the ninety-nine in the open country, and go after the one that is lost, until he finds it? And when he has found it, he lays it on his shoulders, rejoicing. And when he comes home, he calls together his friends and his neighbors, saying to them, 'Rejoice with me, for I have found my sheep that was lost.' Just so, I tell you, there will be more joy in heaven over one sinner who repents than over ninety-nine righteous persons who need no repentance." (Luke 15:1–7)

We have a Shepherd who relentlessly chases after us. We have a Shepherd who is constantly on the lookout for his lost sheep. This is the kind of Shepherd who will prioritize the lost one ahead of the secured ones, the opposite of what the Pharisees would do. We have a shepherd who seeks and saves.

A hired hand may stand out in the pasture, discover that one of his sheep has gone missing, and think, Well, I guess I should cut my losses. At least I still have these ninety-nine. One lost is not so bad.

Not Jesus. He will say, "I've got only ninety-nine here? Where's the hundredth?" And he closes up the pen and gets his hands dirty and runs around, getting out of breath, searching out every rocky path and thorn bush until he finds the one that wandered off.

Jesus follows up this story with two more like it, as if stamping three exclamation points on the Pharisees' foreheads. These would-be shepherds had come to him complaining about the company he kept. They weren't "the right sort" of people—they were the drunk college girls in tube tops and ZZ Top rejects. In response, Jesus hit them with three parables in a row, a great combo punch designed to defeat the most arrogant of opponents. It's as if he was saying, "Do you not get it? Here's the point."

He tells stories of a lost sheep, a lost coin, and a lost son. In "The Lost Coin," a woman turns on every light in the house, pushes aside all the furniture, and sweeps every corner of every room until she finds one little coin that you or I wouldn't stoop to pick up if we saw it lying in the middle of the sidewalk. "The Lost Son," as I'm sure you know, is a masterful story about a father and his wayward heir. This parable captures the radical reconciliation between God and man like almost no other story can.

Friends, we have a Shepherd who seeks us and saves us. He made the inconceivable move of lowering himself to come down here with the sheep and identify with us; and when he's looking for one of us, nothing stops him, nothing gets in his way. He's turning on all the lights in the darkness, he's turning over tables and getting down on his hands and knees, he's peering down every road, because rescuing the lost sheep is what he's all about.

Thankfully, once he's got us, he never lets go.

## A SHEPHERD WHO LEADS

This attribute of the shepherd—leadership—is one that you'd think could go without saying. But even though it may be the easiest to acknowledge, Jesus' leadership is also the hardest part of his shepherding for us to handle. While all of the things discussed so far are things that Jesus the Shepherd does *for* us—his having compassion, making sacrifices, seeking and saving, and now leading—this is the one that requires the most from us in return. We have a Shepherd who leads, but his leadership will not benefit us one bit if we the sheep don't follow.

In John 10:26–28, Jesus warns, "You do not believe because you are not part of my flock. My sheep hear my voice, and I know them, and they follow me. I give them eternal life, and they will never perish, and no one will snatch them out of my hand."

If we don't believe, we are not a part of Jesus' flock of sheep. That's a scary proposition, isn't it? His sheep actually follow him.

The sheep's commitment to following, though—what we'd call in the Christian life "discipleship"—entails another scary idea: *repentance*. Repentance is the first step of our commitment to follow the Shepherd's lead.

Repentance isn't simply a changing of our minds; it's also a turning of our bodies. We usually think of repentance as turning away from something—a sin or a circumstance—but that's not all it is. Repentance is not just a negative action; it's also a positive one. It's not just turning away from something; it's turning *to* someone.

It's not enough to turn away from a cliff. We could easily wander over to another. Instead, we must turn away from the cliff and turn to follow the Shepherd. He will steer us clear of the cliffs altogether.

This doesn't mean that following the Shepherd is without its adventures. Even if we acknowledge that Jesus is the Good Shepherd—who has compassion for us and sacrifices for us and comes looking for us when we go astray—it's a scary thing to follow him, because he goes to some scary places. He takes us to and through some places we don't often want to go. Take a good look at Psalm 23. Our Shepherd makes no bones about having us share meals with our enemies or having us visit the valley of the shadow of death.

Following Jesus requires an inside-out approach to our lives. It requires turning away from ourselves and orienting ourselves to him. In Psalm 23, David says the shepherd's rod and staff comfort him. Do you know what a rod and staff are for? Discipline, usually. A shepherd uses those things to corral the sheep, to whisk them away from the brink of disaster or danger. A shepherd strikes with those things, waves those things around, directs roughly with those things.

If my daughter is running into the street, she may feel as if I'm grabbing her arm too roughly when I pull her back, but she doesn't know that getting smacked by a car would feel much, much worse. If she knew I was only trying to keep her safe, she'd find my rough, abrupt move a comfort.

We've got to get to the place in our "sheepishness" where we trust our Shepherd as he leads us away from what looks to us like great places to graze and laze around. Because what looks good to us often turns out to be looming disaster. We're often oblivious to our own selfishness, ignorant of our own gracelessness. We think of ourselves before others. We're like a leaderless Israel, doing what is right in our own eyes,[16] like stupid sheep transfixed on the small patch of green before us while the ravenous lion sneaks up from behind.

To really and fully embrace the great and perfect goodness of the Good Shepherd, we must repent of our self-satisfaction, our self-wisdom, our self-shepherding. We must stop trying to convince ourselves that we can figure out life by ourselves, because we're wrong. We're idolaters who are too easily satisfied with ourselves and our achievements.

Like sheep, we are dumb and prone to stray. Jesus demands that we own up to our sheepishness and deny ourselves. That's the sort of all-or-nothing following that awaits the Lord's obedient sheep. It's a

16. Judges 17:6.

self-denying, cross-taking enterprise.[17] Both the Old and New Testaments agree that "all we like sheep have gone astray."[18] That's every one of us. At one time Jesus rebuked the arrogance even of his closest followers and warned that they'd perish like everyone else if they didn't repent.

It doesn't matter if you know your Bible, go to church, give money to the poor, and help nuns cross the street. It doesn't even matter if you know all about Jesus, inside and out, and could whip your pastor's butt at *Bible Trivia*. If you don't follow, you will perish. If you don't repent—that is, turn from *your* way and follow the Good Shepherd's way—it will not end well for you.

But there is a promise carried within the command to follow. If you will repent and submit yourself to the leading of Jesus, surely goodness and mercy will follow you all the days of your life.[19] Repent to follow Jesus, and his goodness and mercy will be your traveling companions for eternity. You will have his compassion, his sacrifice, his seeking and saving, his leadership for your entire journey.

17. Mark 8:34.
18. See Isaiah 53:6; 1 Peter 2:25.
19. See Psalm 23:6.

6

# JESUS THE JUDGE

What image comes to mind when you think of a judge? One of those pillars of jurisprudence on the U.S. Supreme Court? One of those sassy yahoos on syndicated television?

Do you think of fairness? Or unfairness?

Do you think of someone powerful? Or someone who's a puppet?

Do you think of integrity? Or corruption?

What comes to mind when you think of judgment or the judging of someone?

Do you think of justice? Or injustice?

Do you think of judgment as a necessary evil? Or an abused virtue?

I suspect that most of us are generally thankful there are people in authority charged with making judgments and executing justice. We just don't like to think about it too much. Oh, we enjoy the entertainment value provided by the state of our modern American justice system—thanks to celebrity trials, "true crime" television shows, and all the blowhards on the cable news networks. But we don't really like to think about judgment with any intellectual depth. And we certainly don't like to think about anyone judging *us*.

Judgment is for all of "those people." We go about our lives every day, making judgments about everyone and everything, yet we're very quick to protest, "Stop being so judgmental!" when someone confronts us with our own shortcomings.

This hypocritical imbalance, and the underlying sense of justice that prompts it, is an innate human characteristic. Even those who would argue there's no such thing as sin or evil will object when someone is interested in breaking into their home, stealing their things, or harming their family. Hypocrisy will kick in and even the staunchest materialist will declare such behavior wrong.

Even small children without being taught have a great sense of equality and justice. Just hang out near a playground for a while,[1] and eventually you'll hear, "That's not fair!" We have this innate sense of justice because we're creatures made in the image of God, and God has a perfect sense of right and wrong, good and evil, fairness and unfairness, justice and injustice. Indeed, he is the very source of this sense, as it emanates from his holiness. Because we get our sense of justice from God, that instinct is good and natural and helpful. But because we're fallen creatures, broken images of God, our sense of justice is corrupted. We're unholy creatures cast in the image of a holy Creator. So despite our knowledge, we revolt, we stray, we "run on for a long time"—in the prophetic words of the late, great Johnny Cash—and sooner or later, our just God must come after us, bringing judgment with him according to his wisdom.

In 1 Kings 13, we encounter an odd story about a prophet whom God directs to pronounce judgment on King Jeroboam, a sinful leader who was perverting Israelite culture with idolatry. The kingdom had become so corrupt that a man of God had to be found from another region entirely to come rebuke what was going on.

So this guy[2] shows up, and he prophesies the birth of King Josiah,

---

1. On second thought, if you're an adult male and don't have children with you, I do not advise hanging out by a playground for a while.

2. The prophet is not identified by name but is called "a man of God" and "a man

who will be a righteous and just leader. He also pronounces judgment on the corrupt sacrificial altar, declaring that God will split it in two. This naturally irks King Jeroboam, and he turns to his goons and does that whole, cheesy movie-villain "Seize him!" thing, but when he extends his arm to point at the man of God, his hand withers up. He has somehow inserted his hand into the aura of God's judgment hovering over the corrupt altar.[3]

So King Jeroboam—with his newly fossilized T-Rex hand, all shriveled and wimpy and basically useless—changes gears very quickly and begs the prophet to ask God for healing. In an act of grace, the man of God obliges, and God restores Jeroboam's arm. Jeroboam is so happy that he says to the prophet, "Hey, come back to the crib and hang out. We got lots of food and drinks. You'll be my guest of honor."

But the man of God had been specifically instructed by God not to eat food or drink water—basically, he'd been commanded to fast—while on his mission. The commanded fast was part of how he was sanctifying himself to God while being God's messenger to the corrupt king. The man of God says to King Jeroboam, "Nope, can't do that. In fact, even if you were to give me half your kingdom, I couldn't be convinced to party with you, because I was commanded by God not to. God was so specific in his instructions that I'm not even allowed to go back the way I came. God gave me detailed directions about what I can and can't do, and as you can see by what happened to your arm, he means business."

And he goes on his way.

He takes a different route home, obviously, because God had told him not to go back the way he had come. After he's gone, word of what he did for the king spreads through the town. Some young morons rush

---

of God from Judah." Because he is essentially a Man with No Name come to execute justice, I like to picture him as Clint Eastwood's cowboy with no name in the Sergio Leone spaghetti westerns.

3. If you don't think this is awesome, there's something wrong with you.

to tell the story to their dad, who is, in the words of the text, an "old prophet,"[4] but who, it turns out, is actually a false prophet. He hops onto his donkey and goes in hot pursuit of the man of God.[5] The old man finally catches up to the prophet and finds him napping under an oak tree. The false prophet moseys on up and says, "Wow, you look beat. Why don't you come back with me and get something to eat or drink?"

"Yeah, sorry. Can't do that," the man of God says. "God told me not to."

The false prophet says, "Oh, but you don't understand. I'm a prophet myself.[6] And God told me to tell you that everything's cool now. Your mission has been accomplished. You can eat all you want. There's an IHOP back the way you came; my treat."

The man of God is fooled. He goes with the false prophet back the way he came, even though God had told him not to do that, and he eats and drinks, even though God had told him not to do that, either. While he's eating, the word of the Lord comes to him at the table and basically says, "Man, you screwed up big time."

After the real prophet leaves the old prophet's home, God sends a lion, and the lion tears the real prophet limb from limb and leaves him in bloody pieces in the road.

This was "the man of God."

This was the guy who went and proclaimed God's message and worked God's power. This was the guy who was obedient right up until the point he got fooled. And because God means business when he tells us to do something, this "man of God" got cut down on his way out of town.

Christians, we worship a holy and righteous God of wrath. "Vengeance is mine," says the Lord, and he means it.[7] Do you want to know how holy God is, how serious he is about this stuff? Read Leviticus

---

4. 1 Kings 13:11.
5. Okay, he was on a donkey, so we'll call it "lukewarm pursuit."
6. I assume he also flashed a fake badge at him.
7. Deuteronomy 32:35; Romans 12:19.

sometime. Any sin we can think of, and a host of ones we can't, are all listed right there. God crosses every *t* and dots every *i*,[8] and he says, "If you violate this stuff, you'll be punished severely." We might even find ourselves executed.

Why is God like this? Is it because he's mean or hateful? Is it because he doesn't like us? Is he the crusty neighborhood curmudgeon who keeps your baseball when it rolls into his yard? And when you dare to wander in to retrieve it, sics a lion on you to tear you to pieces?

No . . . God is like this, because for all he is—loving, gracious, merciful, a caring Father to his careless children—he is also perfectly holy and eternally righteous. And because he is perfectly holy and eternally righteous, our disobedience, sin, corruption, injustice, falsehood, rebellion—all of it—must be punished. A holy God will not let sin stand.

Look at what some hippie philosopher says in Ecclesiastes:

> The end of the matter; all has been heard. Fear God and keep his commandments, for this is the whole duty of man. For God will bring every deed into judgment, with every secret thing, whether good or evil. (Eccl. 12:13–14)

Which deeds will God judge? All of them.

And why the importance of "every secret thing"? It's not just about sins we do in private or keep secret; it's about our integrity, our hearts, our character, our inner lives. Even the stuff we do in our minds—hate, malice, lust, the desire to disobey God—those things will be judged too. God is a completist, is he not?

Because Jesus is everything that God is, and because God is a righteous judge of all creation, we must discuss God's judgment in relation

8. Also every lowercase *j*.

to Jesus. The holiness of God is essential to the person of Jesus Christ. In Revelation 4:8, we see the Lamb (Jesus) being praised with "Holy, holy, holy"—thrice holy, perfectly holy; yet, in the Gospels, we don't see Jesus going around smacking people all the time or siccing lions on them, do we? Is this because Jesus is *yin* to God's *yang*?

An ancient heresy that still persists in some circles today would answer *yes*. In the second century, a guy named Marcion got a flea up his butt about the Old Testament being an outrageous depiction of an inferior god with a tempestuous temper. Marcion decided the Old Testament God was mean and vicious and deceptive, and that the New Testament God was not only different, but a vast improvement. Marcion set up Jesus as the superior redeemer God against the nasty predecessor, and eventually denied the canonicity of the Old Testament altogether. The Marcionite heresy swayed a lot of people back then, and it rears its ugly head today, even in some corners of the church, whenever someone talks about the God of the Old Testament as if he is different from the God of the New, as if the Old Testament shows God being mean, and the New Testament shows God being nice. There is no shadow of turning, however, with God.[9] He is the same today as he was yesterday and will be tomorrow.

The dualistic approach is echoed even in current campaigns against the penal substitution theory of the Atonement. Critics maintain that penal substitution proposes an unloving god essentially inflicting child abuse upon his loving son.[10] They are wrong.[11]

We cannot and must not set Jesus against God, either in our discomfort with God's wrath or in dismissal of Jesus' judgment.

Take a look at John 5:21–23:

---

9. James 1:17.

10. See Alan Jones, *Reimagining Christianity* (Hoboken, NJ: John Wiley & Sons, 2004). Also, Steve Chalke and Alan Mann, *The Lost Message of Jesus* (Grand Rapids: Zondervan, 2004).

11. See Steve Jeffery, Michael Ovey, and Andrew Sach, *Pierced for Our Transgressions: Rediscovering the Glory of Penal Substitution* (Wheaton, IL: Crossway, 2007).

> For as the Father raises the dead and gives them life, so also the Son gives life to whom he will. The Father judges no one, but has given all judgment to the Son, that all may honor the Son, just as they honor the Father. Whoever does not honor the Son does not honor the Father who sent him.

The Christian faith says, "Look to Jesus, and you'll see what God wants you to know about himself." Yet we first see who God is in the pre-Christian narrative of the Old Testament. Jesus is the Old Testament's YHWH made physically manifest, so the proclaiming and delivering of YHWH's righteousness and judgment fall under Jesus' jurisdiction, too.

Does Jesus' judgment make you nervous? Maybe it should.[12]

Maybe when you think of *judgment*, you can't help but think of judgmentalism. So in this chapter, we'll sidetrack briefly to mark out the difference between judging and being judgmental, but our main focus will be on three facets of Jesus' judgment: two things that Jesus the Judge *brings*, and one thing he *takes*.

## JESUS THE JUDGE BRINGS DISCIPLINE

In 1 Corinthians 11:32, Paul reminds us, "When we are judged by the Lord, we are disciplined so that we may not be condemned along with the world."

Followers of Jesus are not bound for hell. The judgment that Jesus brings on us can be most often thought of as *conviction*. By his proclamations and in his presence, we feel guilty about the trajectory of our lives when they are lived out of step with his will. This guilt should be

---

12. Not to make you paranoid or anything, but he *did* see that thing you did yesterday. Tsk, tsk.

momentary, and prompt us to repent, not to despair. When we come under conviction, we turn from the way we're going and follow Jesus the way he's going. This turning encompasses more, however, than just our behavior. It should originate deeper, as a spirit of repentance, and flow outward. The spirit of repentance is about understanding our sinful nature—not just our sinful actions—in the light of God's holiness. In light of Jesus' perfection, we should be convicted of our sin.

Take heart. This is the work of the Holy Spirit within you. In John 16:7–9, Jesus promises the coming of the Spirit, whom he calls the Helper[13] and who, he says, will convict the world of its sin. The Holy Spirit comforts, but also convicts.

*Conviction*. That's a legal term like *judgment*, isn't it? As in, being convicted of a crime. This conviction—that is, God's saying through Jesus, "You are a sinner" or "You are sinning"—is a way of disciplining us. It challenges our deception with the truth, telling us the painful truth about ourselves, which is the first step in being trained toward godliness, in being purified toward holiness. In a heavy, often painful way, Jesus judges our actions and thoughts, which spurs us all the more to work to eliminate those things from our lives.

Keep in mind, though, that Jesus is not a dispassionate, merciless judge, any more than YHWH is a coldhearted judge. YHWH is a loving Father, and Jesus the Son's work of discipline on us is an act of love. Look at what the author of Hebrews says:

> Have you forgotten the exhortation that addresses you as sons?
>
> "My son, do not regard lightly the discipline of the Lord,
> nor be weary when reproved by him.

13. "Helper" in the ESV, "Counselor" in the NIV, "Comforter" in the KJV.

> For the Lord disciplines the one he loves,
> and chastises every son whom he receives."
>
> It is for discipline that you have to endure. God is treating you as sons. For what son is there whom his father does not discipline? If you are left without discipline, in which all have participated, then you are illegitimate children and not sons. Besides this, we have had earthly fathers who disciplined us and we respected them. Shall we not much more be subject to the Father of spirits and live? For they disciplined us for a short time as it seemed best to them, but he disciplines us for our good, that we may share his holiness. (Heb. 12:5–10)

God disciplines us for our good, that we may share in his holiness. Jesus' judgment on us is an act of *discipline*, which is an act of *love*. It is meant to make us more and more like him, to train us. He is whipping us into shape, into a shape that conforms to his image.[14] Discipline is part of the sanctifying process by which God makes us holy as he is holy.

## ARE WE ALLOWED TO JUDGE OTHERS?

Now, of course, we want to sidetrack for a moment and talk about our judging others. In nine out of ten instances, "judgment as discipline" appears to be the motivation of interpersonal judgment among Christians.

Ever employed the phrase "holier than thou"? Ever had it lobbed at you? Many of us grew up in church cultures where judgment was rendered on sins both real and imaginary, both present and past—and those suspected to be future. It's quite true that the judgment we receive from

---

14. Romans 8:29.

fellow believers is not so much disciplinary as it is mercenary. It is more often demoralizing than edifying.

But the question remains: Are we allowed to judge others? Because if iron sharpens iron,[15] and if we are to confess our sins to each other,[16] and if we are meant to rebuke sharply,[17] and if those who are in authority are to be submitted to[18] . . . How does any of that happen without judgments occurring?

Are we supposed to judge each other? If so, in what way?

In John 7:24, Jesus instructs his followers, "Do not judge by appearances, but judge with right judgment."

How do we judge with right judgment?

You're probably familiar with the gospel account of Jesus' encounter with the adulterous woman.[19] Jesus is teaching in the temple courts at dawn, and the religious leaders show up with a woman they've apparently caught in the act. (No word on what they did with the man they caught her with.) They think they're trapping Jesus, the dispenser of forgiveness, because according to the Mosaic Law, when you catch adulterers you're supposed to execute them. So the leaders ask Jesus, "Hey, can we stone this chick?"

Jesus does a very curious thing. He doesn't answer at first. John tells us that Jesus got down in the dirt and started drawing in the dust. This is a great image and, oh, how I wish I knew what he was writing! Was he just doodling while he thought of an answer? Maybe he was drawing the proverbial line in the sand.

The story doesn't tell us what he was writing or drawing, but here's what I think: Take this with a grain of salt, but I think he was down in the dust, and he had all these guys leaning over him looking to see what

15. Proverbs 27:17.
16. James 5:16.
17. Titus 1:13.
18. Romans 13:2–3.
19. John 8:1–11.

he was gonna do or say, and I think he was writing stuff like, "Lusts after women," "Beats his wife and children," "Cheats in the marketplace," "Lies habitually," maybe even "murderer." I imagine Jesus was writing all their sins down there, freaking them out with what he knew, what he knew was in their hearts.

In any event, whatever he was writing, by the time he was done and looked up, there wasn't anybody left. Perhaps his exposure of their sins had convicted them so much they had to flee. You don't mess with Jesus the Judge.

When Jesus looks up, the only person still standing there is the woman. "Where'd they go?" Jesus wants to know. "Is anybody condemning you?"

"Nobody," the woman says.

"Well, neither do I," Jesus answers. "Go . . ."

*But!* Here's the part nearly everyone leaves out when they retell this story of how cool Jesus is with all the junk we do. He says, "Go. But leave your life of sin."

See, Jesus wasn't saying, "You don't deserve to be executed." Jesus knew the Law.

He wasn't saying, "Oh, you didn't do anything wrong." Clearly, she had.

He was saying, "You're a sinner and you need to stop, but I'm not here to condemn you."

Do you recall what John wrote earlier in his gospel? Jesus didn't come to condemn the world but to save the world through himself.[20]

Jesus will convict you, and Jesus will judge your sin. But provided you repent and follow him, Jesus does not bring condemnation. He brings forgiveness.

That is the spirit of judgment we are to have for each other. The Pharisees were within their moral rights under the Mosaic Law to

---

20. John 3:17.

execute a caught-in-the-act adulterer, but they weren't *really* judging according to the standard of God's holiness. They denied the Lordship of Christ—instead, they were trying to trap him—and they were not administering holiness in the context of God's loving sovereignty but in the context of their own hypocritical motives.

Also in John 8, Jesus says, "You judge according to the flesh; I judge no one. Yet even if I do judge, my judgment is true, for it is not I alone who judge, but I and the Father who sent me" (John 8:15–16).

Jesus isn't talking out of both sides of his mouth here. He's saying, "You judge with a fleshly judgment. That's not how I judge. I judge with true judgment, because it comes from a place of perfection and is derived from the authority of the Father, which he has given to me. I don't judge independently, as you do, but in conjunction with the Father's righteous judgment."

Okay, so Jesus judges perfectly—but he's also perfect himself. So does that mean that we—who are less than perfectly holy—aren't to judge at all?

I tread lightly here, but I do think there is a specific, God-sanctioned sense in which we are permitted, and in fact commanded, to judge others. First of all, in 1 Corinthians 5, Paul talks about judging those inside the community of faith, not outside. This tells us two things:

1. We're responsible for our brothers in Christ, to bring discipline and conviction to each other in the hopes of further making the body of Christ holy as God is holy.
2. We have no business judging people who are not Christians.

Look, lost people do lost things. That is just common sense. Treating people who don't know Christ like they should behave as if they do know Christ is just naive, and it says more about our own state of unholiness than it does theirs.

So no judging of non-Christians, but Paul says a certain kind of judgment among the brethren is kosher. What are some parameters for this judgment?

Let's start with a warning from Jesus:

> Judge not, that you be not judged. For with the judgment you pronounce you will be judged, and with the measure you use it will be measured to you. Why do you see the speck that is in your brother's eye, but do not notice the log that is in your own eye? (Matt. 7:1–3)

Rule number one: hypocrisy is out. Jesus says we are not to judge as if we're exempt from judgment ourselves. If you judge someone from a place of being over them and against them, rather than beside them and for them, your judgment is corrupt, and it will come back to bite you. Don't go around pointing out specks while acting as if you don't have planks of your own.

Here's another good rule: "So speak and so act as those who are to be judged under the law of liberty" (James 2:12).

"The law of liberty" means that when we judge ourselves, or others, or a situation, we are to do so guided by the belief that Jesus brings freedom, not condemnation. Our guiding principle for disciplining and rebuking is not malice or jealousy or despair, but love and concern and hope. We judge not to tell people they are going to hell, but to remind them that Christ has brought heaven. It's not to say, "This is where you're going," but to say, "There's a better way." This is just good gospel proclamation.

There are warnings attached to judgment. If you go around acting like the perfect bearer of God's word to those who need to "turn or burn," you will not escape the penalty for your hypocrisy. Paul ominously portends, "Do you suppose, O man—you who judge those who do such things and yet do them yourself—that you will escape the judgment of God?" (Rom. 2:3).

One final parameter I'd offer, in addition to "Don't be a hypocrite" and "Judge according to liberty" is this: "Be very careful." If more Christians practiced judgment of each other that was devoid of hypocrisy and according to liberty, we'd not only all be better off, we'd also have a better view of judgment altogether.

There's a difference between judging and being judgmental. The American church is burned out on judgmentalism, but the American church could use a whole lot more righteous judgment. What's the difference? Judgment says, "This falls short of God's standard and he calls us to a better way." Judgmentalism says, "Everyone but me falls short of God's standard, and thank goodness I'm here to constantly remind you that you are probably condemned."

One is a reflection of God's holiness; the other is a reflection of man's works.

One is in respect of God; the other is in admiration of self.

Remember that judgmentalism will not escape judgment. If we want to participate in God's discipline of his church, we will participate humbly, meekly, and reverently in the administration of judgment as Jesus would judge—a judgment with restoration in mind.

## JESUS THE JUDGE BRINGS JUSTICE

Jesus once told his disciples a curious little parable about a persistent woman and a worn-down judge.[21] In a certain town, there ruled a very selfish judge who didn't fear God and didn't care about anybody else. Every day, a widow would come to him and plead for justice concerning someone's offense against her. And every day, the judge, unmoved, would dismiss her.

21. Luke 18:1–8.

But eventually she wore him down. He got aggravated, basically, tired of having to deal with her. Finally, he decided, "Even though I don't care about God or men, I'm going to give this widow justice, because she's wearing me out with her showing up here every day."

This is an odd analogy for Jesus to give, because his point with this story is that persistence achieves results. He draws a connection between the widow who didn't give up with her pleas to a godless judge and our own petitioning to God for justice. Apparently, he's saying, "Don't give up, keep hoping, keep praying, and God will bring justice."

This is what Jesus says to his followers at the end: "Now you've seen how even an unjust judge will bring justice eventually. And will not God bring about justice for his chosen ones, who cry out to him day and night? Will he keep putting them off? I tell you, he will see that they get justice, and quickly. However, when the Son of Man comes, will he find you faithfully hoping?"

This is his promise: God will bring justice. We live in a world of injustice, unfairness, abuse of power; of corruption in nations, in churches, in families. Evil appears to prevail, and it certainly seems to profit. But God will bring justice. He will not put it off for those who remain faithful.

David puts it lyrically:

> Turn away from evil and do good;
>     so shall you dwell forever.
> For the Lord loves justice;
>     he will not forsake his saints.
> They are preserved forever,
>     but the children of the wicked shall be cut off.
> The righteous shall inherit the land
>     and dwell upon it forever.
>
> (Ps. 37:27–29)

That's a great promise to those of us who've known suffering, who still know suffering. Too many of us have withstood terrible childhoods and personal histories. Maybe you, dear reader, are still in an oppressive, repressive, (God forbid) abusive situation. Maybe you have found the power in Christ to forgive those who've sinned against you, but God is nevertheless promising that justice will be done. Evil does not go unpunished.

And if it isn't punished this side of the afterlife, you can bet it will be on the other side. Don't mistake the inauguration of the kingdom of God on earth for the consummation of it. Don't mistake the prosperity of evildoers on this side of eternity as "getting away with it." That's not going to happen. In the context of eternity, this life is just a blip.

As I first revised this chapter, the news was occupied with the developing stories of church shootings in the Denver, Colorado, area. A young man shot and killed two young missionaries at a Youth With a Mission facility. He then drove nearly two hours to New Life Church in Colorado Springs and murdered two teenage girls and wounded several other people. After being shot by a security guard, the shooter took his own life.[22] These tragic events concluded a week that saw another disturbed young man with firearms murder shoppers at a mall in Nebraska.

The question events like these provoke is "Why?" And when we hear of things like this, when we think of abuse and rape and murder and terrorist attacks, the world (and frequently the church) wants to know, "Where is Jesus when these things happen? Where is the justice?"

What we must remember is that Jesus the Judge is sitting at the right hand of the Father in heaven, storing up wrath for the unrepentant

---

22. We now know that the gunman, Matthew Murray, despite being fired on by the security guard, actually took his own life. See Patrick O'Driscoll and Carolyn Pesce, "Police: Gunman died of self-inflicted gunshot," *USA Today*, December 11, 2007, http://www.usatoday.com/news/nation/2007-12-10-colorado-monday_N.htm.

perpetrators of evil, wrath he will pour out on them in righteous fury and holy vengeance at the end of days. Evil will not go unpunished.

This is the promise of God's kingdom, the kingdom that operates within this brief, chaotic blip but with the rhythm and texture of eternity. In this life, and this earthly kingdom, the unrighteous reign and prosper, might makes right, absolute power corrupts absolutely.

Consequently, this life is full of hurting, broken, stepped on and stepped over, abused, victimized, marginalized people. But we see Jesus saying in the Sermon on the Mount, in that portion called the Beatitudes,[23] "In my kingdom, blessed are those who mourn. Blessed are those who thirst for righteousness. Blessed are the poor. Blessed are the merciful. Blessed are the peacemakers." Because in God's kingdom, justice is delivered. Furthermore, because of all Christ has accomplished, sin and death and those who traffic in them will be utterly demolished.

Take heart and don't give up. Repent and flee from wickedness, and you will be blessed. You will be remembered. Your days of distress will turn into victory. The tears you sow in grief today will be reaped in a harvest of joy.

We have now covered two things that Jesus the Judge brings: discipline and justice.

Now we'll examine one thing that Jesus the Judge *takes.*

## JESUS THE JUDGE TAKES THE PUNISHMENT

Because God is holy, and because we are not, there is a reckoning due. Because evil will be punished, and because we are evil, punishment is deserved. Because we are sinners, and because there is no forgiveness for sins without the shedding of blood,[24] blood must be shed to set things right.

---

23. Matthew 5:3–11.
24. Hebrews 9:22.

If you're one of those who's always concerned about fairness, about whether God is being unfair, about people getting away with evil, let me say this gently but firmly: *you do not want a fair God*. The *fair* thing would be for God to destroy all of us because of our sin, because of our falling short of his glory. Yet that is the very point and definition of grace: it is God *not* giving us what we deserve. We *deserve* punishment for our sins; we *deserve* to have Jesus, the perfect arbiter of right and wrong, say to us, "You don't pass muster. You deserve eternal death."

But instead, our Judge says, "You don't pass muster and you deserve eternal death, but because I'm not logically fair but graciously just, I will take your place."

We find Paul's explication of this astonishing truth in his letter to the Romans:

> But because of your hard and impenitent heart you are storing up wrath for yourself on the day of wrath when God's righteous judgment will be revealed. He will render to each one according to his works: to those who by patience in well-doing seek for glory and honor and immortality, he will give eternal life; but for those who are self-seeking and do not obey the truth, but obey unrighteousness, there will be wrath and fury. (Rom. 2:5–8)

> But God shows his love for us in that while we were still sinners, Christ died for us. Since, therefore, we have now been justified by his blood, much more shall we be saved by him from the wrath of God. For if while we were enemies we were reconciled to God by the death of his Son, much more, now that we are reconciled, shall we be saved by his life. (Rom. 5:8–10)

What an amazing thing! That's the beauty and mystery of the gospel of grace.

We're storing up wrath for ourselves, and for those who don't obey the truth, the result will be wrathful judgment from a furious God. But because God loves us despite our sin, Christ has taken the wrath for us, absorbed that fury for us. God hasn't let sin slide. God hasn't let sin off the hook. He didn't change the rules. Punishment is needed; blood must be shed. But we have a savior—God himself—who takes that on for us. He takes the punishment; he offers his blood.

Do you know what Christ has saved us from? Not just sin, but the due penalty of our sin. Christ has saved us from the wrath of God. Don't go Marcionite on this idea, like those who misunderstand and therefore shortchange the biblical God of wrath. Christ has saved us from the judgment of God.

Jesus is the Provider, who gives himself as the Provision. He's the Shepherd, who becomes the Sacrificial Lamb. He's the Judge, who becomes the punishment itself.

Here again is the notion of penal substitution—*penal*, because it involves justice and punishment; *substitution*, because Christ takes that punishment and fulfills justice by substituting himself in our place. This is not a demonstration of God's being abusive, any more than the incarnation is a demonstration of his being a glutton for punishment. It's a demonstration of a gracious, loving God who inserts himself between his children and the judgment due them.

John elaborates further on the legal motif:

> My little children, I am writing these things to you so that you may not sin. But if anyone does sin, we have an advocate with the Father, Jesus Christ the righteous. He is the propitiation for our sins, and not for ours only but also for the sins of the whole world.

> And by this we know that we have come to know him,
> if we keep his commandments. (1 John 2:1–3)

Check that out: Jesus is not just our Judge, he's also our Advocate. He's like a defense lawyer, arguing on our behalf. For every objection raised by our sin, Christ overrules it by his blood. For every evidence against us—and there is eternal evidence against us—there is an eternal satisfaction in the sin-covering of God's grace.

Jesus is our advocate, our friend, our redeemer.

In Isaiah 53, Isaiah gives a vivid account of the punishment Jesus will take generations later. The punishment is described as being received *for us*. He was pierced for our sins, wounded for our misdeeds. The punishment that we deserved fell on his head and crushed him. By the bloody, mutilated flesh on his back, we find healing.

What an amazing thing that we have in Jesus Christ the holy, righteous, pure wrath of God the Judge, but also the love and the grace and the redemption of God the Savior. We have a judge who brings discipline and justice, but who also takes the punishment on himself.

Do you know much about the Ark of the Covenant in the Old Testament? Maybe, thanks to Indiana Jones and *Raiders of the Lost Ark*, you know that if you take the lid off, an angry angel comes out and melts your face off. Biblically speaking, however, the Ark was a sacred symbol of God's presence with his people. It was, in a transportable altar-type form, emblematic of God's glory. The children of Israel carried it around with awe and care as a way of taking God's tangible glory with them wherever they went.

God was so serious about his glory that anyone who touched this thing would die instantly. There's even a little story in the Old Testament about the thing almost tumbling from an ox cart and some guy reaching out just to catch it.[25] He wasn't trying to sin or do anything

25. 1 Chronicles 13:7–10.

wrong. On the contrary, he just wanted to catch the Ark to make sure it was okay. But as soon as he touched it—*zap!*—homeboy was toast. That's how serious God is about his holiness.

Two thousand years ago, God's glory came into the midst of his people in the form of a Galilean commoner named Jesus. He walked around as one of the people, dusty and sweaty. Human. And yet he was the fulfillment of all the testimonies of glory that God had sent generations earlier.

The temple? Replaced by Jesus.

The Word of God? Incarnate in Jesus.

The Law? Fulfilled in Jesus.

The prophets? Culminated in Jesus.

The tabernacle? Foreshadow of Jesus.

The glory of the Lord? Present in Jesus.[26]

But his fulfillment was unlike the old days when the holiness of God was represented in the glory of the Ark of the Covenant and it could kill you with one touch. No . . . those who reached out to Jesus found healing and restoration. He made blind men see and dead flesh live.

When the glory of the Lord came with the Ark, a guy just doing his duty got cut down simply by touching it. When the glory of the Lord came in person, a woman reached out just to grab the edge of the hem of his robe . . . and she was instantly healed.[27]

In 1 Chronicles, we see a foreshadow of this fulfillment. The people of God are welcoming the entrance of the Ark of the Covenant; this holy emblem, this dangerous object of God's glory, comes into their midst and they are overcome with joy and the spirit of worship. The just judgment of God is in their midst, and they praise him for his might and power, and for his might and power to save.

---

26. The author of Hebrews calls the Son the "radiance" of God's glory (1:3).
27. Matthew 9:20–22.

Let's conclude our celebration of the righteous judgment of Jesus the Judge by reflecting on the Israelites' celebration of the judgment of YHWH:

> Sing to the LORD, all the earth!
> Tell of his salvation from day to day.
> Declare his glory among the nations,
> his marvelous works among all the peoples!
> For great is the LORD, and greatly to be praised,
> and he is to be held in awe above all gods.
> For all the gods of the peoples are idols,
> but the LORD made the heavens.
> Splendor and majesty are before him;
> strength and joy are in his place.
>
> Ascribe to the LORD, O clans of the peoples,
> ascribe to the LORD glory and strength!
> Ascribe to the LORD the glory due his name;
> bring an offering and come before him!
> Worship the LORD in the splendor of holiness;
> tremble before him, all the earth;
> yes, the world is established; it shall never be moved.
> Let the heavens be glad, and let the earth rejoice,
> and let them say among the nations, "The LORD reigns!"
> Let the sea roar, and all that fills it;
> let the field exult, and everything in it!
> Then shall the trees of the forest sing for joy
> before the LORD, for he comes to judge the earth.
> Oh give thanks to the LORD, for he is good;
> for his steadfast love endures forever!

Say also:

> "Save us, O God of our salvation,
> and gather and deliver us from among the nations,
> that we may give thanks to your holy name,
> and glory in your praise.
> Blessed be the LORD, the God of Israel,
> from everlasting to everlasting!"

Then all the people said, "Amen!" and praised the LORD.

(1 Chron. 16:23–36)

Did you read it? I hope you didn't skip it because it's a Bible passage. Read it, you cheater, and when you're done, say "Amen" and "Praise the Lord."

7

# JESUS THE REDEEMER

The story of redemption is Jesus' redemption told in millions of stories. I really believe that, and have experienced it myself, so I hope you won't mind if this particular portrait is painted through storytelling.

The first story I want to share with you belongs to Steve and LaVonne Jones.[1] Steve is my cousin, and I have asked him to tell his story in his own words.

> In March 1999, LaVonne conceived our third child. This was quite a shock because we thought we were done with all the baby stuff, but we soon grew used to the idea of having another child and began looking forward to it. Apparently, our plans didn't fit in with God's plans.
>
> About a month or so later, when LaVonne received the results of her blood work, the doctor was somewhat concerned about a high reading in one of the areas. All he would tell us is that the reading he was getting usually

1. Steve Jones, e-mail correspondence with the author, October 17, 2008.

indicated there was a brain or spine problem, but he didn't get specific. Quite frankly, I was so oblivious to it all that I didn't even give it a second thought.

Several days later, they did an ultrasound to check the baby, and everything looked perfectly fine in the spinal area, but they couldn't get a good view of the head. LaVonne was then scheduled for an ultrasound in Spokane, where they had better equipment.

We met with a genetics counselor to discuss the blood results. LaVonne had an abnormally high amount of AFP in her blood. This is a protein produced by the baby in the uterus. When it gets into the mother's bloodstream, there is cause for concern because it usually indicates there is an opening in the baby and the protein is being released into the amniotic fluid, passing through the placenta into the mother's blood.

From there, we went to Sacred Heart Medical Center and had the ultrasound done. I don't think either of us could have prepared ourselves for what we would see. As clear as day, we could see that the baby's lower back had an opening. The diagnosis was spina bifida. We hadn't thought there would be a spinal problem, because the original ultrasound hadn't picked it up.

One could not imagine the thoughts racing through my head. My first thought was, "Is he going to live?" The reason I thought that was because I work with a man whose wife lost a spina bifida baby when she went into labor at about twenty weeks. At this point, our baby was right about eighteen weeks.

The doctor and the genetics counselor explained to us the range of possible results—everything from dying at birth to growing into adulthood with braces on his legs. That's quite a range! And it wasn't what I wanted to hear. I wanted statistics, odds, histories, and anything else concrete that would help me better understand what we were dealing with. I wanted someone to tell me exactly what we were looking at here so I could get some sort of grasp on it. No one could, and that's because they didn't know.

I felt totally lost and helpless at that moment—and I mean *totally*. Other than wanting to be with my family, the only other thing I could think of was our unborn baby. Mostly, I hurt for him, because he had done nothing to deserve this, and he was going to be faced with living with this for the rest of his life . . . if he lived.

We drove home that evening, crying the whole way. We just didn't understand why this was happening, nor did we like the odds. The doctor led us to believe (we later found out we had misunderstood her) that the baby's chances of survival were slim. We thought our baby would not even make it to full term because of how severe the spina bifida was at eighteen weeks. But when we got a few things clarified, we found out that he had just as good a chance of doing as well as any other spina bifida case.

I am ashamed to admit that at one point we were tempted to end the pregnancy. We thought the baby had no chance of survival at all and figured we would just get the pain of losing him over with. LaVonne was in such a state of pain and shock, she couldn't think clearly at all, nor could I, for that matter.

I e-mailed my family that night and told them the news—and that we were really torn apart about what to do. I remember mentioning that if we decided to terminate the pregnancy, I knew God would forgive us, but I honestly didn't think that I could ever forgive myself.

One night, I couldn't sleep. I would like to blame it on the stress and shock of the whole situation, but I knew then and I know now, that I couldn't sleep due to the temptation of ending the pregnancy. I kept trying to justify my thoughts by trying to convince myself that I would just take care of what God had already chosen for this child: no life. I had never felt so miserable! Here I was tempted to go along with something I had been so adamantly against all my adult life, and I was so torn up about it I couldn't eat for fear I would just vomit.

God really began to convict me. This was conviction like I had never felt before in my life. I went into my room sometime late in the morning on July 2, fell face down on my bed and cried. I'm not talking about shedding a few tears. I bawled. I wasn't only weeping over the turmoil going on in my head, but for the baby. I asked God why he was doing this.

Of all the things I didn't know, one thing was for certain: God was not going to let me rest easy until I changed my mind. So I did. The next afternoon, I told LaVonne that we were going to have this child as long as God saw fit. It didn't take much to convince her, and we were in agreement. I now realized what I had known deep down inside all along: God had given this baby life and we had no right whatsoever to undo what God had done. I firmly believe that we would have gotten all the way over to Spokane and we would have turned back. I know in my heart that even though I had considered abortion, I never could have followed through with it. Now I know, firsthand, the temptation others have faced, and will face, in similar situations.

The Devil really tries to convince you, at times through other people, that the child will have no "normal" life, will take up all your time and resources, and will deprive the existing siblings of their needed love and attention—all of which are complete lies. We even had one person try to convince us that we would be doing it out of love. Love for whom, or worse yet, for what? Love for myself? My wife? Our children? Our families? Our finances? Our current standard of living? Our way of life? It certainly would not have been out of love for the baby.

For reasons unbeknownst to us, God had chosen us to bring a child with spinal bifida into the world.

Since we decided to keep him until God sees fit to take him (or us) home, I haven't been happier. LaVonne says I'm too happy. I just know that for the first time in my life my faith was really tested and we did what we felt God would have us do.

We realize that by choosing to have this baby we could be facing a lifetime of caring for him. At this point, I would welcome it. I just want him to live; and if God decides to take him home soon after he's born, I just want to see him as long as God will allow. If God chooses to let us keep him, I don't care if he has to ride around in a wheelchair or walk with braces. I don't care if he doesn't grow up to be a scholar. I don't care if he isn't the captain of the football or baseball team. I don't even care if he can't play Little League baseball or learn to swim.

I just want him to feel sunshine on his face, snow on his tongue, a cool rain, the soft fur of a cat or dog on his hands, a kiss on the cheek, a hug, God's salvation. I want him to see a campfire, a rainbow, the ocean, a beautiful sunset, a magnificent lightning storm, his parents and siblings and, eventually, God. I want him to taste a hamburger, a hot dog, a good chicken fried steak, the sourness of a lemon, ice cream and dewberry pie. I want him to smell a fresh summer rain, a wet evergreen forest, a rose, a skunk. I want him to hear a dog bark; a wave crash; a waterfall; thunder; his parents say, "We love you"; and God's Word. I want to hear him laugh, cry, scream, call me *Daddy* and call God *Father.* That's what I want for this child and that is what we ask God for. His whole family will definitely love him in the same manner God loves us . . . unconditionally.

LaVonne gave birth to Colton on November 2, 1999. Steve later wrote,

About an hour and a half after Colton was born, the neurosurgeon informed us that his cerebellum and brain stem were much lower in the neck than they should be and didn't seem to be making a good connection with the brain. He told us that the condition Colton had was "incompatible with life," and that his chances of survival were extremely low. The main problem was that Colton was not voluntarily breathing and was on a ventilator. And the prognosis was that he

> probably would not breathe on his own. Needless to say, this devastated us.
>
> We got LaVonne to her room, and when we got a few minutes to ourselves, we began to pray . . . again. This time, it wasn't for healing in his legs, but rather healing in his head. Suddenly, the fact that his legs worked didn't matter anymore, and we couldn't understand why God had chosen to heal his legs only to turn around and allow this to happen.
>
> At that moment, I felt what thousands of other fathers had felt before me. I was losing a child and there was nothing in my physical being that could do anything about it. I felt more helpless now than when we had initially found out he had spina bifida. At the same time, I felt even closer to God.

In looking back at their experience with Colton during his lifetime, Steve adds,

> To say the last nine years have been a roller coaster ride would be an understatement. Our lives have been filled with joy and sorrow, happiness and sadness, achievement and disappointment. A good portion of the first three years of Colton's life was spent in the hospital, with most of it being during his first year. It seemed that when one issue would get taken care of, another would surface.
>
> There have been sleepless nights in uncomfortable hospital room chairs; hours of tears and prayer; feelings of loneliness when you think no one understands or cares what you're going through; and countless trips to a city one hundred miles away for appointments that

lasted only fifteen minutes at times. There have been many moments of feeling like our hearts were getting ripped out when Colton would come out of surgery, cry out for comfort and all we could do was stroke his face, whisper his name, and try to convince him it would be all right. There have been moments of trying our best not to cry in front of him as he was being prepped for a surgery so risky and sensitive that we didn't know if we would ever speak to him again. Kyndra and Cody, Colton's older sister and brother, have had to deal with the stress of saying good-bye to him before he headed off to another surgery, and then staying home and not knowing whether their little brother was going to come back.

But we have also seen God work in ways that we would never have seen otherwise. We've seen a newborn baby breathe without the aid of a ventilator only two days after we were told that his condition was "incompatible with life." We've seen a cyst in a six-year-old's brain stem disappear without a trace of existence the day he was going to have surgery to have it drained. We've been able to use all of these experiences to teach our children about the goodness of God and to watch them have the opportunity to witness it firsthand. Others have been touched and have shared our tears and our joy.

The amount of time and dedication required to raise and care for a child with a disability such as this is more than we could have ever expected. Many, I'm sure, can relate, and many have cared for children whose conditions were more severe. My wife, LaVonne, has essentially put her whole life aside to care for Colton. Is it hard? Without

> question. Is it rewarding? Without a doubt. She adores that child and he adores her. I honestly don't think I could do what she does as well as she does it. Colton's wonderful spirit is a direct reflection of how much he is loved, and evidence of what God has given him.
>
> Because of all we've been through, our family is close, our faith has grown, and our trust in God has deepened. I don't think there's anything that builds as much faith as having absolutely no control over a situation you care so deeply about and realizing that God is the only one who can do anything about it. That's where we were and still are. We didn't know if we would ever see our baby alive; and if we did, we didn't know to what extent. We still don't know if he will outlive us; but then again, we don't know that about any of our children.
>
> God is good. And I don't say that lightly. I know without a doubt that God loves us, cares for us, and wants what is best for us. I am still in awe of all he has done in our situation. We are blessed more than we deserve and it's truly humbling. To be the recipient of such acts of grace has been more than a blessing—it has been an honor.

I'll be honest in saying that I don't know how someone gets to that point. There are clues, of course. Steve talks about prayer and about perspective. But to endure under such weight and say, "We are blessed" and "It has been an honor" is not sentimentality—it is supernatural. Steve's story is not a testament to learning lessons or finally being able to breathe a sigh of relief. His story is a testament to the real-life weight of, and real-life victory in, redemption. He is honest enough to admit his doubts and sins, but he focuses not on what Colton has "cost" their family, but on the invaluable treasure that Colton is to their family, and to the world.

I haven't been through anything one-fourth as difficult as Steve and LaVonne have. Yet even though I see God's refining me in my pain and struggles, I'd certainly go back and change a whole bunch of stuff if I could.

Redemption is something that only those who've been through it can understand. Explaining a redemption like Steve and LaVonne have experienced is like explaining grace to someone who's never experienced it. It's a scandal. It's foolishness. But you who have been through intense times of trial, or the testing of your mettle, know from experience that keeping the faith brings you out on the other side stronger, more faithful, more in love with God.

That is the power of Jesus the Redeemer. When we talk about redemption, we could—and should!—talk about redemption from sins or redemption from God's wrath. The word *redeem*, in a biblical context, has connotations of paying a ransom, as Jesus did with his life, or of rescuing someone. Those ideas play heavily in the narrative approach I mean to take in this chapter. But because there's plenty of space in other chapters to highlight our salvation from sin, in this chapter I want to feature God as Storyteller and demonstrate how *redeem* can also mean "re-make." I want to show you how committed God is to taking our checkered pasts, replete with flaws and failings and mistakes and misfortunes—and using them to mold our lives and our hearts into something beautiful.

We are impatient, shortsighted people, though, aren't we? God may be telling a great story of redemption with our problems and pains, but very often he doesn't tell it *quickly* enough to satisfy us. We are sitcom people serving the God of epic novels. While we are day in and day out concerned about relief, God sees through infinite eyes in the scope of eternity. The hurts of our lives, the lingering darkness we cannot see beyond, he may see as mere shadows in the otherwise brilliant eternal portrait he is painting of his dominion over our lives. We typically see this portrait, albeit in a limited way, after we've passed through the redemptive journey. Imagine hacking your way through a dismal valley, then the next day you view it from a scenic overlook and realize how beautiful it is. But the key to experiencing the sustaining power of Jesus the Redeemer in our lives is experiencing him by trusting him precisely *in* those long valley crossings.

How do we get to that other side? How do we see God's method in the madness, God's providence in our pain, before we get there?

To be honest with you, I'm not sure. I'll offer (respectfully) some applicatory advice at the end of this chapter, but I'm generally reluctant to hand out a patented set of Several Steps to Whatever-the-heck,[2] especially when the steps we're taking are taken under the heavy weight of real-life struggles—illnesses and injuries, betrayals and infidelities, distances and deaths. These aren't "How to Succeed at Work"–type experiences.

Do you know the story of the invalid at the Sheep Gate pool? Here's a portion of it from John's gospel, a little something to further whet your appetite for redemption:

> Now there is in Jerusalem by the Sheep Gate a pool, in Aramaic called Bethesda, which has five roofed colonnades. In these lay a multitude of invalids—blind, lame, and paralyzed. One man was there who had been an invalid for thirty-eight years. When Jesus saw him lying there and knew that he had already been there a long time, he said to him, "Do you want to be healed?" The sick man answered him, "Sir, I have no one to put me into the pool when the water is stirred up, and while I am going another steps down before me." Jesus said to

2. Unlike thousands of preachers in American churches this weekend.

> him, "Get up, take up your bed, and walk." And at once the man was healed, and he took up his bed and walked. (John 5:2–9)

This man had waited thirty-eight years for his healing. Thirty-eight years![3] You don't need me to tell you, that's a long time. (And, of course, some people go their entire lives enduring excruciating pain that is never healed until they are received into God's presence after their death.) Day after day, for "a long time" the passage tells us, this man watched while others ignored him, even stepped over him, to get their own healing. Day after day, for a long time, this man lay paralyzed, mere inches from hordes of people celebrating the joy of the pool's healing power. Day after day, for nearly forty years, I imagine this man had to fight feelings of resentment, jealousy, and despair. But he didn't give up.

Heck, how could he? He was paralyzed, right? What other choice did he have? This, I submit, is beside the point. The point is that the man could have decided, "This will never happen for me." In his spirit, he could have abandoned all hope. He might not have been able to flee the pool's tantalizing vision, but he could have given up hope he'd ever make it into the water himself.

In the end, of course, it wasn't the pool he needed. It was Jesus. How often do you or I believe material substitutes will cure what ails us? We hold out hope for a new job, a new home, a new relationship, a new whatever, believing that when we finally accomplish this or that, we'll finally be free of our doubts or fears or struggles. Rarely do we embrace that only the grace of God in Jesus is sufficient for our needs.

Do you think Steve and LaVonne could have given up? They could have "easily" terminated their pregnancy, or begrudgingly taken to the

---

3. Perhaps not coincidentally, as forty years in Jesus' time generally constituted a generation.

care of Colton as an insufferable burden and curse from God. We've all known people who have served merely out of obligation. Even if Steve and LaVonne had merely "done their duty," do you think they would have emerged on the far side of the journey seeing their traveled path with redemption-colored glasses?

Here's one tiny truth I'll offer on how to see your painful journey as an act of God consecrating your life to his will: during the journey, work at consecrating each moment to faith, hope, and love. By faith, I don't mean "believing in yourself." By hope, I do not mean "hoping for the best." By love, I do not mean "following your heart" or some such vague nonsense. We, like invalids, are incapable. We, unlike God, do not really know what's best for us. We, unlike Jesus, have hearts that are deceitful above all things.[4]

No, we will endure, we will prevail, we will persevere, we will be redeemed, both during the process and in the culmination of a Christ-centered faith, hope, and love. Day in and day out, we consider our options to endure or despair, and we choose *endure*, because to despair is no more valid an option for us than getting up and running away is for a paralyzed man. We consider our lot and declare, in the spirit of Simon Peter, "To whom shall we go?"[5] Because opting for anything other than proximity to Jesus is no option at all.

One of the most interesting books of the Bible is a collection of complaints, but even Lamentations does not suggest despair as a reasonable alternative for God's people. Take a look at one passage, and savor the poetic transition from breathless desperation to incredible hope:

> Our enemies shout abuse,
>     their mouths full of derision, spitting invective.

4. Jeremiah 17:9.
5. John 6:67–69.

We've been to hell and back.
    We've nowhere to turn, nowhere to go.
Rivers of tears pour from my eyes
    at the smashup of my dear people.

The tears stream from my eyes,
    an artesian well of tears,
Until you, God, look down from on high,
    look and see my tears.
When I see what's happened to the young women in the city,
    the pain breaks my heart.

Enemies with no reason to be enemies
    hunted me down like a bird.
They threw me into a pit,
    then pelted me with stones.
Then the rains came and filled the pit.
    The water rose over my head. I said, "It's all over."

I called out your name, O God,
    called from the bottom of the pit.
You listened when I called out, "Don't shut your ears!
    Get me out of here! Save me!"
You came close when I called out.
    You said, "It's going to be all right."

You took my side, Master;
    you brought me back alive!

(Lam. 3:46–58 MSG)

In the English Standard Version, the last verse is translated, "You have taken up my cause, O Lord; you have redeemed my life."

Been there, done that? Enemies closing in, nowhere to turn. Your eyes are an "artesian well of tears." You're at the end of your rope. You're scraping the bottom of the barrel. Life stinks, basically. Yet in a flash of redemptive glory, God rescues you from the pit.

Or maybe you're there right now, wondering where God is, wondering if he even plans to show up.

Because God is a storyteller, I want to share one of his great stories, perhaps his greatest. It is a multigenerational family saga, an epic drama that's part Hallmark Channel movie, part *Desperate Housewives*.

A very long time ago, there was a man named Judah, who had three sons. His oldest son married a woman named Tamar.

We don't know much about Tamar's first husband other than his name—Er—and that he was so terrible a person that God just killed him. *Zap!* You've got to be pretty evil for God to pull a backward rapture on you like that.

In any event, Tamar was widowed. By custom, she was owed marriage by her first husband's next oldest brother.

The apple doesn't fall far from the tree, however, and Judah's second son, Onan, married Tamar but would not conceive a son with her. Because of this disobedience, God killed Onan too, making Tamar a widow twice over.

By custom, Tamar was now owed the next son, Shelah, but by now Judah was tired of handing over his sons only for them to be killed by what he likely assumed was the Black Widow. Tamar, grieving and abandoned, was denied yet again. Judah tried to smooth things over. He told Tamar to go back and live with her parents, reasoning that Shelah was too young to marry anyway. If Tamar would wait patiently for a few years, Judah promised, Shelah would marry her later.

So Tamar returned to her home and waited. And Shelah grew up. But he never came to take her hand in marriage. Tamar got tired of waiting. She was getting older, too. She'd already lost two loser husbands and she was childless. In that culture, a childless widow was a disgrace. So she did something very desperate.

She took off her widow's garments and put on a veil and went to hang out by the gate where Judah would pass while tending his sheep. Eventually, Judah came along and, not recognizing Tamar and believing her to be a prostitute, he solicited her for sex.

For payment, Tamar asked Judah how much he had on him. He said that he would give her a kid from his flock of sheep. Tamar knew that Judah wasn't a promise keeper, so she asked him for his signet, his bracelets, and his staff. Judah agreed to this, and he and Tamar, his daughter-in-law, had sex together.

Judah later sent a servant with a kid from his flock of sheep to give to the prostitute in exchange for his signet, his bracelets, and his staff. But when the servant got to the gate, the woman was nowhere to be found. When he asked some of the locals about her, they said they'd never seen her before. As far as they knew, there had never been a prostitute in that place.

Three months later, Judah heard that his daughter-in-law, Tamar, had been running around town and got pregnant. Naturally—but hypocritically—upset, Judah ordered that Tamar be brought to him so he could order her execution.

Tamar was retrieved, and in a scene worthy of any great suspense thriller, she showed Judah his signet, bracelets, and staff. She told off Judah: "The jerk who would make my unborn son a bastard is the owner of this stuff."

Judah freaked. Beyond that, however, he repented and gave Shelah to be Tamar's husband, which I'm sure Shelah was totally stoked about.[6]

The sordid intrigue for this family doesn't end there, however. About five generations down the line, another woman had a hand in

6. Ah, welcome back, old friend Sarcasm. We missed ye.

soiling the family name. Rahab didn't merely pretend to be a prostitute; she made it her career choice. But when some righteous men sought refuge in her city, she protected them and, like the fabled Hooker with a Heart of Gold, helped them escape their pursuers.

Rahab the prostitute eventually had a son, an awesome son. His name was Boaz, and he was given the opportunity to redeem a woman like those in his own family history who were at risk of dishonor and disgrace. The woman's name was Ruth, a widow who not only needed a husband to continue her dwindling family lineage, but also so that she and her mother-in-law, who was also widowed, could survive.

Naomi is the name of the mother-in-law, and she's a wily chick. Picture her played by Kathy Bates or Grace Zabriskie in full-on delightfully devious mode. Naomi tells Ruth that she has a relative she should check out. Enter Boaz (in the Hollywood version, probably with glistening abs), the kinsman redeemer.

Boaz is attracted to Ruth, but as there is another man who is a more direct relative, he must first get this man's permission to take Ruth's hand in marriage. After getting that guy's okay, and after a little pseudo-seduction from Ruth at incorrigible Naomi's urging,[7] Boaz takes Ruth to be his wife.

It's a happy ending to a romantic subplot, but a romance of another sort is waiting just down the generational line. Boaz and Ruth's great-grandson threatened to screw everything up. He was the most powerful man in the land. So powerful that one night as he's spying on another man's wife taking a bath, he gives orders to have her brought over.

You probably know this story. It's about David and Bathsheba, and their adultery doesn't just end in a messy family history; it ends in the murder of Bathsheba's husband.

---

7. I'm compelled to admit here that I, along with many Bible commentators, do not believe this "seduction" to have included any sexual impropriety.

This sordid family saga, full of sex and murder and disgrace and dishonor, is spread out through the Old Testament.[8] The New Testament retells this little soap opera in the form of a genealogy.[9] Matthew's gospel caps off the genealogy with a tale of teenage pregnancy.

That tale begins, "The book of the genealogy of Jesus Christ, the son of David, the son of Abraham . . ."

Tamar, Rahab, Ruth, Bathsheba. And Mary. This "desperate housewives" thing is basically Jesus' family tree.

Matthew didn't have to include the stories of these women. Culturally speaking, genealogies typically showed the male lineage of their subjects. Ancient Jewish genealogies were about forefathers. Women were not included. Matthew, who wrote specifically for a Jewish readership, bucked tradition to include five women. And not just any five women. He included five women with questionable backgrounds, women with clouds of suspicion hanging over them (whether or not innocent like Ruth and Mary). Why would Matthew risk scandalizing his readers by reminding them of this scandalous past?

As our own cultural prophet, Bono, sings, "Grace makes beauty out of ugly things."[10]

Out of this line of sin and salaciousness arrives Jesus the Christ, the sinless savior and redeemer of all our sordid, scandalous pasts. The redeemer of history is himself the redemption of a family history ripe for redemption! Did I tell you God was a great storyteller, or what?

This is a vivid picture of how God can use our sins for his own ends, drowning out our evil by funneling it into his own conquering goodness. It's like Joseph said to his brothers at the end of a very hard

---

8. I've drawn from Genesis 38, Joshua 2, the entire book of Ruth, and 2 Samuel 11.

9. See Matthew 1:1–17.

10. "Grace," words by Bono, music by U2, from the album *All That You Can't Leave Behind*, Interscope, 2000.

road, the one that began with their attempt to murder him, "What you meant for evil, God meant for good."[11]

Paul writes in Romans 8:28, "We know that for those who love God all things work together for good, for those who are called according to his purpose."

Now, it's all well and good to get to the other side of a difficult time and say, "Ah, I see what that was all about now." It's entirely different to be in the muck and in the confusion but say, in the spirit of the persevering invalid at the Sheep Gate, "God, I don't know how, but I trust you are using this for my good. I trust you have a plan."

The key to living in a redemptive way, to trusting Jesus the Redeemer, is to trust him to redeem you *in* the circumstances and situations, not after the fact. Anyone can get to the end of something and in a "Phew!" moment, say "Well, I'm glad God got me out of that. Looking back, I can see he meant something with all that." It's something entirely different to look forward into the invisible future, clouded by all that assails and assaults you, and still see Jesus the Redeemer. Trusting Jesus the Redeemer to bring you out of a trial while you're still in the trial requires not just waiting for redemption, but also living redemptively. You can live redemptively by committing yourself and disciplining yourself to do these three things:

1. Take heart.
2. Hold hope.
3. Have faith.

It takes a tough faith to be in the middle of an ongoing, no-end-in-sight crisis and think, "I'm glad you're doing something with this, God." But faith is exactly for such circumstances. There'd be no need for faith if we could always see difficulty, or the end of difficulty, coming.

---

11. See Genesis 50:20.

What is faith anyway? It's not retrospect. Look at how the author of Hebrews defines it: "Faith is the assurance of things hoped for, the conviction of things not seen" (11:1). This conviction of things not seen isn't just about trusting God to use our messes for his glory; it's about trusting that he's in control and that there's no escaping his steadfast loving-kindness. In other words, conviction is trusting that both our stumbling and our sinning cannot prevail over his lordship.

This wonderful truth is essentially what Jesus the Redeemer made it his business to announce. Everywhere he went, Jesus made it his mission to redeem everything in sight. Just look at what he says in Revelation's retrospect: "Behold, I am making all things new!"[12] And just in case the people he encountered didn't believe it, he freed demoniacs from their spiritual prisons, restored leprous limbs, and made dead people come to life.[13]

Why do you think Jesus took dirt and spit and put it in a guy's eyes to heal his blindness?[14] Because it'd be a neat thing to do? Because there was some healing mineral in the dirt? Have you ever thought about that? Why did Jesus do that?

I think it was a conscious echo of creation. In the story of our first appearance on the redemptive scene, God made man out of the dust of the ground.[15] He made man out of dirt, and blew his own breath into him to give him life. Here, then, Jesus is re-creating the creation story—redeeming fallen creation—by using dirt and his mouth to give a man a new lease on life.

Jesus the Redeemer even refashioned the Jews' thinking about the Law, about the way it related God's will to ours, about the way it related

---

12. Revelation 21:5, and you gotta read it feeling that exclamation point!

13. And not in some zombie-like "walking dead" sort of life. This was actual life he was restoring. That's much cooler than zombies, which is pretty awesome because, as everybody knows, zombies are pretty cool.

14. John 9:1–7.

15. Genesis 2:7.

us to our neighbors. His take on the Law is why the Sermon on the Mount is often thought of as Jesus' take on Moses bringing the tables of the law down from Mt. Sinai.

Jesus wasn't abolishing the Mosaic law. But in fulfilling it, he certainly created bridges between two points nobody else was seriously connecting. How is the redemption of God's people made manifest in the land? In large part, Jesus proclaimed, by adhering to a merging of the traditional Shema[16]—"You shall love YHWH with all your heart, soul, mind, and strength"—with a bit from Leviticus 19:18—"Love your neighbor as yourself."[17] Jesus took this redemptive outlook even further, commanding a clear reversal of Pharisaical gracelessness:

> You have heard that it was said, "You shall love your neighbor and hate your enemy." But I say to you, Love your enemies and pray for those who persecute you. (Matt. 5:43–44)

When you commit to living a life of grace toward others—blessing your enemies, praying for those who hate you, forgiving those who keep hurting you—you're demonstrating that your faith is in something hoped for, that your convictions are about things not seen. Living a life of grace and hope and joy is really living a life of faith. And when you go around redeeming the moments and being God's instrument in bringing redemption to others, you are participating in the grand story God is telling about Jesus the Redeemer. You are a vital character in the story of redemption that God is telling about you, the ones you live with and around, and about the church and the world itself.

---

16. The Hebrew Shema, from Deuteronomy 6:4–5, is a prayer of devotion to YHWH that faithful Jews recited twice a day.

17. For a great exploration of Jesus' amended Shema, please see Scot McKnight, *The Jesus Creed: Loving God, Loving Others* (Brewster, MA: Paraclete), 2004.

Isn't that exciting?

Living that way takes a hard-core faith, though. A radical faith. Any Christ-follower who's lost something dear—whether it's a loved one who's died or a hope that's died—knows the beautiful agony of such trust.

You likely know Job's story. Ponder this passage from his prayers of lament:

> My bones stick to my skin and to my flesh,
> and I have escaped by the skin of my teeth.
> Have mercy on me, have mercy on me, O you my friends,
> for the hand of God has touched me!
> Why do you, like God, pursue me?
> Why are you not satisfied with my flesh?
>
> Oh that my words were written!
> Oh that they were inscribed in a book!
> Oh that with an iron pen and lead
> they were engraved in the rock forever!
> For I know that my Redeemer lives,
> and at the last he will stand upon the earth.
> And after my skin has been thus destroyed,
> yet in my flesh I shall see God.
>
> (Job 19:20–26)

That, friends, is a living hope. That is a hope that says, "God you've taken everything, but I still trust you."

Elsewhere Job says—remarkably, astoundingly—"Though he slay me, yet will I hope in him."[18]

18. Job 13:15 NIV.

As Grace, my five-year-old daughter, would say, "Thumbs up on that."

I wonder if Job had that kind of faith before the waste matter hit the ancient fan. I like to think he did but didn't realize it. That's something those of us who've been through extreme trials of faith realize too—it takes going through the valley, one step at a time, to realize we've got the strength to take the steps.

But Job's faith here is not a pie-in-the-sky, wake-me-when-I'm-in-heaven kind of faith. And when I offer the admonition to "take heart, hold hope, have faith," I'm not saying, "Pull yourself up by your bootstraps and make yourself feel better, bigger, stronger, *whatever.*" The glorious goodness of the gospel isn't that Jesus died to make us feel better. Nor is faith in Jesus about avoiding problems.[19] Job cries, "Even though this body will be destroyed, in my flesh I will see God." He knows that God will redeem his very body, give him new flesh, new eyes to see, new ears to hear, a new tongue to taste how good God is.

That's what Jesus will do in the resurrection to come, in that final, forever redemption.

Someday, Jesus the Redeemer will return to redeem *everything.* Fully. Completely. Eternally. He's going to come to finish what he started. This life will be redeemed, this earth will be redeemed, these very bodies will be redeemed, and so our hopes and dreams and fears and failings will all be redeemed as well.

Revisit the Apocalypse with me:

> Then I saw a new heaven and a new earth, for the first heaven and the first earth had passed away, and the sea was no more. And I saw the holy city, new Jerusalem, coming down out of heaven from God, prepared

19. Don't believe the liars on religious television stations who tell you differently.

> as a bride adorned for her husband. And I heard a loud voice from the throne saying, "Behold, the dwelling place of God is with man. He will dwell with them, and they will be his people, and God himself will be with them as their God. He will wipe away every tear from their eyes, and death shall be no more, neither shall there be mourning, nor crying, nor pain anymore, for the former things have passed away."
>
> And he who was seated on the throne said, "Behold, I am making all things new." Also he said, "Write this down, for these words are trustworthy and true." (Rev. 21:1–5)

Thumbs up on *that*! I'm counting on that. I'm "all in" on that.

Behold! He is making all things new. And he's doing it now. So whatever you're going through, whatever you've been through, trust that the God who loves you is in control and is redeeming your life in and through your circumstances. Trust that the God who loves you will sustain you as you seek to live redemptively with and toward others. Trust that the God who loves you will not forget you, that he's crafting beauty out of your darkness, that he's telling a great story in your life, an epic one that places you in a vital role in the story of the body of Christ.

Your heart, soul, mind, and strength yearn for their redemption. Believe it is coming, deep down in your bones, for it is your bones that Jesus is promising to redeem. Believe it not as inspirational but as *factual*. I'm reminded of something Thomas Schmidt writes in his wonderful little book *A Scandalous Beauty*. Throughout several short meditations on the cross of Christ, Schmidt crafts brilliant and penetrating images of the gospel, none as penetrating as when he reflects on the loss of his young daughter, Susanna. In the conclusion of his book, in the postscript to his collection of redemptive stories, Schmidt reflects on Revelation's promise of a new heavens and a new earth:

> It matters to me that this is true, not merely interesting, not merely comforting. The chaos of this life, the flood waters, have closed over my head. Yet I choose against despair. I believe that death will one day die, that the love of God will prevail. In the meantime, even if the rest of my path lies in shadow, I will follow the Lamb in trust and in hope—until I see Susanna again. It may be that faith is no more and no less a choice between the words "it may be so" and "I will live as if it is so."
>
> Not far from my apartment, on a bluff overlooking the heaving sea, there is a marker on a new grave that bears the name of my only child and the following inscription:
>
> With joy still deeper than pain
> Gently flows the River
> Where we shall meet again.[20]

That is sentiment born of conviction, of hope in things unseen. And my hope is that you can share it. My hope is that somehow in the storms of your life, even if you—or someone you love—are at the brink of death, you are seeing the light of redemption in the Son of God who died to redeem life and who rose to conquer death.

Whatever you're doing, wherever you are, trust that the former things are passing away. Jesus the Redeemer is making all things new.

---

20. Thomas Schmidt, *A Scandalous Beauty: The Artistry of God and the Way of the Cross* (Grand Rapids: Brazos, 2002), 126.

8

# JESUS THE KING

There can be no serious talk about Jesus without reckoning with the idea of him as king. There can be no serious talk about Jesus' message without reckoning with his announcement that "the kingdom of God is at hand."[1] His kingship is perhaps the primary thing we must know about Jesus, the primary way to see him. Up to now, all the ways we've looked at Jesus—as a prophet, as a shepherd, as a redeemer, as a judge—have been his vocations or facets of his ministry. But from the beginning to the end of the Gospels, the idea that Jesus came to usher in the kingdom of God runs throughout and remains at the forefront. Even at Jesus' birth, the angels proclaimed that the Lord of the people had arrived.[2] The wise men went to seek out that king, and Herod tried to have that king killed.

At the inception of his public ministry, as Jesus took over for his cousin John the Baptizer, he continued proclaiming, as John had proclaimed, "Repent, for the kingdom of God is near." Nearly every New Testament scholar and commentator today agrees that the thrust of

1. Mark 1:15.

2. Luke 2:10–11. Even before Jesus' birth, the angel promised Mary that her son would sit on the throne of David and reign over the house of Jacob in an endless kingdom (see Luke 1:32–33).

Jesus' ministry was the proclamation of the gospel of the kingdom of God. He didn't go around inviting people to say a prayer to get him into their hearts, or setting up social justice activist groups or twelve-step programs—although those things, and others, can be valid applications of his teachings. No, Jesus went around proclaiming, explicitly and implicitly, that the kingdom of God had now arrived *by* him and *in* him. And he went on to demonstrate the realities of that kingdom in a culture that knew only the yoke of kingdoms of godlessness.

Let's not get ahead of ourselves. We must first step back and ask, "Just what is the kingdom of God?" What does that phrase mean? Explaining the kingdom of God is a difficult task, because the Bible speaks of it in myriad ways, and the amount of biblical material on the subject can make for overwhelming study. The kingdom of God has consequently been considered a mercurial subject, hard to pin down, open to interpretation.

So we begin our study of Jesus the king, brief though it may be, by explaining what the kingdom of God is *not*.[3]

## THE KINGDOM OF GOD IS NOT HEAVEN

Heaven, in the context of the Gospels—and in the Jewish cosmology from which the Gospels draw—is not a pie-in-the-sky outer-space lounge with angels playing harps. It is best thought of, even if it's hard to envision, as the place where God lives, the dimension of God's tangible presence. But when Matthew's gospel speaks of "the kingdom of heaven," it's not referring to this place, but rather to this *thing*: the kingdom of God, which is no less real.

Matthew was written primarily for Jewish readers, and because Jews considered it taboo to write or read the name of God, Matthew, as

---

3. On the subject of the kingdom of God, here and elsewhere I'm most indebted to George Eldon Ladd, *The Gospel of the Kingdom* (Grand Rapids: Eerdmans, 1959); and George Eldon Ladd, *The Presence of the Future* (Grand Rapids: Eerdmans, 1996). Also, Tom Wright, *The Original Jesus* (Grand Rapids: Eerdmans, 1997).

a sign of decorum and reverence, substituted "heaven" for "God." In literary terms, this kind of substitution is called *circumlocution*. It's a way of saying something by getting around actually saying it. So Matthew's "kingdom of heaven" is synonymous with "the kingdom of God" in the other gospels.

In any event, the kingdom of God (or the kingdom of heaven) is not the *place* called heaven, as if Jesus were announcing there was a new location where everybody could now go. That would have made little sense, given that he said he was bringing this "place" with him, that his very presence signaled the very presence of this place.[4] And if this "place" was meant to be understood as the heavenly rest, Jesus would have had a lot of explaining to do to his followers, who suffered many things during and after his public ministry.

## THE KINGDOM OF GOD IS NOT THE CHURCH

Another common interpretation of the kingdom, one that has gained a lot of traction among Christians today, is the idea that the kingdom is synonymous with the church. Evangelistically speaking, we may talk about "bringing someone into the kingdom" when he or she comes to salvation and becomes a part of the church. Or we might think of ourselves as the kingdom, as the populace of the institution that is the kingdom of God. But the kingdom of God in the Gospels is not the community of believers called the church. The kingdom is not a place with borders and boundaries.

Although, under the Old Covenant, the kingdom of God was manifested on earth in the political nation of Israel, even Paul intimates that the kingdom then was not about geography or ethnicity.[5] And when Jesus came inaugurating the New Covenant, he basically blew the doors

4. Actually, because heaven is the place of God's personal presence, Jesus, as God incarnate, *was* kind of bringing that place into history.

5. Romans 9:6b: "For not all who are descended from Israel belong to Israel. . . ."

off that way of seeing the kingdom. He removed nationalism, class, and race as prime players in the kingdom movement. He transferred the kingdom borders from inhabitable land to inhabitable hearts. In other words, the kingdom might be *in* you, but it is not *you*.

So what is the kingdom of God? If it's neither place nor people, what can it be?

## THE KINGDOM OF GOD IS THE MANIFEST PRESENCE OF GOD'S SOVEREIGNTY

The kingdom of God, when we factor in all the ways the New Testament proclaims and explicates it, is the reign of God, the manifest presence of the sovereignty of God. It's not a place or an institution, but a *status*, a dynamic reality. It's the expression of God's sovereignty. The kingdom is God's system of order.

Because of this, it's easy to spiritualize the kingdom, to misinterpret it by metaphorizing it,[6] to make it intangible. But this is why Jesus came: to make the reign of God vitally present, *really real*, actually here. And as we'll see, the arrival of the kingdom of God, with Jesus as the kingdom's arriving king, causes real damage in rival systems and brings real hope to those caught in those systems. This is not a symbolic kingdom, any more than Jesus was a symbolic king—or to put it another way, any more than Lazarus was symbolically resurrected.

Let's get in the way-back machine and witness the cataclysmic quality of the kingdom's arrival as prophesied by Daniel.[7] King Nebuchadnezzar

---

6. Some scholars fall into the "misinterpretation by metaphor" trap when they insist that the kingdom of God is a "symbol." There's a grain of truth to this, of course, but the farther we go down the trail of symbolism, the farther we may get from the quite obvious facts that the incarnation is the very antithesis of "symbol," that Jesus was neither a symbolic person nor a symbolic God, and therefore he was not a symbolic king of a symbolic kingdom. That his kingdom did not look like all the other kingdoms of the earth doesn't mean it wasn't "real." This difference in appearance was kind of the point of his kingdom in the first place.

7. Daniel 2:31–43.

has just had a troubling dream involving a statue made of different metals, kind of a gigantic Frankenstein's idol. Only Daniel could interpret the dream, and he shocked Nebuchadnezzar by relating the events to the rise and fall of the successive kingdoms of the future. At the end of Daniel's astonishing prophecy, he foretells the glorious coming of the kingdom of God:

> "And in the days of those kings the God of heaven will set up a kingdom that shall never be destroyed, nor shall the kingdom be left to another people. It shall break in pieces all these kingdoms and bring them to an end, and it shall stand forever, just as you saw that a stone was cut from a mountain by no human hand, and that it broke in pieces the iron, the bronze, the clay, the silver, and the gold. A great God has made known to the king what shall be after this. The dream is certain, and its interpretation sure."
>
> Then King Nebuchadnezzar fell upon his face and paid homage to Daniel, and commanded that an offering and incense be offered up to him. The king answered and said to Daniel, "Truly, your God is God of gods and Lord of kings, and a revealer of mysteries, for you have been able to reveal this mystery." (Dan. 2:44–47)

In the context of this particular story from the book of Daniel, the arrival of a new kingdom that shall never be destroyed is an earth-shattering event. The breaking in of God's kingdom will smash to pieces all of the world's other kingdoms and bring them to an end.

This violent imagery carries right on over to the Gospels, when Jesus proclaims the arrival of the kingdom in himself. He says and does things that hearken right back to Daniel's description of the kingdom as a stone cut from a mountain by an inhuman hand that crushes the opposition.

> Jesus said to them, "Have you never read in the Scriptures:
>
> 'The stone that the builders rejected
> has become the cornerstone;
> this was the Lord's doing,
> and it is marvelous in our eyes'?
>
> Therefore I tell you, the kingdom of God will be taken away from you and given to a people producing its fruits. And the one who falls on this stone will be broken to pieces; and when it falls on anyone, it will crush him." (Matt. 21:42–44)

The rock imagery gets frequent play in Jesus' teaching—especially when he starts talking about the temple, and when he says things like, "If you build your life on me, you are like the wise man who built his home on rock instead of sand."[8] But, wow, here's Jesus also saying that the kingdom of God is like a stone that, if you stumble over it, will break you, and if it falls on you, will squash you like a bug. Is it any wonder, then, that Jesus elsewhere said, "The kingdom has been forcefully advancing, and forceful men lay hold of it"?[9] (Some translations read "violence" and "violent.")

What did Jesus mean by that? What did this decidedly nonviolent man, who went around instructing people to turn the other cheek and bless those who persecute them, mean with this violent imagery? In

8. See Matthew 7:24.
9. Matthew 11:12 NIV.

a time when some men really were trying to usher in the kingdom of God on earth through military insurrection and violent zealotry, what could Jesus have been getting at?

I think he really meant that the kingdom comes in and smashes up worldviews and systems, and tears apart the bondage created by sin and Satan. The kingdom coming into this world, in the arrival of Jesus the King, wreaks havoc among those opposed to it.

The proclamation of the kingdom's arrival even begins with a battle—in the wilderness, as Jesus withstands the temptations of Satan.[10] And at the end, he dispatches the Devil, banishes him. Later, Jesus tells a story to his followers, outlining the way to plunder someone's house by invading it and binding the strong man.[11] This is Jesus alluding to what he's doing to the sinful corruption of the prevailing system. He's come in, whupped up on the Devil, hogtied him, and now he's taking all his stuff. He's rescuing everyone and everything held captive by fallenness.

If you look at what Jesus goes around doing in his ministry, it indeed reflects this invasion-and-rescue idea. He makes sick people well, he makes paralyzed people get up, he makes the dead live. And perhaps most vividly connected to the notion of spiritual invasion, he goes around casting demons out of people. He literally frees them of their spiritual possession. He releases the captives.

Like any new king, he's issuing pardons.

This is a pretty violent arrival for this kingdom. In Luke 10:18, Jesus tells the disciples, "I saw Satan fall like lightning from heaven." Now, a lot of people believe that Jesus is referring to the fall of the Devil way back at the beginning of time, when he was an angel ousted from heaven by God for his insurrectionist pride. Jesus' words may indeed refer to that event, but in the context of this incident, the

10. Matthew 4:1–11.
11. Mark 3:27.

disciples are marveling at their ability to cast out demons, and Jesus is basically saying, "No duh. I gave that guy the boot. His power is subject to mine."

So that's what the kingdom does. Its arrival is violent, cataclysmic, shaking strongholds, putting the fear of God into rulers and religious leaders. It knocks out the enemy and sets the enemy's prisoners free. It turns over the tables in the worldly culture. It turns almost everything upside down—which is to say, in God's view, right side up.

So Jesus goes around making these kingdom proclamations, announcing and flat-out demonstrating that a new king is in town—but he also makes some declarations. His actions demonstrate the new reality of the kingdom's presence—but his teachings tell us what life is like in the new kingdom. These are sort of like his first royal declarations. His unfurling of the new constitution. "This is how things used to be," he tells us, "but now that there's a new king in town, things are gonna be like this . . ."

We can fill in those ellipses with all of Jesus' teachings, but most notably with those found in the Sermon on the Mount. Like Moses presenting the delivered Law to the children of Israel, Jesus brings a new law that fulfills the promise of the old. He lays out a blueprint overview of what the kingdom of God looks like on earth. "Here's what happens now," he tells us, and he gives us the glorious gospel of the Beatitudes:

> Blessed are the poor in spirit, for theirs is the kingdom of heaven.
> Blessed are those who mourn, for they shall be comforted.
> Blessed are the meek, for they shall inherit the earth.
> Blessed are those who hunger and thirst for righteousness, for they shall be satisfied.
> Blessed are the merciful, for they shall receive mercy.
> Blessed are the pure in heart, for they shall see God.

> Blessed are the peacemakers, for they shall be called sons of God.
> Blessed are those who are persecuted for righteousness' sake, for theirs is the kingdom of heaven.
> Blessed are you when others revile you and persecute you and utter all kinds of evil against you falsely on my account.
> (Matt. 5:3–11)

These aren't just feel-good promises for some future fulfillment.[12] Truly, none of us will really know eternal relief and feel total blessedness until the kingdom is consummated at the end of time, but in the kingdom now present, under the reign that Jesus brought with real-world impact, this blessedness has arrived, as well as a furious foretaste of the glory to come. Some may argue that Jesus was only foretelling the kingdom's arrival, not really heralding its arrival in himself, suggesting that when he said the kingdom was at hand, he only meant it would come someday soon. This is a bit like saying the light at dawn isn't really sunlight.

Jesus personally brought—and bought—the victory that secures blessedness then, now, and for all time. This is entirely why Jesus didn't go around just making promises, but actually went around *doing things.* Extraordinary things. We call them now, as the crowds called them then, miracles. He didn't just promise miracles someday, in the by and by. He wasn't hinting at a future heavenly life, he was ushering it in, *living it* out as if it was already present. The full spectrum of the import of God's kingdom crashing into existence burst through in Jesus' ministry as he taught, fellowshipped, wept, suffered, healed, rebuked, judged, prophesied, loved, comforted, cursed, and blessed.

---

12. I know of no more enlightening—which is to say, insightful and helpful—writer on the Beatitudes than Dallas Willard. See especially Dallas Willard, *The Divine Conspiracy: Rediscovering Our Hidden Life in God* (San Francisco: HarperCollins, 1998), 97–128.

The fullness of God's plan for the redemption of Israel was inaugurated entirely in the arrival of Jesus the King.[13] Eschatologically speaking, then, the "end times" don't begin sometime in our future; they began about two thousand years ago when Jesus showed up. In the kingdom of God, those who've been waiting forever for God's righteousness to prevail have their patience rewarded. Those who give mercy to others find their efforts rewarded. Blessed even are those who have been hurt in the line of duty, being reviled and suffering evil on the King's account.

This is the new order of the kingdom. In all other kingdoms, the operating system runs on Cobra Kai ethics, right? "Mercy is for the weak; the weak deserve no mercy."[14]

Life sucks, then you die.

Just working for the weekend.

All is meaningless.

We're just cogs in a machine.

Life is futile.

Whoever dies with the most toys wins.

Get yours while you can.

Money makes the world go around.

These and a host of other messages and life-values are what other kingdoms prop up as realities best grasped for real living. But in the kingdom of God, all that stuff is rubbish. The kingdom of God is like the huge stone in Nebuchadnezzar's dream that smashes all that junk to bits by declaring a new order.

People who live according to the blueprint of the Sermon on the Mount see, as the fruit of life in Jesus' kingdom, the discombobulating

---

13. See Mark Saucy, *The Kingdom of God in the Teaching of Jesus* (Dallas, TX: Word, 1997), 328–29.

14. If you were born before 1960 or after 1986, that's a *Karate Kid* reference. If you were born between those years and still didn't get it, please stand by. Johnny Lawrence is coming to sweep your leg.

effects of this shift in character on competing worldviews and ethical paradigms. That, by the way, is the place of the church in the kingdom of God. What does Paul call the church? The body of Christ. And what did the real body of Christ do on earth? He went around living out the kingdom and testifying to its presence. So that's what the church, as the body of Christ, should do: live out the kingdom life and testify to the world about the kingdom's presence.

In Matthew 5:13–16, Jesus expounds on the role of his followers in the kingdom:

> You are the salt of the earth, but if salt has lost its taste, how shall its saltiness be restored? It is no longer good for anything except to be thrown out and trampled under people's feet.
>
> You are the light of the world. A city set on a hill cannot be hidden. Nor do people light a lamp and put it under a basket, but on a stand, and it gives light to all in the house. In the same way, let your light shine before others, so that they may see your good works and give glory to your Father who is in heaven.

Salt preserves. It saves. It gives flavor. What happens when it doesn't do those things? It gets trampled. But Jesus has already set up the kingdom as the thing that does the trampling. So how do we make sure the kingdom continues doing damage against evil in the spiritual world and liberating the hearts of those in bondage? By getting up on a hillside and turning the lights on. By shining the truth of God onto the lies and corruption of the world. And not doing so to our own credit, or to just be rabble-rousers and troublemakers, but to give God glory. To proclaim loudly and brilliantly, "Jesus is the king, and look what his kingdom does!"

Jesus says we do this proclaiming when our good works glorify God, not ourselves. We do it by living kingdom lives in the midst of those living earthly lives captive to worldly kingdoms. We believe differently, we trust differently, we hope differently, we love differently—therefore we live differently.

We are too used to living as if the church were a subculture, filling a niche in society, when instead we ought to be living as a countercultural force against society as a whole. We should be subverting the larger culture, subverting worldly beliefs and ethics, just as Jesus subverted expectations in his day. What the world expected was a warrior king on a horse with a military envoy. Instead, they got a servant King on a donkey, heralded by women and children singing. The world expected a king who would throw out the Roman occupation and assume the throne; instead, they got a King who submitted himself to Roman execution and death on a cross. Because the world didn't understand that in the kingdom of heaven you die to live, they missed the whole point. That's what "take up your cross" was all about.

That is so upside down! That is so crazy. It makes no sense, which is why it's so revolutionary. The beauty and brilliance of the kingdom of God can't be grasped practically without grasping it spiritually. You can't do one without seeing the other—and seeing it requires being set free by God. In order for us to really experience the kingdom, to taste and see the glory of the kingdom life, the king has to burst open the prison of our hearts and minds, and give us new eyes to see and new ears to hear.[15]

To those who can hear with new ears, the community of believers really living the kingdom life is like a beautiful symphony played with the music written by God. But to those whose ears have not been renewed, the community of believers living out the kingdom life is like nails on a chalkboard. It's stupid, dumb, naive. It's like shards of bone scraped against each other (to borrow a favorite image from C. S.

15. Check out Matthew 13:11–16. How's your mind? Blown?

Lewis). In Psalm 48:4–5, the city of God astounds and panics the kings of the world. The spiritually blind just don't get it.

And so the community continues, in the midst of skepticism and opposition and persecution, living as if the visible kingdom of the world has no hold on us, living right inside it and beside those captive to it, "in it but not of it,"[16] praying and hoping and testifying to the glory of God with our actions and our words, doing the best we can to proclaim freedom to as many as we can until the end of time.

Jesus himself spoke of this countercultural living every time he told a parable. Did you know that's what parables do, really? The modern church has tended to dilute them, as we have done with the Old Testament stories. We have Sunday schooled the parables into moral lessons or tidy religious fables, but they are, in fact, explosive, transformative stories that illustrate the incongruity of the kingdom of God lived out in the world. As I first revised this chapter, I was also preparing a message series on selected parables for the community I pastor. We called this series "Postcards from the Revolution: The Parables as Sabotage," because that's just what the parables are: kingdom narratives that sabotage cultural, worldly, and even religious narratives.

Look at the parable of the weeds, in particular, which illustrates the countercultural blueprint for the kingdom:

> He put another parable before them, saying, "The kingdom of heaven may be compared to a man who sowed good seed in his field, but while his men were sleeping, his enemy came and sowed weeds among the wheat and went away. So when the plants came up and bore grain, then the weeds appeared also. And the servants of the master of the house came and said to him,

16. See John 17:15–16; Romans 12:2; 1 Corinthians 5:9–10.

> 'Master, did you not sow good seed in your field? How then does it have weeds?' He said to them, 'An enemy has done this.' So the servants said to him, 'Then do you want us to go and gather them?' But he said, 'No, lest in gathering the weeds you root up the wheat along with them.'" (Matt. 13:24–29)

The wheat and the weeds grow side by side, because even as the kingdom continues to bring people into its fold, the enemy continues to deceive others. So the kingdom of God and the kingdoms of the world coexist for a time. But not for long.

The tagline in the preceding paragraph might seem to refer to the misconception we talked about earlier—about the kingdom of God's being merely a future reality, something that happens or appears in the so-called end times. That's only partially true. The radical reality is that Jesus ushered in the kingdom himself, in his ministry and message. The kingdom was already present in him. This dynamic reality proposes that we rethink our modernist eschatology, the "last days" sort of thinking, which today we take for granted as tradition but which is really only about a hundred years old.[17] A proper biblical and contextual understanding of the end times is that there is an "already" sense, and a "not yet" sense.[18]

Eschatology should encompass more than just apocalyptic, end-of-the-world type stuff. Eschatology is really about salvation history,

---

17. I'm thinking here mainly of classic dispensationalism of the Scofield/Ryrie sort and of its modern ideological heir, pretribulational premillennialism of the Walvoord/LaHaye sort. Many staunch adherents of these schools of thought are shocked to discover that these views are relatively new innovations in the long history of Christian theology.

18. Again, I must recommend the indispensable works of George Eldon Ladd on this subject. And this time I will also add Anthony Hoekema, *The Bible and the Future* (Grand Rapids: Eerdmans, 1994), 68–77.

about God's unfolding plan of redemption, from promise to fulfillment, from Genesis to Revelation. Jesus' inauguration of the kingdom was the beginning of the end, a creation of the ongoing tension between *already* and *not yet*, in which *already* gradually expands and *not yet* gradually vanishes into the already.

The already-and-not-yet theme is echoed in the life of salvation.[19] We are saved, yet we still sin. But God is at work within us, his Spirit purifying us, disciplining us, gradually conforming us more and more to the image of Christ, bearing fruit in our lives until that final day, in that great Someday at the kingdom's consummation, when we won't sin anymore. That part of salvation is the process called sanctification. When we live in God's literal presence, when we enter the God dimension called heaven, we'll finally be sanctified. For now, although we're reckoned righteous by our faith, we still dabble in unrighteousness every day.

This same duality applies to the kingdom. It is present, and yet it is future. For now, the wheat and the weeds coexist. But it won't always be so.

Notice, though, what Jesus says to do: leave the weeds—don't try to pull them. For now, leave the weeds. Because in the reality of the kingdom, the dead come back to life. Goats become sheep, weeds become wheat. When we see with kingdom eyes, we don't write anyone off or leave anyone for dead. Instead, we do the radical, revolutionary, countercultural thing—bear with the unbearable and minister with grace to those who don't have what we have. We coexist with the weeds—peacefully, humbly, lovingly—in the hopes that more and more stalks will come into the light and be transformed into wheat.

There's a promise connected to this command to leave the weeds alone. We see it in another illustration that Jesus offered about the kingdom:

---

19. This is why a good eschatology deals with soteriology. And if you know what those words mean, that's why you don't have many friends.

> He said therefore, "What is the kingdom of God like? And to what shall I compare it? It is like a grain of mustard seed that a man took and sowed in his garden, and it grew and became a tree, and the birds of the air made nests in its branches."
>
> And again he said, "To what shall I compare the kingdom of God? It is like leaven that a woman took and hid in three measures of flour, until it was all leavened." (Luke 13:18–21)

Jesus the King promised that the kingdom would grow and spread, that the invasion would proceed and take over, that it would infiltrate. This is a promise that the Christian counterculture will see completed in the end. All other cultures and countercultures will fade away, having been shown to be vanity and the Christless aspirations of humanity. But the kingdom of God, as Daniel told Nebuchadnezzar, shall never be destroyed. It's like leaven, or yeast, that spreads throughout the flour and lifts it, expands it, makes it fuller. It's like a tiny seed that becomes a complex tree with hundreds of branches that provide refuge.

That's what the kingdom does. And as the kingdom does that, it sets the captives free; it gives us new eyes to see the world in the light of God's glory; it brings satisfaction and fulfillment to the grieving and the victimized and the marginalized; it brings hope and peace and love; it challenges everyone with a radical grace; it grows, expands, takes over. The invasion that began with Jesus the King's triumphal entry into Jerusalem continues every day when those in the kingdom crucify their flesh and humble themselves before a world that revels in the flesh and is staunchly opposed to humility. As that happens, the kingdom of God takes over.

Throughout the church's spotted history, however, some have been tempted to usher in God's kingdom in worldly ways, whether through moralistic politicking or with sword and shield. Look at what Jesus pops the Pharisees with: "The kingdom of God is not coming with signs to be observed, nor will they say, 'Look, here it is!' or 'There!' for behold, the kingdom of God is in the midst of you" (Luke 17:20–21).

It's *in* you. It's not something you wield like a hammer. It's not something you institutionalize or politicize or showboat. The kingdom is Jesus the King reigning in hearts and minds. So every chance Jesus got, he continued to transfer his spotlight from things like the temple and the Law to things like the state of our hearts and minds. Our bodies are now the temple of the Spirit of God.[20] Our character and the quality of our hearts—not our showiness in legalism—demonstrate our faithfulness and obedience.[21]

The heart and mind thing is the real difficulty with something like the Sermon on the Mount. We have this misguided notion that Jesus somehow made things easier by refocusing the Law, making things more "touchy feely" and less legalistic. But let's be honest: it's a whole lot easier not to murder someone than it is not to hate someone in our hearts. It's a whole lot easier not to commit adultery than it is not to lust after someone in our minds. Controlling behavior is relatively easy compared to taming sinful hearts and minds, which is why the Pharisees could be so outwardly holy but so inwardly disgusting.

The actions of kingdom people testify to the kingdom, but those actions won't work to further the kingdom—they won't be a true testimony that glorifies God and sets people free—if they don't flow from hearts ruled by the King. Right behavior must come from right character. Without right character, right behavior is hypocrisy.

But in the area of being set free, we also have a promise. We are promised that Jesus the King really has accomplished what he set out

20. See John 2:21; 1 Corinthians 6:19.
21. As in 1 Samuel 16:7.

to do, that he really has achieved victory. He has, in effect, taken the throne and started handing out pardons, as when an outgoing president leaves office, typically pardoning people as a last hurrah of grace and good tidings. These pardons usually rankle those who oppose the president. Maybe you recall when President Clinton handed out a host of pardons that a lot of people took exception to. In the eyes of some, he was setting free people who didn't deserve it.

Without commenting on the legitimacy of Clinton's pardons—and I'm sure our current president will ruffle just as many feathers with his pardons when he gets to them—this is nevertheless a comparable picture of what Jesus does. He sets free people who don't deserve it, and in the process, he scandalizes people who don't get it, who oppose it.[22]

Now we know that the kingdom of God is God's sovereignty brought to bear, that it has been made manifest in Jesus, and that it maintains presence in the hearts of his followers. We know that the church, like Jesus, is supposed to be proclaiming the kingdom and becoming a living witness of its power and presence. What sort of king is Jesus, then?

Christ's lordship encompasses so many aspects, we could fill several volumes exploring them all. I'm going to offer two in brief, the two that I think most encapsulate the gospel of the kingdom that Jesus the King proclaims.

## JESUS IS A CONQUERING KING

First, we must never be fooled by Jesus' mercy and mistake it for weakness. We must never mistake his peace for passivity. And we must never mistake his sacrifice of himself for defeat. On the contrary, Jesus the King is the strongest, most powerful king to have ever lived.

22. This will likely be the last time I compare the actions of an American politician with those of Jesus.

Hundreds of other kings may save or take lives, but only Jesus the King can save or take lives on the supernatural scale of eternity. It should come as no surprise, then, that Paul urged the church to give "thanks to the Father, who has qualified you to share in the inheritance of the saints in light. He has delivered us from the domain of darkness and transferred us to the kingdom of his beloved Son, in whom we have redemption, the forgiveness of sins" (Col. 1:12–14).

What a tremendous way to put it! He has "delivered us from the domain of darkness."

Jesus the King may not yet have physically vanquished all other kingdoms, but he has set us free from their spiritual hold. He has ransomed us, rescued us, redeemed us. He has stolen us from Satan's power, saved us from the wrath of God, and made us citizens of his kingdom,[23] a heavenly kingdom that will outlast all others.

## JESUS IS THE SOVEREIGN KING

> He is the image of the invisible God, the firstborn of all creation. For by him all things were created, in heaven and on earth, visible and invisible, whether thrones or dominions or rulers or authorities—all things were created through him and for him. And he is before all things, and in him all things hold together. And he is the head of the body, the church. He is the beginning, the firstborn from the dead, that in everything he might be preeminent. For in him all the fullness of God was pleased to dwell, and through him to reconcile to himself all things, whether on earth or in heaven, making peace by the blood of his cross.
>
> And you, who once were alienated and hostile

23. Philippians 3:20.

> in mind, doing evil deeds, he has now reconciled in his body of flesh by his death, in order to present you holy and blameless and above reproach before him, if indeed you continue in the faith, stable and steadfast, not shifting from the hope of the gospel that you heard, which has been proclaimed in all creation under heaven, and of which I, Paul, became a minister. (Col. 1:15–23)

We have a king who is YHWH incarnate. He is a king who, through great power and control, draws us, woos us, and captivates our hearts and minds. He steers the lost and the wayward and brings them back into the fold, reconciling them to himself. He is a king who looks out at every single person in other kingdoms, sees them doing sinful things, and says to himself, *I want that person.* He is a king who goes after people and offers them his blood as a peace offering and a covering, like God covered Adam and Eve with animal skins.

The first part of the passage above from Colossians speaks of Christ as God, as the sovereign power of the universe. The second part speaks to this Almighty God stooping to become a human king in order to fill his kingdom with lost family members.

This is the entry point to the kingdom, too, by the way: acknowledging God's sovereignty and submitting to Jesus as the sovereign ruler of the kingdom. Repentance, salvation, entering the kingdom—all those things are euphemisms for embracing the yoke of God's sovereignty.

Embracing that sovereignty is not just about behavior; it's something Christ does for us. Jesus defined it for one fellow as being "born again." I don't mean to go all Calvinist on you, but spiritually speaking, we have no more choice in conceiving our new birth than a baby does in being conceived by his parents. Dead people cannot will themselves to life. Maybe that line of thinking irritates you, and it probably breaks down at some point, as all analogies do, but let us never for one second resent the notion itself that Jesus may be in sovereign control over all things. Whether it's true or not theologically may be up for debate,[24] but the idea of Jesus the King having supreme power over all things, having dominion over all things, owning every corner of the world and every microbe in it, should not by itself bother a heart turned toward him. Why would we want it any other way?

Seeing Jesus' sovereignty this way—where we do not bristle at his yoke and burden but find them ironically easy and light[25]—requires a total revolution of the heart and spirit. This is something Jesus does for us and in us, something that prompts us to turn away from all idols, all former lives, all ways of living that are against or inferior to the heavenly kingdom, and submit to the lordship of Jesus Christ, to the kingship of Jesus Christ. When you submit to—embrace!—Jesus' sovereignty, you have taken the glorious first leap into the life of the kingdom of God.

As the author of Hebrews reminds us,

> This phrase, "Yet once more," indicates the removal of things that are shaken—that is, things that have been made—in order that the things that cannot be shaken may remain. Therefore let us be grateful for receiving a kingdom that cannot be shaken, and thus let us offer to God acceptable worship, with reverence and awe, for our God is a consuming fire. (Heb. 12:27–29)

As weak and weary as you may get, as assailed upon and as targeted as you may feel, as victimized and marginalized as you may be, remember that you have received a kingdom that cannot be shaken—as

24. Well, for me personally, it's not up for debate, but I'm trying to be charitable to all my less-Calvinist friends.

25. Matthew 11:30.

Daniel warned Nebuchadnezzar, and as the author of Hebrews reminds us. Our God is a consuming fire; and though the kingdom of God is already here, we know it's also "not yet," which means it will someday come crashing—literally—into this world, into this dimension, where it will drown out every fear, every flaw, every problem, every sin, every grief, and every worry. When the kingdom arrives completely, we will apprehend universally the full-fledged, fall-on-your-face glory of God that we only glimpse now.

We are a part of a kingdom that will demolish all pretenders. It will fulfill, in furious fashion, the promise of redemption that is already sealed for us through the atoning work of Jesus Christ.

# 9

# JESUS THE SACRIFICE

It's a messy thing, sacrifice. Bloody and messy.

You could say that the history of God's people is covered in blood. The shedding of their own blood, their shedding of the blood of others, the regular and required ceremonial shedding of the blood of animal sacrifices. God established this vivid demonstration to depict for us both the grossness of unholiness and the extreme cost of making the unholy holy. God has said, and is saying, through the institution of sacrifices, "This gulf between men and me can only be bridged by death."

"Indeed," Hebrews 9:22 tells us, "under the law almost everything is purified with blood, and without the shedding of blood there is no forgiveness of sins."

It was like this from the beginning. Remember that Adam and Eve were frolicking in the garden, innocent and naked and unashamed of their nakedness. When they gave in to temptation and initiated the fall of mankind by eating the forbidden fruit, their eyes were opened. Suddenly they realized, "We ain't got no clothes on!" and they covered themselves with leaves.

How does God respond? He kills some animals and covers them in skins.[1] "For your shame to be covered," he is saying, "it takes death to make up for the death you've created."

From then on, we see throughout the Old Testament that the history of God's people has been a bloody mess, with sacrifices offered throughout the journey. For example, take a look at this description from Ezekiel 43:19–20:

> You shall give to the Levitical priests of the family of Zadok, who draw near to me to minister to me, declares the Lord God, a bull from the herd for a sin offering. And you shall take some of its blood and put it on the four horns of the altar and on the four corners of the ledge and upon the rim all around. Thus you shall purify the altar and make atonement for it.

Blood everywhere! On the four horns and on the four corners. All over the altar. The priests killed a bull, which would have had a heckuva lot of blood pumping through it, and covered the altar with blood. They purified the altar by basically making a mess of it in blood.

And this is one of the prophetic books. Take a look at a book like Leviticus, where the Law is explicated and sacrifice is required for nearly everything. It takes a lot of blood to cover a growing people who can't stop sinning.[2]

This legacy of bloody sacrifice is the tradition and history in which Jesus grew up. His was a religious family, devoutly Jewish. When he was a child, his family traveled to Jerusalem when it was required. They honored the Passover and the other holy days. We can see that, even in his adult years, Jesus observed the feasts and festivals. Jesus grew up

1. Genesis 3:21.
2. There will be more on the subject of blood, from a slightly different angle, in chapter 10, "Jesus the Provision."

not only knowing a working class dad and a loving mom who followed God, but also amid a religious system that required the slaughter of animals to make atonement, to enact forgiveness between the nation and God.

And as the awareness grew in Jesus that he was God's Son, that he was indeed the Messiah sent to take away the sins of the world, surely the realization also grew that his identity meant taking on the burden of sacrifice. I mean, you don't go around pointing to yourself as the fulfillment of the Prophets and the Law and the temple and the covenant and somehow conveniently forget about sacrifices. Jesus had to have known, as soon as he grasped his mission, that he would have to fulfill—indeed, *embody*—the ceremony of sacrifice.[3]

How did this sacrifice happen? In the aftermath of Mel Gibson's popular film *The Passion of the Christ*, new discussions and debates have ensued about Jesus' betrayal, arrest, and execution. Who was responsible? How did the whole thing go down? Let's look briefly at what events and actions led to, or conspired to lead to, his execution.

## JESUS WAS NO MERE MARTYR

First of all, we must dispense with the notion that Jesus got killed because he taught love and peace while others taught hatred and intolerance. Historically speaking, it makes no sense. The Pharisees and Sadducees wouldn't have bothered. A hippie peasant who went around telling people just to love each other and be happy would not have caused the waves Jesus did. It just wouldn't have happened. No one got killed simply by preaching love.

But people did get killed, under Old Testament law, for being a

---

3. I'm not trying to propose a weak self-consciousness for Jesus in this discussion, only to generally accommodate the vague truth that Jesus apparently grew in wisdom and stature (see Luke 2:52), by which I assume the Scriptures mean that his adult thinking was more developed than his infant and adolescent thinking.

false prophet. For preaching blasphemy. And this is where Jesus got into trouble with the religious leaders and those they had duped. What we see in the Gospels, time and time again, is not someone upset that Jesus is calling for love and grace. We see religious leaders who are upset that Jesus is claiming authority that only God is supposed to have, performing miracles that he says demonstrate forgiveness of sins, and violating man-made traditions that man-made traditions had elevated to equal status with God's law itself.

The forgiveness of sins thing was huge. As good followers of YHWH, the religious leaders and observant Jews knew that only God can forgive sins, so in the Pharisees' eyes, if someone is claiming to do this, he's making himself out to be God. Jesus *was*, of course, making himself out to be God, but the Pharisees couldn't make that leap. They instead charged him with blasphemy.[4]

Also, they reasoned, how could he forgive without a sacrifice? Even if Jesus were going to forgive sins on God's behalf, where was the blood to ceremonialize it? They didn't know that Jesus planned to make that sacrifice himself, once for all.

Here's another big violation in the eyes of the Pharisees: Jesus healed on the Sabbath. You weren't supposed to do much of anything on the Sabbath. The religious sticklers had, in fact, developed a system that told you exactly what you could do—for example, exactly how many steps you could take, and exactly what constituted work that would violate the Sabbath command. But Jesus went around doing what he pleased, as if the Sabbath restriction didn't apply to him, or worse still, as if he was the real authority over what one could or couldn't do on the Sabbath. We, of course, know that he is. But the leaders saw this, again, as blasphemy.

As Jesus developed a sizable following, his "heresy" would have

---

4. Mark 2:7.

become more and more distressing to the religious powers that be. It wasn't so much that he was teaching so many people about love and peace and grace, but that he was teaching so many people that he was the long awaited ruler while simultaneously making himself out to be God. That second part was not expected. The Messiah was anticipated as God's messenger and deliverer of the people, but an incarnate YHWH was beyond the realm of Jewish messianic belief.[5] We can assume, then, the conspiracy began on behalf of the Jewish religious leadership because blasphemy cannot go unpunished, and popular blasphemy, especially, must be snuffed out.

Now the religious leaders had the authority to decide that Jesus *deserved* to die, but legally they didn't have the authority to carry out such a punishment. Only the Roman government could do that. To convince the Romans to execute Jesus, the religious leaders invented a sort of capital crime, a trumped-up charge that connected to Jesus' words and actions surrounding the temple. Keep in mind that even though the temple was the Jews' sacred spot, it was technically Roman property on Roman land. So if the Romans could be convinced that Jesus meant harm against the temple—and they could infer just such a thing when he says stuff like, "Not one stone here will be left unturned,"[6] and, "Destroy this temple and I will raise it up"[7]—they could be convinced that Jesus was a dangerous insurrectionist. Given his popular following and the way he kept referring to himself as a king, the Roman authorities would certainly be interested in this guy, Jesus of Nazareth. The Romans didn't take kindly to would-be kings and self-appointed lords, even so-called "kings of the Jews," because in their eyes, Herod was the

5. To be clear, I'm not saying that Jesus the Messiah was not God himself. I'm saying that the Jews of Jesus' day did not expect the Messiah to be God in the flesh. On this point, see N. T. Wright, *Jesus and the Victory of God* (Minneapolis, MN: Fortress, 1996), 477–78.

6. See Matthew 24:2.

7. See John 2:19.

king over the Jews and Caesar was the lord of lords. Rows of crucified Jews outside Jerusalem provided vivid testimony to the Romans' intolerance of upstart kingdoms and would-be kings.

The awkward converging of these often competing forces—the Jewish religious leaders and the Roman authorities—resulted in the targeting of Jesus, the betrayal of Jesus by a friend, and the arrest of Jesus. His arrest led to his trial in a first-century kangaroo court, and culminated in his torture and eventual execution.

That was the way the world worked then. It was the way the world worked for anyone who made implicit claims to be God or made explicit claims to be the true king of Israel. Such an upstart was wished dead by the Jews and executed by the authorities of the governmental kingdom. *And Jesus knew this.* He knew it from the beginning on. So we can't bother with talk of Jesus the naive peasant getting chewed up and spit out by forces out of his control. Before politics and religion were conspiring to take him to Golgotha, he already knew that's where his path would lead. In Matthew 26:2, he flat-out tells his disciples that the Son of Man must be handed over to die. He says near the beginning of his ministry that he has a "baptism to suffer through,"[8] and he's understandably anxious about undergoing it. Jesus knew that in order to go about giving life to the spiritually—and physically—dead, and in order to speak words of life to everyone, he must die to make it happen. He was, quite literally, born to die.

So let's be clear about this. Though Jesus was in a very real sense victimized by friends and countrymen, he was not a victim.

## JESUS WAS A WILLING SACRIFICE

> For this reason the Father loves me, because I lay down my life that I may take it up again. No one takes

---

8. Luke 12:50 NCV.

> it from me, but I lay it down of my own accord. I have authority to lay it down, and I have authority to take it up again. This charge I have received from my Father. (John 10:17–18)

Nobody takes Jesus' life from him. He's the king of the universe. He had all the frailty of man, but if he so wished, he could have called legions of angels to his command. He could have hopped down off that cross, as the onlookers taunted him to do. When Satan tempted him in the desert to show his power in a way that might save him from the will of his Father, Jesus could have done those things. At any point, he could have said, "You know what? Forget this," and taken up a sword and laid waste to all who opposed him. He had that power.

But he chose to lay down his life. Nobody took it from him.

This is important today because of a divisive and hurtful argument that some boneheaded Christians have made. It has to do with that perennial question reignited in the wake of *The Passion* film: "Who killed Jesus?" Was it the Jews or the Romans?

Focusing on the Jewish role in the political collusion to kill Jesus has led to an insidious anti-Semitism in some corners of the church. The Gospels don't seem to help, really, because they depict Jews as thirsty for Jesus' blood and the Roman officials acting as if their hands are tied.[9] This is historically accurate because, when confronted with no evidence that Jesus really meant to physically overthrow the government, Herod and Pilate saw no cause to execute him, even though the Jewish religious leaders and their followers continued to beg for his murder.

But the Jews had no authority to execute anyone, so in the end, the Roman government is guilty of actually murdering Jesus.

---

9. Matthew 27:24–25.

Regardless of the apparent players in the drama, we have to remind ourselves that nobody took Jesus' life. He gave it of his own free will. Nobody took anything from him that he wasn't willing to give. So focusing on who killed Jesus is the wrong question and winds up with beside-the-point answers. The answer to the question of who killed Jesus is found in three truths about his death: (1) Jesus himself said that he gave his life willingly; (2) Jesus forgave his executioners while he was on the cross; (3) the guilt Jesus took to the cross belongs to everyone.

The great power of the betrayal and execution of Jesus is that he went into it with his eyes wide open, with his heart ready to endure the agony submissively, willingly—like a lamb led to the slaughter. Do you remember what he said in the garden of Gethsemane on the eve of his crucifixion? "Father, . . . not my will, but yours, be done."[10] That's Jesus saying, "I know what lies ahead, and I'm up for it."

## JESUS WAS AN INNOCENT SACRIFICE

Let's back up a bit to the point about the government officials' not finding just cause to execute Jesus. They heard some witnesses, they got a few words from Jesus, but Herod and Pilate were not convinced. The charges the Jews wanted Jesus convicted on weren't sticking. Pilate's wife even had a dream about the mess, according to one of the gospels, and she warned her husband, "Don't mess with that dude."[11] Pilate said, "I'm innocent of this man's blood," and he ceremoniously washed his hands of the situation.[12]

For all of his talk of being a king of a new kingdom that had arrived, Jesus had no plans to raise a militia and take the throne by force. That's because his kingdom, as we discussed in chapter 8, is one that reigns in hearts and minds. So he wasn't guilty of plotting the physical overthrow

10. Luke 22:42.
11. Matthew 27:19, author's paraphrase.
12. Matthew 27:24. And, really, what a sissy.

of the government. At the same time, he was also not guilty of blasphemy. When he claimed to be God and to speak for God and to have authority over the Law and authority to forgive sins, it was all true. So Jesus was not only a willing sacrifice; he was an innocent one.

And he was innocent from top to bottom, by which I mean not only was he innocent of the specific charges brought against him, he was also innocent of any sin that anyone could ever bring against him. Jesus was utterly and totally sinless. Hebrews 4:15 tells us that he was tempted in all the same ways we are, and yet was without sin. Why is that important?

First, by never sinning, Jesus redeemed the sin of Adam. As the New Adam, it was Jesus' mission to pull a huge do-over on the fall of mankind, to right the wrongs of our ancient parents Adam and Eve. Thus, he had to live a sinless life to redeem the lives of sinners.

Second—and most applicable to the subject at hand—Jesus had to be a sinless man, an innocent man, because by God's command, and thus by Jewish law, any sacrifice offered for the forgiveness of sins must be pure and unblemished. An inappropriate or corrupted sacrifice wouldn't work. Only the blood of something pure could cleanse the hearts of the impure.

And so we see Jesus referred to as a spotless lamb.[13] By offering himself as a sinless sacrifice, Jesus met the demands of ritual purity.

What happened in the sacrifice? As we saw in the beginning of our discussion, sacrifices were bloody and messy. Jesus' sacrifice was no different.

If you don't know already, crucifixion was designed to be the cruelest, most agonizing, most humiliating form of execution imaginable.[14] Crucifixion was essentially torturing someone to death on autopilot.

---

13. 1 Peter 1:19, for example.

14. The best concise survey of crucifixion in the ancient world I know of is Martin Hengel, *Crucifixion in the Ancient World and the Folly of the Message of the Cross* (Minneapolis, MN: Augsburg, 1977).

Typically, crucified prisoners were first beaten or scourged, as Jesus was, in order to weaken them. Then they were usually stripped naked. This is something you don't see, obviously, in most artistic depictions of crucifixion, which preserve a shred of dignity for the condemned with a well-placed bit of cloth. But in real life, the prisoners were stripped naked to expose them completely to the elements and to expose them completely to humiliation.

In the crucifixion itself, the condemned's wrists, and sometimes their legs, were nailed to a pole. Sometimes their wrists or hands were nailed to a crossbeam that ran perpendicular to a pole, and sometimes their wrists or hands were nailed above their head to the length of pole above them. A popular notion today is that Jesus must have been nailed through his wrists because there's not enough cartilage or bone in one's hands to support body weight. But hands could have been nailed, actually, if the arms were tied to the crossbeam with lashes for support. In addition, stakes or crosses sometimes had little ledges for the condemned's feet—which might seem to offer the prisoner some relief, but were actually designed to prolong the pain and agony. The real cause of death from crucifixion wasn't from pain or the loss of blood—although those things often did people in—but from suffocation. The condemned were mounted on the cross or stake in such a way that their chests expanded. Eventually they would tire out to the point where it was impossible to contract and expand the lungs to breathe. In a complex physiological exercise, prisoners often had to push up their bodies with their legs to be able to fill their lungs with air. However the cross was constructed, the purpose was to create as long and excruciating a death as possible. But if for some reason the executioners wanted to hasten death, they'd often take a stick or a club and break the prisoners' legs so they couldn't push up anymore and they'd suffocate and die.

Crucifixion looked like this: a prisoner, torn to pieces from Roman scourging, who'd had rocks and other items thrown at him, would be hoisted onto a cross and nailed to it, naked and exposed to the hot sun and elements. The naked man would hang there—humiliated, agonized—until his lungs gave out and he died. Carrion birds might come and pick at his eyes or at exposed bits of flesh. Prisoners often lost control of their bowels, so their blood and sweat and tissue and feces would pool up at the base of their crosses. They'd be dying of thirst and pain and gasping for breath.

It was a horrifying, ugly, messy, revolting scene.

It was so awful, in fact, that even though one could walk a few steps around the city and see this very thing happening without cover, it wasn't discussed in polite society. The word *crucifixion* itself was considered impolite, improper. It was meant to be—and it was—a shameful, undignified death.

A messy, bloody death. Like a messy, bloody sacrifice.

Yet Jesus underwent it innocently and willingly.

Why? Because plunging into the depths of shame was the only way to achieve glory. Crucifixion for Jesus not only epitomized the whole "die to live" dynamic of Christian faith, it also epitomized the very foundation of the kingdom call: empty yourself, humble yourself, crucify yourself, pour yourself out, sacrifice yourself.

## JESUS WAS AN ATONING SACRIFICE

What does the word *atonement* mean? It means making amends, setting things right, achieving forgiveness. It means cleaning, cleansing. Just as a priest would bring up a spotless animal to sacrifice for the sins of Israel, Jesus gave himself up to achieve forgiveness of sins. There is no more beautiful meditation on Jesus as sacrifice than that found in the letter to the Hebrews.

> Therefore he had to be made like his brothers in every respect, so that he might become a merciful and

> faithful high priest in the service of God, to make propitiation for the sins of the people. (Heb. 2:17)

Here, Jesus is cast in the role of high priest, the guy who intervenes between God and sinners and offers a sacrifice to make that connection possible. And yet Jesus, himself the priest, became that sacrifice.

This stunning role reversal is the real crux of the incarnation, by the way. Jesus was God who became man. Jesus was a king who served . . . a shepherd who became a sheep . . . a judge who took the punishment. And now a priest who not only offers a sacrifice, but a priest who *becomes* the sacrifice.

The Hebrews passage says it this way: "to make propitiation for the sins of the people." That word *propitiation* is just a highfalutin way to say "payment." Because of our sin, there is a blood debt owed. And remember, without the shedding of blood there is no forgiveness of sins. In order to overcome spiritual death, a sacrifice of physical death must be made. "The wages of sin is death," Paul tells us in Romans 6:23. Sin requires death for payment. And Jesus, as both priest and unblemished sacrifice, makes that payment for us.

Here's Paul again, in another well-known passage on sin:

> For all have sinned and fall short of the glory of God, and are justified by his grace as a gift, through the redemption that is in Christ Jesus, whom God put forward as a propitiation by his blood, to be received by faith. This was to show God's righteousness, because in his divine forbearance he had passed over former sins. (Rom. 3:23–25)

God offered Jesus as a propitiation—a payment for satisfaction—for the wages of sin. This is the debt that we are unwilling and unable to pay, and that Jesus was both willing and able to pay on our behalf. Through Christ's sacrifice, we who have fallen short of God's glory are now justified, brought before God with Jesus' work applied to us. We have been given Christ's righteousness. We have been atoned for.

What does *atonement* really mean? There's a clue in its spelling: "at-one-ment." We are made "at one" with God.[15] The other word for this is, of course, *reconciled*. Like wayward sheep, or estranged children, we were lost and in need of being brought back. Jesus' atoning sacrifice reconciled us to our Father. The division that sin caused, because we are sinful and God is holy and perfect, has been covered, broken down, overcome, destroyed by the atoning payment of Christ's sacrifice.

> Remember that you were at that time separated from Christ, alienated from the commonwealth of Israel and strangers to the covenants of promise, having no hope and without God in the world. But now in Christ Jesus you who once were far off have been brought near by the blood of Christ. For he himself is our peace, who has made us both one and has broken down in his flesh the dividing wall of hostility. (Eph. 2:12–14)

We who were once far off have been brought near by Christ's blood. His blood reconciles us to God. His sacrificed flesh breaks down the dividing wall.

Remember what happened in the temple when Jesus was crucified? The heavy, huge, indestructible veil that hung between the outer courts and the holy of holies, the great symbol of the divide between

15. Okay, it's kinda simplistic and cheesy, like one of those corny messages on a church sign, but I like it.

the perfect and holy presence of God himself and us, the unwashed riffraff, was ripped right in two. It tore from top to bottom.[16] That's an amazing picture of what Christ's sacrifice has done. It has torn in two the division between God and man, because the God who became man *for* man threw his beaten body into the gears of time and ended forever the otherwise endless process of making amends. The system of alienation, of estrangement, of irreconcilable differences has been vanquished by Christ's sacrificial body. He has made atonement for us, done the dirty work we couldn't and wouldn't do to restore us to right relationship with God.

Look at the language Paul uses in Ephesians 2: we were *brought near* by Christ's blood; we have been *made one* by his flesh. That's an accomplished work, an effective sacrifice. And that's why we can't have any of this wishy-washy stuff about Christ's death making *a* way to God, or Christ's death making salvation *potential*, or Christ's death being "a good example." What God sent Christ to do, Christ did. What Christ's death was meant to accomplish, it accomplished. He made atonement. He saved us by his blood. He brought us near. He didn't just show us the way. He blazed the trail, picked us up, and ran us down it.

He didn't perforate the veil. He didn't put a dotted line on the veil so we'd know where to use our scissors. He didn't put a "tear here" label on the veil and add a ziplock enclosure so we could seal it back up if we wanted. He absolutely ripped the thing in half. One act. Fully complete.

Revel in this: *Jesus has made atonement for* your *sins.* And because he has made real atonement, he has put an end to the need for animal sacrifice. Never again. Don't need it, don't want it. Isn't required. Jesus fulfilled the law with his new covenant; he fulfilled the prophecies of the prophets; he rendered the temple null and void by bringing the

16. Matthew 27:51.

presence of God to us in person; he fulfilled the sacrificial system by saying, in effect, "Oh, you need a sacrifice? I'm your sacrifice right here."

## JESUS WAS A FINAL SACRIFICE

With his willingness, in his innocence, and by his atoning work, Jesus was a final, once-and-for-all sacrifice.

> For it was indeed fitting that we should have such a high priest, holy, innocent, unstained, separated from sinners, and exalted above the heavens. He has no need, like those high priests, to offer sacrifices daily, first for his own sins and then for those of the people, since he did this once for all when he offered up himself. For the law appoints men in their weakness as high priests, but the word of the oath, which came later than the law, appoints a Son who has been made perfect forever. (Heb. 7:26–28)

We are now done with imperfect priests enacting an imperfect system for imperfect people. It used to be that the high priests had to offer daily sacrifices to cover the people's daily excursions into sin. No longer. Jesus Christ, being sinless and blameless and holy himself, offered himself as a once-and-for-all sacrifice. Which means no more animal sacrifices in the temple. Don't need to do it anymore. Don't need any more blood to cover our sins. Christ's blood did the job—forever. His blood was more than sufficient. His blood atoned for our daily sins—and then some. As our forever perfect sacrifice, Jesus, in giving himself for us, ascribed to us that same "forever perfection." His holiness is eternal, not symbolic or finite like an animal's. So when his blood is applied to us, it makes any other attempts at holiness unnecessary, incomplete, flawed. Christ accomplished the perfect sacrifice *once and for all.*

And just so we wouldn't forget it, Jesus confirmed it from the cross: "It is finished."[17]

It's done! It's complete! It's accomplished!

The expiration date of the sacrificial system was a dark day in A.D. 33 (give or take). But while Christ's sacrifice was the last one needed to cover our sins, it is not the last sacrifice required. We don't have to offer animals anymore, and there's certainly no other sacrifice we can make of any kind to cleanse us from our sins. But now our mandate, powered by the freeing blood of Jesus, is to go around embodying that sacrifice in our daily lives. To live our lives the way Jesus died his death—humbly, submissively, sacrificially.

Here is Paul's encouragement:

> I appeal to you therefore, brothers, by the mercies of God, to present your bodies as a living sacrifice, holy and acceptable to God, which is your spiritual worship. Do not be conformed to this world, but be transformed by the renewal of your mind, that by testing you may discern what is the will of God, what is good and acceptable and perfect. (Rom. 12:1–2)

Paul asks us to present ourselves as living sacrifices, and thus we become walking, talking ambassadors of Jesus' sacrifice on behalf of all mankind. This, according to Paul, is spiritual worship. Not singing songs or listening to preaching, but presenting our lives, in church and out of church, to the will of God and the needs of our fellow man in the same way that Christ did. In Philippians 2:17, Paul talks about

17. John 19:30.

pouring himself out as a drink offering. It's the same concept—a life of sacrificial living; a me-third lifestyle,[18] a commitment and attitude and behavior that says, "I submit to God; I serve others."

Do not be conformed to this world, Paul says, echoing Jesus. This world tells us that sacrifice is stupid, foolish. That turning the other cheek is dumb. That blessing those who hate us is ridiculous. That giving up our own needs for someone else's is unhealthy and unsatisfying. That's not what the kingdom life says, though. It says we find our lives when we lose them, when we give them up. The way to life is death, so we must take up our crosses daily and become living sacrifices.[19]

Why? Because it's nice? Because it will get us the gold star in Sunday school?

No, because the kingdom life is about reconciliation. It's about reconciling us to God. It's about dying to ourselves, just as Jesus died to himself when he came to earth—and dying to ourselves for the same reasons that Jesus died to himself: to glorify God and to redeem those around us.

Paul calls this life "the ministry of reconciliation."

> Therefore, if anyone is in Christ, he is a new creation. The old has passed away; behold, the new has come. All this is from God, who through Christ reconciled us to himself and gave us the ministry of reconciliation; that is, in Christ God was reconciling the world to himself, not counting their trespasses against them, and entrusting to us the message of reconciliation. (2 Cor. 5:17–19)

---

18. Using the Great Commandment's assumed prioritization of God first, neighbor second.

19. Luke 9:23; Romans 12:1.

Through Christ's sacrifice, God has reconciled us to himself. He's made us new people. We were aliens, strangers to him. Now we're sons and daughters of God. But being "in Christ" is not about getting our own personal Jesus. It's not about putting Jesus in our pockets—like My Buddy, wherever I go, he goes.[20] Being in Christ is about conforming to his sacrifice so much that our entire lives now are oriented around this amazing work of reconciliation. The ministry of reconciliation is essentially the same concept as living redemptively—filling every moment with the good news of Christ's atoning work for others.

We tend to make excuses for our failure to fulfill the ministry of reconciliation, pleading busyness and emotional baggage. The truth is, we in the Western world have it pretty darn easy.

Let's compare ourselves, just for example, with Christians in Sri Lanka, where twenty years of bloody civil war have left them as constant targets for religious and ethnic violence. I first learned of the persecuted church in this tumultuous nation in 2003, thanks to an incredible article in *Christianity Today* by Tim Stafford, called "The Joy of Suffering in Sri Lanka." Here's an excerpt:

> Bernard is slight, almost delicate in his appearance. He said his captors beat him and threatened him with execution for two days, then threw him into an 8-by-8-foot room with 40 other men. The room was too crowded to sleep lying down, but "I shared Jesus Christ with many people," he told me in his high, soft voice. "It was a good place to tell about Jesus."
>
> Eventually he was moved to a rehabilitation center, where he found two other born-again believers. At a

20. If you were born before 1983, think of My Buddy as the boy version of Cindy Brady's Kitty Carry-all, and marketed to the effeminate sons of sensitive Baby Boomers.

> daily chapel, "Hindus were in the middle, the right corner was for Buddhists, Roman Catholics were in the left corner." Bernard's fellowship of three grew as others came to faith. Eventually, some of the prisoners complained to the authorities that Bernard's group induced conversions with offers of money or other favors. This is a frequent complaint against Christians in Sri Lanka, that they pursue "unethical conversions."
>
> "The captain called me in and asked me who gave me the authority to lead this group. I said that God gave me the authority. He made me kneel down on the floor, and he beat me.
>
> "He told me to bring all the new believers, and he beat them. That was very hard for me to see. He told them that they could not pray anymore. He ordered them to go back to their old religions."
>
> "We were very glad of this, because of Christ," Bernard told me with absolute, deadpan seriousness. "I told the others to go back [to their old places in the chapel], just as the captain had ordered them, but not to worship. 'You know the Truth now,' I told them."
>
> Bernard was released after 16 months and returned immediately to Bible school. Of his time in prison he says, "It was a very useful experience for me. I learned how to communicate with people, how to counsel."[21]

Are you as blown away as I am? "We were very glad of this"? "It was a very useful experience"? Not a whiff of complaint.

---

21. Tim Stafford, "The Joy of Suffering in Sri Lanka," *Christianity Today*, October 2003, http://www.christianitytoday.com/ct/2003/october/5.54.html.

Stafford tells another Sri Lankan's story that is equally powerful:

> Lalani was holding her son when she heard a gunshot. Lionel [her husband] came back into the bedroom, covering his face with his hands. Right behind him was a man with a knife, who repeatedly stabbed him. Lalani tried to shelter her son. She heard another gunshot. The intruder disappeared.
>
> "They brought his body home, and I held onto his feet. He had received an award from Lanka Bible College for distinguished students. I prayed, 'I'm not a distinguished person like him, but I'm not going to leave here.'"
>
> Afraid of further violence, her landlord asked her to vacate. When she moved to another small house, people threw stones at it day after day, frightening her son. Letters came telling her she would be killed like her husband unless she left by a certain date. Protests were organized against the church; the roof was burned.
>
> "God became very close to me during that time. I would tell him everything. I said, 'If you want me to die, I'm ready, but I'd prefer not, because I have work to do here. But if I die, I want to write on the wall with my blood, 'Jesus is alive.'"[22]

Wow. These persecuted believers in Sri Lanka are paying for their faith with their safety, their security, their very lives. They are living sacrifices, prepared to be literal sacrifices, and yet they find joy in this struggle and see providence in the pain and the danger. As a result, they

---

22. Ibid.

continue to spread the faith. As the church father Tertullian is thought to have said, "The blood of the martyr is the seed of the church." That's a fancy way of saying that the more Christians you kill, the more Christians you make. The more sacrificially you live, the more lives you will affect with the radical reconciliation of Jesus Christ.

The sacrifice works; the sacrifice is effectual.

Do you see what sacrifice does? It changes things. It throws a wrench into the works. It stops time and starts a new day. It reflects a new creation. That's what it means, by the way, to be a new creation. Not just becoming a changed man or woman. It means we—you and I—are now new people who live according to the order of a new creation. We live not according to this life, but according to eternal life. We respond to the rhythms of the kingdom now, not the rule of the world. And just as Christ's sacrifice accomplished such a radical reconciliation for us, living our lives as sacrifices devoted to God for the beauty of redemption means we can tear open the veils between others and God. We get to participate in a life here and now with the quality of eternity. When we get down into the dirty, messy, gritty, humiliating, sometimes agonizing life of sacrificing ourselves, we proclaim to the world that Jesus has accomplished atonement.

> "It is finished."

But what about Christ's other words from the cross?

> "My God, my God, why have you forsaken me?"[23]

If you grew up in church, as I did, you may have heard a hundred variations on these words, and a lot of ways to explain them or even

23. Mark 15:34.

dismiss them. When pastors and writers focus on these words of Christ, they often start filling in all kinds of gaps that don't exist—about God abandoning Jesus; that the sin Jesus bore was so ugly that God had to depart; that God couldn't look at his Son; that Jesus had to know what it was like to be spurned by God; blah blah blah. Growing up, I wrestled with this for years, because all these stabs at interpretation never made much sense to me. They didn't seem to grasp what Jesus was saying. If you take him at his word, he is saying, "God, why have you forgotten about me?" And you can't spin that. You can't interpret that to mean something other than what it says. So I was troubled by what it said, and I was troubled by everyone's inability to explain it adequately, and at how all the attempts seemed disingenuous.

I went for years not realizing that Jesus wasn't just uttering some random, painful lament, but that he was actually quoting Scripture. Of all the people I'd heard who'd tried to explain this cry of Jesus, none ever mentioned that. So imagine my surprise when I finally followed a long-overlooked cross-reference in my Bible one day and saw the full scope of what Jesus was calling to mind.

Keep in mind, also, that the passage he quotes is one that most of his Jewish listeners, and most of those who would hear the story later, would recognize. When Jesus said, "My God, my God, why have you forsaken me?" they wouldn't be scratching their heads wondering what the heck he was talking about. They would say, "Ah, he's quoting David." And not just any words of David, but the opening line of a messianic psalm, a song that prophesies the very thing Jesus was now going through.

> My God, my God, why have you abandoned me?
>   Why are you so far away when I groan for help?
> Every day I call to you, my God, but you do not answer.
>   Every night you hear my voice, but I find no relief.

Yet you are holy,
 enthroned on the praises of Israel.
Our ancestors trusted in you,
 and you rescued them.
They cried out to you and were saved.
 They trusted in you and were never disgraced.

But I am a worm and not a man.
 I am scorned and despised by all!
Everyone who sees me mocks me.
 They sneer and shake their heads, saying,
"Is this the one who relies on the LORD?
 Then let the LORD save him!
If the LORD loves him so much,
 let the LORD rescue him!"

Yet you brought me safely from my mother's womb
 and led me to trust you at my mother's breast.
I was thrust into your arms at my birth.
 You have been my God from the moment I was born.

Do not stay so far from me,
 for trouble is near,
 and no one else can help me. . . .

My life is poured out like water,
 and all my bones are out of joint.
My heart is like wax,
 melting within me.
My strength has dried up like sunbaked clay.

My tongue sticks to the roof of my mouth.
You have laid me in the dust and left me for dead.
My enemies surround me like a pack of dogs;
an evil gang closes in on me.
They have pierced my hands and feet.
I can count all my bones.
My enemies stare at me and gloat.
They divide my garments among themselves
and throw dice for my clothing.

O Lord, do not stay far away!
You are my strength; come quickly to my aid!
Save me from the sword;
spare my precious life from these dogs.
Snatch me from the lion's jaws
and from the horns of these wild oxen. . . .

For he has not ignored or belittled the suffering of the needy.
He has not turned his back on them,
but has listened to their cries for help.

I will praise you in the great assembly.
I will fulfill my vows in the presence of those who worship you.
The poor will eat and be satisfied.
All who seek the Lord will praise him.
Their hearts will rejoice with everlasting joy.
The whole earth will acknowledge the Lord and return to him.
All the families of the nations will bow down before him.

For royal power belongs to the Lord.
He rules all the nations.

Let the rich of the earth feast and worship.
Bow before him, all who are mortal,
all whose lives will end as dust.
Our children will also serve him.
Future generations will hear about the wonders of the Lord
His righteous acts will be told to those not yet born.
They will hear about everything he has done.
(Ps. 22:1–11, 14–21, 24–31 NLT)

God didn't abandon Jesus. And don't ever think for a second that he did. And don't ever think for a second that he will abandon you. The author of Hebrews affirms that God has promised us, "I will never leave you nor forsake you."[24] Do you think he was lying? Do you think God would do to his perfect, sinless Son what he wouldn't do to us miserable creatures?

Of course not!

Jesus wasn't saying from the cross, "God has abandoned me." He was quoting Psalm 22, which is actually a psalm about God *not* forsaking him, about God *not* forsaking his people, whom he loves and desires to redeem. And if you read the whole thing, you'll see that while Jesus laments the weight of sacrificial death, he also heroically cements a promise, marks a solemn occasion, and signals the finality and fulfillment of the prophecy that God's kingdom would be brought near and made victorious by the messy, dirty, sacrificial death of its King.

When we live sacrificial kingdom lives, we tell the watching world

24. Hebrews 13:5.

that Jesus "has done it." His sacrifice for us doesn't mean that God has forsaken us; it means that God has accomplished his purpose! Let us now commit ourselves to become living sacrifices in the ministry of reconciliation, declaring to ourselves, to our Christian brothers and sisters, and to everyone with whom we come into contact that God is not a great abandoner, but that he redeems, reconciles, and rescues. That God, in the sacrifice of Christ, *has done it!*

10

# JESUS THE PROVISION

The twelve tribes of Israel were in disarray, the nation divided. In the north, the largest portion—still called Israel—had slipped into idolatry. King Jeroboam had set up golden calves in certain parts of the kingdom to keep his subjects from traveling to Jerusalem—which, at that time, was in the southern kingdom of Judah—to worship YHWH.[1] Years later, Israel's wicked king Ahab led a more complete abandonment of worship to YHWH, and the northern kingdom officially offered allegiance to Baal.[2]

God is a jealous God. Angry with the nation for this spiritual infidelity as well as for their murder of many of God's priests, God sent the prophet Elijah to tell Ahab to prepare himself for three and a half years of terrible drought.

After delivering this terrifying news, Elijah went into hiding, and God sent ravens to feed him. Elijah drank water from a brook, and the ravens brought him food twice a day. But when the drought covered the land, the brook dried up. God told Elijah to head to a place called Zarephath, and he told him that he would find a woman there, a widow,

1. Read the full story in 1 Kings 11:26–13:10. Also, see 2 Chronicles 10:1–13:20.
2. This was, of course, before Ahab bought that boat and went looking for Moby Dick.

who would take care of him.[3] Elijah obeyed, and when he reached the gates of Zarephath, he saw the woman. She was gathering sticks. Elijah asked her for something to drink,[4] and as she left to oblige, he called after her, asking her also for some bread.

This the woman couldn't do. "I have no bread," she said to Elijah. What she did have was a small bit of meal in a barrel. And she also had a little bit of oil in a bottle. In fact, she was collecting sticks so she could cook this last little bit of food for herself and her son. After that, they planned to just lie down and wait for death. It was all they had, and they had given up hope of finding more food anywhere else because of the terrible toll taken by the drought.

Elijah was not deterred. He told the widow to take up the little bit of meal she had, and the little bit of oil, and make a little cake for him first. After that, she could make a meal for her son and herself. Then he made an incredible promise: he told the woman that if she followed his instructions, God would allow her meal and oil to last until the end of the famine.

Amazingly, the woman obeyed. She made Elijah a little cake first. Then the prophet, the woman, and her son ate from a handful of meal and a bit of oil like it was an all-you-can-eat buffet. They were fed for days and days, until the end of the famine.

But that's not the end of the story. Even after this brief tale of miraculous provision, God came through with an even greater miracle of provision. Check this out:

> After this the son of the woman, the mistress of the house, became ill. And his illness was so severe that there was no breath left in him. And she said to Elijah, "What have you against me, O man of God? You have

3. Read the full story in 1 Kings 17.
4. Where else have we seen a scene like this? Try John 4:7.

> come to me to bring my sin to remembrance and to cause the death of my son!" And he said to her, "Give me your son." And he took him from her arms and carried him up into the upper chamber where he lodged, and laid him on his own bed. And he cried to the LORD, "O LORD my God, have you brought calamity even upon the widow with whom I sojourn, by killing her son?" Then he stretched himself upon the child three times and cried to the LORD, "O LORD my God, let this child's life come into him again." And the LORD listened to the voice of Elijah. And the life of the child came into him again, and he revived. And Elijah took the child and brought him down from the upper chamber into the house and delivered him to his mother. And Elijah said, "See, your son lives." And the woman said to Elijah, "Now I know that you are a man of God, and that the word of the LORD in your mouth is truth." (1 Kings 17:17–24)

Several concepts, or motifs, here are bound up together time and time again in Scripture under God's provision; his provision of food, of the truth of God's word, and of the gift of life. Those three are consistently connected throughout the Bible's chronicle of God's provision for his people.

Why?

Well, there's the literal sense in that God provides daily bread for his children, and, of course, we need to eat to keep our bodies alive.[5] But then there's this other idea, this sense in which God's words of truth are said to be sustenance; God's promise itself is said to keep us alive.

5. Although "life" is a relative concept for the young adults in my community who appear to subsist on pizza, Sixlets, and Red Bull.

This is perhaps no more explicit than in Jesus' words to Satan in the desert:

> Then Jesus was led up by the Spirit into the wilderness to be tempted by the devil. And after fasting forty days and forty nights, he was hungry. And the tempter came and said to him, "If you are the Son of God, command these stones to become loaves of bread." But he answered, "It is written,
>
> 'Man shall not live by bread alone,
> but by every word that comes from the mouth of God.'"
>
> (Matt. 4:1–4)

So it's not just physical bread that we need to live, but God's Word itself. It is God's Word that sustains us, that gives us nourishment. It is his promises that give us hope; his decrees that give us guidance; his blessings that give us joy; his laws that keep us safe. And it's his declaration over us—"I will provide for you, for I am your God"—that keeps us alive, keeps us going, gives us strength to move. "In him we live and move and have our being" (Acts 17:28).

All of this amounts to a spiritual life that cannot be compartmentalized away from our "real life." This repeated scriptural motif of provision points consistently to a spiritual life that correlates to our physical life. We learned in elementary-school science class that oxygen, water, and food make us able to live and move. But the Bible tells us, "No, it's in God that you are able to do those things."

## JESUS' PROVISION DOESN'T IMPROVE LIFE—IT *GIVES* LIFE

It's imperative we see that God is not interested in making our lives *better*. He'll have nothing to do with being a supplemental enhancement to support our personal goals and ambitions. He's not a sidekick, co-pilot, or self-help guru, and we should stay far away from a so-called Christianity that presents God as a way to improve our lives.

God is life itself. Christ is life itself. We cannot live apart from God.

Jesus took this truth, and in his Jesusy way made it provocatively about himself. He irked all kinds of people by taking all the stuff God had done and said in the Hebrew Scriptures and saying, "Yeah, that's about me." His saying that he was fulfilling the Law, and his exercising authority over the temple system, appropriating the prophets, and assuming the mantle of high priest and sacrifice made the "owners" of this spiritual heritage very angry. And he really hacked off some people when he took one of their most sacred memories of God's provision for his people—the manna in the wilderness—and made it, too, all about himself.

Surely you know the story of the Israelites' subsistence on manna. (You can refamiliarize yourself with the story in Exodus 16.) It's basically about the needy Israelites, newly escaped from slavery in Egypt and wandering in the desert. They were hungry, and like all hungry children, they whined.

I sort of sympathize with them, to be honest with you. Not just because I see my own sinful impetuousness and easy idolatry in the story of their wanderings, but also because their being hungry in the desert makes absolute sense to me. I don't know if you've noticed, but it's hard to come by food in the wilderness. It's kinda hard for thousands and thousands of people to sneak up on an animal.[6]

They were hungry, and they needed to eat to live. Just to live. But also for the energy to, you know, walk around the desert for forty flippin' years. So God sent manna, a flaky breadlike substance that tasted like honey. The Israelites found it on the ground each morning, and they were able to scoop it up for their daily sustenance. God sent this heavenly

---

6. I'm assuming this is how hunting works. The closest I've come to hunting is playing *Duck Hunt* on the 8-bit Nintendo.

food, not only so the people could eat, but also so they would continue to connect their daily provision of life with the breath of God itself.

The word *manna* in Hebrew literally means "what is it?" or "what is this stuff?" What it was, actually, was God's provision for his people. Manna was God's daily bread, given as a consistent, tangible reminder that his word is true and his word gives life.

Jesus took this sacred story and applied it to himself. But let's back up just a bit. In John 6, right before Jesus declares himself to be the bread of life, John tells a story in which Jesus provides food for a large crowd. This, too, is a great echo of YHWH's Old Testament provision. Jesus takes five loaves of bread and two fish that some kid had in his Pokémon lunchbox and turns it into a never-ending meal for five thousand people. There were twelve baskets of leftovers!

Let's reflect on that for just a minute. What a beautiful picture of God's provision. As with the widow's limited meal and oil, from one small offering—the meager loaves and fish—comes food aplenty, with much left over. In Jesus we find abundance. That's actually a great word for what I'm talking about here: *abundance*.

In the modern evangelical church landscape, "abundance" tends to mean things like having extra money or more stuff. You may hear prosperity gospelists, and those influenced by them, talking about "the abundant life." By which they mean being happy and receiving material blessings and finding the right parking place.

But that's not really abundance. Anyone who mistakes "health and wealth" for true abundance is, in fact, like the ignorant child C. S. Lewis writes about "who wants to go on making mud pies in a slum because he cannot imagine what is meant by the offer of a holiday at the sea." Lewis concludes, "We are far too easily pleased."[7]

---

7. C. S. Lewis, "The Weight of Glory," in *The Weight of Glory* (San Francisco: HarperCollins, 1980), 26.

No, abundance is not lots of stuff. Abundance is God's all-surpassing, all-sufficient provision for his people. It's about having so much life that it overflows. It's about being more than provided for; it's about God's giving us not just the bare minimum or just enough to live on for a few days or weeks, but enough to sustain us every day of our lives—and then, after our lives on earth are done, into the eternal day of the life to come. That's abundant life. It's not a three-car garage with a Mercedes in every slot. It's living forever.

## JESUS' PROVISION IS HIMSELF

After the miraculous feeding of the five thousand, there's this little matter of Jesus' walking on water, which we'll look at in our next chapter. But if we can set that dramatic vignette aside for the moment, I'd like to focus our attention on the subsequent exchange between Jesus and some very eager and very frustrated people:

> When they found him on the other side of the sea, they said to him, "Rabbi, when did you come here?" Jesus answered them, "Truly, truly, I say to you, you are seeking me, not because you saw signs, but because you ate your fill of the loaves. Do not labor for the food that perishes, but for the food that endures to eternal life, which the Son of Man will give to you. For on him God the Father has set his seal." Then they said to him, "What must we do, to be doing the works of God?" Jesus answered them, "This is the work of God, that you believe in him whom he has sent." So they said to him, "Then what sign do you do, that we may see and believe you? What work do you perform? Our fathers ate the manna in the wilderness; as it is written, 'He gave them bread from heaven to eat.'" Jesus then said to them,

> "Truly, truly, I say to you, it was not Moses who gave you the bread from heaven, but my Father gives you the true bread from heaven. For the bread of God is he who comes down from heaven and gives life to the world." They said to him, "Sir, give us this bread always."
>
> Jesus said to them, "I am the bread of life; whoever comes to me shall not hunger, and whoever believes in me shall never thirst. . . ."
>
> So the Jews grumbled about him, because he said, "I am the bread that came down from heaven." . . . Jesus answered them, . . . "I am the bread of life. Your fathers ate the manna in the wilderness, and they died. This is the bread that comes down from heaven, so that one may eat of it and not die. I am the living bread that came down from heaven. If anyone eats of this bread, he will live forever. And the bread that I will give for the life of the world is my flesh."
>
> The Jews then disputed among themselves, saying, "How can this man give us his flesh to eat?" (John 6:25–35, 41, 43, 48–52)

Apparently these yahoos had never heard of the Roman Catholic doctrine of transubstantiation, which I will now elucidate for you over the next six pages, using only the most technical of theological jargon . . .

Still there? Yeah, we're both glad I'm just joking.

Basically, Jesus says to them, "Look, you're looking for signs and wonders, which I've been happy to give you, but you're missing the point. The point is not the signs and wonders, but what the signs and wonders point to. The manna given to your ancestors wasn't about Moses or about having a great story to tell. It was about God—to point you to God, to make you rely on God, to have you connect the provision of life itself to God himself. I'm now giving you a never-ending meal of bread so that you'll remember manna and see *me* as your manna now."

Jesus says, "You know that manna your ancestors needed to live? Yeah, that was *me*. I am the bread you need to live. I am your daily bread."

*Ex-squuuze me?* His incredulous listeners are like, "Um . . . what? Did he just say what I think he said?"

And, yeah, he kinda did.

They were grumbling about him because he said he was the manna from heaven, and that they have to eat his flesh to live. They have to consume him to live.

We have to have him *in us* to live.

I'm going to give you something from the teacher's answer key right now.[8] I believe the concept of "being in Christ" is the key to Christianity. It's not rules or regulations or quiet times or listening to worship CDs or having Bible knowledge or listening to the best preachers or doing good deeds, although all those things are good things and can help you grow along the way. The key to Christian faith is found in the little recurring biblical phrase "in Christ." Or "in him."

This is another feature of Jesus that we Christians have diluted into practical incoherence. Have you ever seen this phrase at the end of a letter or note? "In Him, Aunt Joanie."

I especially love it (not really) when I receive an angry letter with an "in Him" sign-off. Having written some fairly opinionated and occasionally provocative stuff in the Christian blogosphere over the last several years, I've occasionally received e-mailed diatribes resembling the following fabricated missive:

---

8. Don't tell anyone; it'll be our little secret.

> You're a sorry excuse for a Christian. You're a jerk and you obviously don't know about the subject at hand. You probably kick puppies and taunt babies. How can you be so narrow minded? You are so condescending and judgmental.
>
> In Him,
> Jerky McJerkison

*In Him*. We see it and use it all the time. Do we know that it's biblical? Are we using it biblically . . . or absentmindedly? At the risk of stepping on some toes, I'm compelled to mention that, for all the evangelistic usefulness we may get out of inviting people to get Christ into their lives (or into their hearts), the Bible is more emphatic and more direct about our being in Christ's life. Strictly speaking, we don't find life by accepting Christ into our lives and hearts, but by repenting of our lives and awakening to Christ's acceptance of us into *his* life.

Jesus did talk about being *in us* but, again, this was about sustenance, not enhancement.

> Abide in me, and I in you. As the branch cannot bear fruit by itself, unless it abides in the vine, neither can you, unless you abide in me. I am the vine; you are the branches. Whoever abides in me and I in him, he it is that bears much fruit, for apart from me you can do nothing. (John 15:4–5)

Jesus artfully fuses his living in us with our living in him, but the bottom line is his unequivocal assertion that without him there is no life. We can do nothing without him. Nothing. Achievements, successes, family legacies, charitable donations, the helping of old ladies across the street—all are nothing apart from Christ.

Look . . . if we didn't know any better, we'd really think Jesus was an egomaniac, wouldn't we? You can just imagine one of those great, self-righteous, pharisaical jerks saying, "Look, it's not all about you, Jesus."

And Jesus is all like, "Um, yeah, it kinda is."

Apart from him we can do . . . nothing. There is nothing outside of Christ but death. But no, we say there are lots of adventures to be had, and lots of fun activities to participate in, and lots of people to know and love, and lots of pleasures to partake in, and lots of good to do, and lots of other religions that facilitate a connection between people and whatever other spiritual realities are out there. Nope. Those aren't life. They are poor, poor substitutes. Even good things, things that God has graciously given to us—family, friends, work, money, talents—can become idols when we turn to them for the spiritual sustenance that only God can give. In comparison to the daily manna that is Christ, feeding on anything else is like eating dog poop. Now, dog poop can be eaten. But it's not bread. It's not life.

Lest we mistake the symbolism in Jesus' offer of bread and water with that of a widow's handful of flour or a boy's lunchbox meal, we cannot forget that Christ's meal is the only meal that gives life. This is not a meager prisoner's meal, a crust of moldy bread and a tiny cup of brackish water. Jesus is no mere bowl of daily gruel. He's the bread of life and the living water, a veritable feast, a meal of abundance. Look at how Paul describes the gift of life in Christ:

> If, because of one man's trespass, death reigned through that one man, much more will those who receive the abundance of grace and the free gift of righteousness reign in life through the one man Jesus Christ. (Rom. 5:17)

There's that great word again! It is an *abundance* of grace. It is *reigning* in life. It is enough, in Christ, to have an abundant life and to be a part of the only kingdom that will outlast the world and reign forever. This is the picture Jesus gives when he acts out his provision.

## THE PASSOVER MEAL AND THE LORD'S SUPPER

I don't know if you've noticed, but food is a really big deal throughout the New Testament, just as it is in the Old Testament. Lives are bought and sold over meals.[9] Major decisions are made over food. God's trustworthiness is related to being given a feast.[10] Trusting God is related to sitting at a table in the midst of our enemies.[11]

The Old Testament is chock-full of sacrificial meals, commemorative meals, symbolic meals, promises of meals, and the withholding of meals. Then there's the dietary law itself.

In the Gospels, Jesus presents some wonderful culinary word pictures of God's provision. Remember his first recorded miracle? John 2 tells us the great story of Jesus, at his mother's request, turning water into wine. And he doesn't turn to Mary and say, "Drinking wine is a sin, Mother; I'll just make more water." He doesn't offer Crystal Light or Sam's Choice ginger ale.[12] No, it's a *party.* It's supposed to be festive. The kids are breaking open the piñatas, the grown-ups are playing Scattergories, and Jesus says, "I'll bring the wine. The good stuff."

The Gospels tell us too, you'll recall, that one of the things that angered the religious leaders so much was Jesus' *dining* with the wrong people. The wrong sort. He sat at tables and ate and drank with sinners. With tax collectors and other yucky people you weren't supposed to consort with.

But because Jesus was about rescuing the lost, he sought out the lost. And because Jesus was about providing himself as the sustenance

9. Genesis 25:29–34; 37:25–27.
10. Psalm 36:7–8.
11. Psalm 23:5.
12. If you are Baptist, please disregard this paragraph. You and I both know that when the Bible says "wine," it means "unfermented grape juice." Except when it's speaking negatively of wine, in which case it means "wine."

for eternal life—chew on that (pardon the pun)—he sat down and had dinner with the lost. This is a great and recurring picture of kingdom reconciliation. Just like when the prodigal son came home and his father called for a fatted calf to be killed and a big feast to be made, Jesus talks about the kingdom life being a big banquet, a big wedding feast, a big party where everyone is welcome to the table. There's a seat for the worst of sinners because God is providing the meal, and he can take small supplies and make a forever-course meal.

One of the last things Jesus did with his followers before he ascended to heaven was have breakfast. And, of course, one of the last things he did with them before his arrest and execution was have dinner. It was the Passover meal for them. We commemorate it today as the Lord's Supper, or Communion, or the Eucharist. Whatever we call it, we must observe it not just as a ritual that reminds us of Christ's crucifixion, but as an act of worship. An act of worship in which we say to God—just as we speak to God when we worship in other ways—that *we need Jesus to live*. We need the provision of his sacrificed body to live. Apart from him, we have no life. So, when we prepare to partake of the elements of Communion, we must have in our minds to say from our hearts, "I need this to live. I need this flesh and blood to live."[13]

> And when the hour came, he reclined at table, and the apostles with him. And he said to them, "I have earnestly desired to eat this Passover with you before I suffer. For I tell you I will not eat it until it is fulfilled in the kingdom of God." And he took a cup, and when

---

13. Preparation for the elements is serious business, indeed. "Whoever, therefore, eats the bread or drinks the cup of the Lord in an unworthy manner will be guilty concerning the body and blood of the Lord. Let a person examine himself, then, and so eat of the bread and drink of the cup. For anyone who eats and drinks without discerning the body eats and drinks judgment on himself" (1 Cor. 11:27–29).

> he had given thanks he said, "Take this, and divide it among yourselves. For I tell you that from now on I will not drink of the fruit of the vine until the kingdom of God comes." And he took bread, and when he had given thanks, he broke it and gave it to them, saying, "This is my body, which is given for you. Do this in remembrance of me." And likewise the cup after they had eaten, saying, "This cup that is poured out for you is the new covenant in my blood." (Luke 22:14–20)

In partaking of Christ's broken body in this meal, we also identify with his sacrifice. Eating and drinking the elements is a commitment that we will die to ourselves. That is how we signal our entrance into the kingdom, remember? Die to live.[14]

Now the great news that is the Good News is that salvation is achieved by Jesus' effort, not ours. So partaking of the sacraments does not save us. But the grace that they depict does. The church in Galatia had trouble keeping this distinction straight, and it sort of drove Paul batty. He had proclaimed the gospel to them and thought he had established them in its assurance. But a group called the Judaizers were causing trouble among the Galatians, leading them astray. They confused many by convincing them that observing the Law—specifically, observing the old covenant sacrament of circumcision—was necessary for justification.

Paul's short letter is a masterpiece of gospel-centered polemic. The very signs that our flesh tends to trust for salvation—circumcision, baptism, Communion—cry out to us as we practice them that salvation is not of ourselves but of God's grace.

---

14. The clearest picture of this die-to-live entrance is, of course, the other required new covenant sacrament—baptism, which, in reenacting Christ's burial and resurrection, proclaims our death to sin and rising to new life.

> I have been crucified with Christ. It is no longer I who live, but Christ who lives in me. And the life I now live in the flesh I live by faith in the Son of God, who loved me and gave himself for me. I do not nullify the grace of God, for if righteousness were through the law, then Christ died for no purpose. (Gal. 2:20–21)

But Jesus did die for a purpose. He died to give life. It's not us living; it's Christ doing the living. And the life we live in our flesh and blood is made abundant by the flesh and blood Christ provided for us. That abundance is the grace of God. We who are dead have been raised by the provision of Christ's life. Partaking of this provision requires that we repent of our sinfulness (death) and place our faith in Jesus (life).

So when we sit down with our brothers and sisters at the Lord's table to partake of his body and blood, we're saying firstly, "I need this to live." And we're saying secondly, "I commit to sacrifice."

## JESUS' PROVISION MAKES SACRAMENTS OF US

We are—just like the bread and the wine—ordinary, earthy things declared sacred because of what they signify in relation to God's grace. Like the elements of Communion, we ourselves are vehicles of grace. Therefore, we are made sacraments. When we take our flesh and blood and sacrifice ourselves, we are made sacred in God's life-giving work. We carry the import of holiness when we make ourselves walking, talking bread and wine. We are human sacraments. And this is why Paul gives such stern warnings about taking the elements of Communion:

> Therefore, my beloved, flee from idolatry. I speak as to sensible people; judge for yourselves what I say. The cup of blessing that we bless, is it not a participation in

> the blood of Christ? The bread that we break, is it not a participation in the body of Christ? Because there is one bread, we who are many are one body, for we all partake of the one bread. Consider the people of Israel: are not those who eat the sacrifices participants in the altar? What do I imply then? That food offered to idols is anything, or that an idol is anything? No, I imply that what pagans sacrifice they offer to demons and not to God. I do not want you to be participants with demons. You cannot drink the cup of the Lord and the cup of demons. You cannot partake of the table of the Lord and the table of demons. (1 Cor. 10:14–21)

In the same way that Paul says we can't drink from two cups or partake of two tables, Jesus said we can't serve two masters.[15] We're either consecrated to God or we're not. We either love Jesus or we don't. We're either crucified with him or we're not. And we can't keep one foot in this world and one in the other. We have to put our whole selves on the altar, our whole beings in the place of sacrifice. Look at verse 18 again: "Are not those who eat the sacrifices participants in the altar?" Paul is talking about how eating the sacrifice is the same as participating in the sacrifice. To partake of the offering is to identify with the offering itself.

Our partaking is, by the way, a great echo of the incarnation.

In our examination of Jesus' roles and vocations, we have seen an echo, a reflection, of the incarnation. The incarnation is the template for all the stories about Jesus, the metanarrative for all the narratives. The incarnation is the incomprehensible wonder that God inhabited flesh and became man. So we see in Jesus a shepherd who became a sheep, a king who became a servant, a priest who became the sacrifice,

15. Luke 16:13.

a judge who became the punishment, and now a provider who becomes the provision. We, in a mini-echo, perhaps, receive the bread and wine in such a way that we are committing to being bread and wine ourselves, to being, as we've seen before, living sacrifices.

Our commitment to being living sacrifices is why Paul says we can't have it both ways. We can't sacrifice for God but remain committed to idolatry—of any kind. The sacrifice must be pure.

Thank God we have Christ's righteousness given to us.

## THE GOSPEL OF JESUS' PROVISION

We take Communion because it is a powerful way to confess with our mouths that we are sinners in need of life. We take Communion because it is emblematic, a confession of our finding the life we need. The meal is both an admission of our guilt and a testament to our new life in Christ.

Here's Jesus, once again, talking about our eating him:

> So Jesus said to them, "Truly, truly, I say to you, unless you eat the flesh of the Son of Man and drink his blood, you have no life in you. Whoever feeds on my flesh and drinks my blood has eternal life, and I will raise him up on the last day. For my flesh is true food, and my blood is true drink. Whoever feeds on my flesh and drinks my blood abides in me, and I in him. As the living Father sent me, and I live because of the Father, so whoever feeds on me, he also will live because of me. This is the bread that came down from heaven, not like the bread the fathers ate and died. Whoever feeds on this bread will live forever." (John 6:53–58)

Is this cannibalism or what?

Not really. Maybe . . . kinda . . . sorta. It's the eating and drinking of his flesh and blood, but it's the consuming of these things as true food, true drink. It's eating them as a testimony to the eternal life that he gives us.

Under the old covenant, consuming blood was an abomination. Anyone who ate blood was to be excommunicated from the covenant people.[16] Under the Law, then, the consuming of blood is a curse. Under the new covenant ushered in by Jesus, the consuming of his blood is a blessing. Because Jesus has authority over the Law, his command to us to drink his blood is just one more provocative reversal of our condemnation under the Law.

What we're eating, friends, is the gospel itself. The meal symbolizes both our need and God's provision for that need. When we eat and drink the gospel, we make the Good News of eternal life by grace through faith in Jesus Christ a part of us. Even deeper than that, we make life in Christ our very life itself—our lifeblood. Flesh of my flesh, blood of my blood. It's important, then, that the Communion meal be taken only by those who know their need and acknowledge Jesus as the only provision for it.

You may already know that the Corinthian church Paul was writing to was seriously messed up. They got drunk on the Communion wine, shut out the poor and needy from partaking in the meal, and even incorporated the pagan practice of orgies in their services.[17] It was a wild scene, man.

Paul basically writes, "You know, the gospel is only good news when you're on the receiving end of it, on the belief end of it" (see 1 Cor. 1:18). Because the first part of the gospel message is that we are sinners

---

16. Leviticus 7:27.

17. Now that I think about it, this actually sounds like any television show on the CW network.

who deserve death,[18] if we take part in the gospel meal without having partaken of the belief that Christ gives us life, we end up not eating and drinking the good news of the full gospel, but imbibing the judgment of the half gospel. Here's Paul again, in a sublime ranting about the sinful supping in the Corinthian church:

> For I received from the Lord what I also delivered to you, that the Lord Jesus on the night when he was betrayed took bread, and when he had given thanks, he broke it, and said, "This is my body which is for you. Do this in remembrance of me." In the same way also he took the cup, after supper, saying, "This cup is the new covenant in my blood. Do this, as often as you drink it, in remembrance of me." For as often as you eat this bread and drink the cup, you proclaim the Lord's death until he comes.
>
> Whoever, therefore, eats the bread or drinks the cup of the Lord in an unworthy manner will be guilty concerning the body and blood of the Lord. Let a person examine himself, then, and so eat of the bread and drink of the cup. For anyone who eats and drinks without discerning the body eats and drinks judgment on himself. (1 Cor. 11:23–29)

Cue ominous music. Pass the plate. All you sinners, roll the dice now. Take the meal and take your chances. Right?

The passion of my life is the scandalous gospel of God's amazing grace in Jesus Christ. The Holy Spirit cultivated this passion in me

18. I consider this part of the gospel an incomplete gospel, but still good news, because it's finally someone being honest with us about what our real problem is.

through the Scriptures, in which I see Jesus chastised and criticized for proclaiming the gospel by eating with sinners and giving himself to sinners. My encouragement to you—my call to you—is to partake of that gospel, to acknowledge and confess and believe that you are a sinner in need of God's grace, and that Jesus Christ died and rose to manifest that grace to you, and that you can't live without Jesus. You cannot do it. Acknowledge that truth, grab hold of the gospel, and then you can approach the throne of grace with confidence to have your needs provided for.[19]

## JESUS' PROVISION IS THE PROVISION TO END ALL PROVISION

> But when Christ appeared as a high priest of the good things that have come, then through the greater and more perfect tent (not made with hands, that is, not of this creation) he entered once for all into the holy places, not by means of the blood of goats and calves but by means of his own blood, thus securing an eternal redemption. For if the blood of goats and bulls, and the sprinkling of defiled persons with the ashes of a heifer, sanctify for the purification of the flesh, how much more will the blood of Christ, who through the eternal Spirit offered himself without blemish to God, purify our conscience from dead works to serve the living God.
>
> Therefore he is the mediator of a new covenant, so that those who are called may receive the promised eternal inheritance, since a death has occurred that redeems them from the transgressions committed under the first covenant. (Heb. 9:11–15)

19. Hebrews 4:16.

There's that bloody mess again. Blood. Flesh. Gory altars. We've already covered why it has to be that way, so I won't rehash it again—except to reiterate that without death there is no life. A blood debt is owed because the wages of sin is death. And thank God that Jesus, God in the flesh, offered himself as the provision for this sacrifice. He provided his own flesh and blood. The old covenant saw a constant succession of animals slaughtered. The new covenant issued the once-and-for-all provision of Christ's sacrifice.

His blood over our lives, in our hearts. His blood purifying us.

YHWH sent Moses to deal with Pharaoh and get the Israelites freed from Egyptian bondage. God kept sending plagues as judgment upon the land, in order to demonstrate his power and to sort of coerce Pharaoh to release God's people.[20] The first nine plagues were no cakewalk,[21] but the tenth plague was a virtual horror movie.

God said to Moses, "I'm sending an angel of death who will take the lives of every firstborn in the land. Every firstborn. From Pharaoh all the way to the lowliest slave. But you can avoid this judgment by taking a spotless lamb, slaughtering it, and putting its blood over your doorpost. And when the angel of death comes in the night, he will pass over the households that are marked with blood."[22]

This "pass over" is the first big foundational image of God forgoing the judgment of death because of the sign of blood. And this momentous occasion—life granted because of the blood of the lamb—became the basis for an ongoing holiday and feast for the Jewish people. Observant Jews today still celebrate the Passover.

Jesus and his followers sat down to celebrate this meal at the appointed time, to recall, as all good Jews would, that somber day when

20. Exodus 7:14–12:32.

21. When I was a kid, I participated in a very confusing cakewalk at a school fair and won a horrible carrot cake. Let me tell you, that cakewalk was no cakewalk.

22. Author's summary and paraphrase of Exodus 11:1–12:13.

God passed over his people because they were covered in blood. They had a blood covering that marked them for life. And Jesus, in his inimitable way, made it all about himself. He wasn't being presumptuous. The Passover *was* about Jesus. All the things that Jesus appropriated were not originally about something or someone else. They were always about him. The Old Testament was the foreshadow; Jesus is the light. The Passover meal, and the Last Supper meal that fulfilled it, was about needing Christ's blood—his flesh and blood—to escape death.

In Ephesians 2:14, Paul says that Jesus himself is our peace. Paul will not let us believe for a second that there's any virtue, or any value worth having, outside the person of Jesus Christ. Peace is not a general feeling or a universal moral virtue. Jesus Christ himself is peace. Just as love is not mere niceties or altruistic kindness; God himself is love.[23] This is something the Bible does to us over and over again—it continually points us to the triune Creator as the epitome of, the manifestation of, the giver of, and the gift of, all the things we think of as good and right and necessary. The Provider *is* the Provision.

Think back to Job. He was trusting God not to give him his stuff back. He was trusting God *to be God*. Job cried out that even if God killed him, he'd still trust God. He was trusting God to give himself, not just a bunch of stuff. And that is the same provision for which we must trust Christ—for the provision of Christ himself, not the provision for successful lives. Because Jesus himself—and Jesus alone—is abundant life.

The Communion meal that Jesus gave to us, and the crucifixion it recalls—and by extension the bloody sacrifices his crucifixion recalls—are an immense, insurmountable, unavoidable enemy of self-help, self-feeding, self-supporting spirituality. The cross of Christ is foolishness

---

23. 1 John 4:8.

to those who are perishing,[24] which is a stinging indictment of so many self-appointed "Christian" spokespeople who have conveniently forgotten all about that cross. The cross is a foreign concept to the religious hucksters on television, and those in the pulpits and in publishing, who would ask you to take Jesus without taking his cross.

My friends, Jesus is not a pop song, snuggly sweater, affectionate boyfriend, a poster on your wall, self-help book, motivational speech, warm cup of coffee, ultimate fighting champion, knight in shining armor, or Robin to your Batman. He is blood.

And without blood, you die.

24. 1 Corinthians 1:18.

# 11

# JESUS THE LORD

The introduction to this book recalled perhaps the most important question Jesus asked. It's the single most important question anyone can ask him- or herself, and the answer illuminates the chasm between life and death.

> Now when Jesus came into the district of Caesarea Philippi, he asked his disciples, "Who do people say that the Son of Man is?" And they said, "Some say John the Baptist, others say Elijah, and others Jeremiah or one of the prophets." He said to them, "But who do you say that I am?" (Matt. 16:13–15)

We'll cover the disciples' responses later, but let's not pass over the power of the question itself. We've considered the assertion that the key to Christianity is the little phrase, which we throw around so carelessly, "in him" or "in Christ." This question that Jesus asks—"Who do you say that I am?"—is one that we also answer very easily, very flippantly, without realizing the weight and the importance our answer should and must convey.

We know how the world answers this question. "Jesus, if he even existed," they say, "was a very good man who loved people very much; and he was a very good teacher, perhaps even an enlightened man who was in touch with the supernatural world, if it exists, and so he's probably the most perfect role model we could ever have." Even people who will not believe *in* Jesus as Christians do come rather close to saying that Jesus was the most perfect man ever to live. Where they get this information, I don't know, because the evidence for Jesus' goodness and enlightenment is found in the same place as the evidence for his being the God of the universe.

Christians can answer the question easily enough: "Who's Jesus? Well, he's the Son of God. He's God." But too many of us have no idea how we know that, where Jesus asserted that, where the Bible confirms that. The reason many in the church still admire a varnished portrait of Jesus is the same reason many in the church couldn't tell you how they know that Jesus is God: biblical illiteracy. We just do not know our Scriptures.

"Who do you say that I am?"

To answer this question, we must go beyond theological shorthand. To answer this question we must go beyond creeds—as important as they may be—or tactical apologetics—as helpful as they may be. To feel the weight of this question in our hearts, we must find the answer in the gift we've been given that best reads and reveals our hearts—God's written Word.

In his book *Surprised by the Power of the Spirit*, Jack Deere recalls examining a straight-A seminary student who was applying for a doctoral program. Deere asked him what he believed about the deity of Jesus Christ. The young man said that he affirmed the full deity of Jesus. But when Deere asked him why he believed that and where the Bible teaches it, Deere was amazed to find his theological wunderkind struggling to answer.

> He hesitated a moment and then asserted, "The deity of Jesus is everywhere in the New Testament."
>
> "Could you be just a little more specific? Tell us one text that teaches his deity unambiguously."
>
> After hesitating for what seemed like a full moment, he finally blurted out, "I and the Father are one."
>
> I told him that it was true John 10:30 did say that, but did that actually mean that Jesus was God? I could say, for instance, that he and I were one, but that wouldn't prove that we were the same, let alone from the same family. Jesus could have meant that he and the Father were one in purpose.
>
> At that point he gave up trying to use John 10:30. He didn't know enough to cite the next few verses that showed clearly that the Jews understood this to be a claim to deity. If he had done that, I would have granted that this passage taught the deity of Jesus, which it does unambiguously. In the end he could not give us one clear passage from the Bible on the deity of the Lord Jesus Christ. Here was a man who had completed four years of Bible college and four years of seminary. He had a master's degree in theology, and had taught for one year at a conservative biblical seminary. Yet he could not produce and defend one unambiguous reference in the Bible to the deity of Jesus![1]

We could dog on this poor guy all day, but what about you? Would you fare any better? Say a couple of Jehovah's Witnesses come to your

---

1. Jack Deere, *Surprised by the Power of the Spirit* (Grand Rapids: Zondervan, 1993), 48–49.

door. Let's assume you don't turn off the TV and lower the blinds so they think no one's home. And let's assume you actually engage them in conversation. Know in advance the key difference, among plenty of differences, between orthodox Christianity and the Watchtower cult: they say Jesus wasn't God, but was *a* god.[2] Other than a few changes to the Bible text—such as in John 1:1, the passage just cited—to make the Scriptures better fit their heresy, they have a Bible like yours and mine. If you wanted to open that Bible to show them where, in their own book, Jesus is God, where would you turn?

## PAUL'S TEACHING ON THE INCARNATION

Well, you could go to Romans 9:5, where Paul refers to Christ as "God over all." That's pretty unambiguous. Or you could go to the famous incarnational hymn in Philippians 2, in which Paul says (though he may have been quoting another source) that Jesus was "in the form of God."[3]

Those are a couple of pretty clear references to Jesus as God. And throughout the New Testament Epistles, we see Jesus called *Lord*, from the Greek word *kyrios*, which is sometimes translated "master," but sometimes references "YHWH God."[4] The Greek word *theos* is translated "God," not "Lord," but many of the New Testament's references to Jesus as Lord (*kyrios*) do so either in conjunction with *theos* (as in Thomas's confession in John 20:28) or carry the linguistic import of the Old Testament's use of the all-caps LORD for YHWH. On this point, scholar F. F. Bruce writes,

2. John 1:1 in The Watchtower's *New World Translation*.
3. Philippians 2:6.
4. See Murray J. Harris, *Jesus as God: The New Testament Use of Theos in Reference to Jesus* (Grand Rapids: Baker, 1992). Also, Craig L. Blomberg, *Jesus and the Gospels* (Wheaton, IL: Broadman and Holman, 1997), 408–9.

> It might not be appropriate to reword "Jesus Christ is Lord" as "Jesus Christ is Yahweh"; but nothing less than this is involved. This usage did not originate with Paul (if the Christ-hymn is pre-Pauline), but repeatedly he ascribes to Jesus Old Testament texts and phrases in which the word "Lord" represents the Hebrew Yahweh. "The day of the Lord" (the great day of judgment) in the Old Testament is the day of Yahweh; what Paul understood by it is shown by the way in which he calls it variously "the day of the Lord," "the day of the Lord Jesus," or "the day of Christ."
>
> In Joel 2:32, "whoever calls on the name of the Lord will be saved," "the Lord" is Yahweh; but when Paul quotes this passage in Romans 10:13, the context makes it plain that for him "the Lord" is Jesus.
>
> Other New Testament writers share this usage with Paul; they did not derive it from him. The writer to the Hebrews applies to Christ the words of Psalm 102:25, which were originally addressed to Yahweh. He knows what he is doing, for the Greek version which he quotes adds the word "Lord," which is not present in the Hebrew text of this verse: "Thou, Lord, didst found the earth in the beginning" (Hebrews 1:10).[5]

Here's one of the best, most comprehensive, least loopholey passages from the New Testament declaring Jesus as the God of the universe:

> He is the image of the invisible God, the firstborn of all creation. For by him all things were created, in

5. F. F. Bruce, *Jesus: Lord and Savior* (Downer's Grove, IL: InterVarsity, 1986), 203.

> heaven and on earth, visible and invisible, whether thrones or dominions or rulers or authorities—all things were created through him and for him. And he is before all things, and in him all things hold together. And he is the head of the body, the church. He is the beginning, the firstborn from the dead, that in everything he might be preeminent. For in him all the fullness of God was pleased to dwell. (Col. 1:15–19)

Jesus is the image of God. We were made in the image of God, but Jesus *is* the image of the invisible God, which is to say, all that is God the Spirit is present in Jesus. When we look at ourselves, you and me, we see the image of God—or we would if the fall hadn't broken us so radically. But when we look at Jesus, we see God himself. When Paul says that Jesus is the firstborn of all creation, it doesn't mean that Jesus was created or made like you and I were. Likewise, the phrase "only begotten Son" in John 3:16 doesn't mean that Jesus was made (without pre-existence), but rather that Jesus is the premiere image of God, the image of God we might have been if our image had not been broken. In the Old Testament, the firstborn son is the chief heir, the family's honor and virtue. Thus, Jesus is referred to here as the honored Son.

Colossians 1:16 tells us that Jesus created everything; we know from Genesis 1:1 that God created everything. We see in verse 17 that Jesus controls everything; we know from the Old Testament record of God's sovereignty, that God controls everything. We know that God is the only one who existed before the beginning, and yet Paul says Jesus was there. Then, in the last verse of this passage, Paul tells us explicitly that Jesus wasn't just a little god, he didn't have a little bit of God in him, he wasn't a demigod, but that the fullness of God dwelled in him. He was, according to Paul, God in the flesh.

Now that's all well and good, but what if Paul, as some scholars insist, was just giving his own interpretation here? Is the incarnation a Pauline invention? Where in the Gospels do we see Jesus acting as, or referring to himself as, God?

## JESUS' ASSERTION OF HIS DEITY

Some of the things that we think connect Jesus to God don't do so exactly. The miracles, for example. Moses and the prophets performed miracles, the apostles performed miracles, heck, even Pharaoh's sorcerers and assorted Devil worshippers performed miracles. We don't say that any of them were God.

On the flip side, some of the things we don't often think of as evidence of Jesus' divinity actually are good examples. The most obvious, of course, is that Jesus went around forgiving sins.

> And when Jesus saw their faith, he said to the paralytic, "Son, your sins are forgiven." Now some of the scribes were sitting there, questioning in their hearts, "Why does this man speak like that? He is blaspheming! Who can forgive sins but God alone?" (Mark 2:5–7)

The scribes knew that only God has the power to forgive sins. For Jesus to do it meant that he was assuming the authority of God. If he were not God, the scribes would be correct in saying that Jesus was blaspheming.

Over and over, if not verbally or explicitly, at least practically and implicitly, Jesus went around placing himself at the center of the God-life, at the center of God's kingdom, at the center of one's faith in God. He was asserting himself as the one to orient your life around if you really want to be faithful to God. And, folks, a normal man doesn't do that. These days, we put people in mental institutions when they claim to be God.

So though we don't have examples of Jesus explicitly saying, "I am God incarnate," we do see him making the equation. He says, for example, that God's elect are his elect, God's angels are his angels, and God's kingdom is his kingdom.[6] If he were not God—what an egomaniac; what an idolater! The Pharisees would have been right in wanting to get rid of him—if he had really been lying. If he was not who he claimed to be, his call to people to leave everything to worship him was leading people away, leading them astray. In those days, when someone in the Jewish culture and religion took worship away from YHWH God, he was spurned, denounced, and perhaps executed, provided the Roman authorities could be convinced to facilitate it or could be convinced to look the other way.

Another example of Jesus' divinity was how he rewrote and reinterpreted commandments. "A new command I give to you."[7] Well, who are you, Jesus, to give us commandments? Who are you, Jesus, to tell us what the greatest commandment is? To rewrite the Shema with this touchy-feely, love-your-neighbor stuff? Who are you to come into our world and redefine, reinterpret, and realign around yourself everything we look to, participate in, and put our trust in to be right with God? Who are you to say the temple is you, the sacrifices are you, the Law is you, the Prophets are you, the Word of God is you, the Creator is you?

We cannot read what Jesus says and does in the full context of the Gospels and say honestly, "What a good teacher." "What a nice boy that Jesus is." "What a guy in touch with the spiritual plane of the universe."

No. We cannot see the works and words of Jesus as they really are and come to such a lame, tame, comfortable conclusion. He didn't leave that option open.

---

6. See, for example, Matthew 24:22–24; 13:41; 16:28.
7. John 13:34.

In the indispensable *Mere Christianity*, C. S. Lewis presents his classic "trilemma":

> I am trying here to prevent anyone saying the really foolish thing that people often say about Him: "I'm ready to accept Jesus as a great moral teacher, but I don't accept His claim to be God." That is the one thing we must not say. A man who was merely a man and said the sort of things Jesus said would not be a great moral teacher. He would either be a lunatic—on a level with the man who says he is a poached egg—or else he would be the Devil of Hell. You must make your choice. Either this man was, and is, the Son of God: or else a madman or something worse. You can shut Him up for a fool, you can spit at Him and kill Him as a demon; or you can fall at His feet and call Him Lord and God. But let us not come with any patronizing nonsense about His being a great human teacher. He has not left that open to us. He did not intend to.[8]

He hasn't left the "good teacher" option open. Anyone taking this ubiquitous third route—he was a good man, an enlightened teacher, a prophet perhaps, but not as the Christians believe, God in the flesh—isn't being honest with the evidence.

## THE CRITICAL TRUTH OF THE DEITY OF CHRIST

I will allow that the unintended danger of the so-called search for the historical Jesus is the minimization or avoidance of the deity of Christ. This academic quest involves a mixed bag of scholars and writers, some liberal and some conservative, some orthodox Christians and some

---

8. C. S. Lewis, *Mere Christianity* (New York: Macmillan, 1952), 45.

atheists, some committed to the historical accuracy of the Gospels and some staunchly opposed to the idea. It will do no good, however, to throw out the idea of researching the historical Jesus. That would be like throwing out the proverbial baby with the bathwater. Nevertheless, we must acknowledge that the inability, or unwillingness, of some in the church to honestly weigh the research and untangle the good from the bad has perhaps led to the influential stream in Western Christianity that appears to proclaim a predominantly human Jesus. When truth is deemed relative and the infallibility of Scripture deemed too "static," it's no wonder that many today, younger folks mostly, claim to follow a Jesus who appears to be the love child of John Lennon and Ralph Nader.

At the same time, perhaps out of fear of diminishing Christ's deity, the church has for all intents and purposes *de*humanized Jesus. We've made his manhood merely aesthetic, iconic. We don't spend much church time contemplating Jesus the Man, at least not in any substantive sense that would help our discipleship, because we don't want to seem as if we're denigrating his God-ness.

Mark Driscoll assesses this unfortunate dichotomy in the church this way:

> Over the centuries, various Christian traditions have been prone to emphasize either the incarnation/humanity of Jesus or the exaltation/divinity of Jesus at the expense of the other. Liberals and their Emergent offspring generally prefer the former, while conservatives and fundamentalists generally prefer the latter. On this matter we must be careful to avoid reductionism whereby we embrace only part of the truth and in so doing undermine it altogether. . . .
>
> Once we have the incarnation and the exaltation clear in our Christology, we are then sufficiently ready

> to contend for the truth of the gospel and contextualize it rightly for various cultures and subcultures of people, as Jesus did and commands us to do.[9]

This contending for, and contextualization of, truth is part of our aim here. And a large part of this effort, of course, has been to look afresh at the person and the personality of Jesus of Nazareth. What was his culture like? What was his world like? What do his means and motivations say about him, not as a figure or character or icon, but as a *person*?

As we focus on that, it may escape us that we are actually doing a personality profile on the God of the universe. This is important for us to realize. Because even if we were to choose whether to focus on his incarnation *or* his exaltation, there remains one constant in both aspects: Jesus is God. So regardless of which aspect we choose to focus on, it's not really a choice of whether or not to reflect on his deity. Jesus did not *become* God, he did not graduate into godhood, and he didn't have godhood thrust upon him. Jesus is and always has been God.

## JESUS THE GREAT I AM

> In the beginning was the Word, and the Word was with God, and the Word was God. He was in the beginning with God. All things were made through him, and without him was not any thing made that was made. (John 1:1–3)

This is such a great passage, not just because of the unequivocal way its states equality between God and Jesus Christ—"the Word was

9. Mark Driscoll, "The Church and the Supremacy of Christ," *The Supremacy of Christ in a Postmodern World*, ed. John Piper and Justin Taylor (Wheaton, IL: Crossway, 2007), 127, 133.

God," not "a god," as the Jehovah's Witnesses' (per)version says—but also because it places Jesus at the beginning, the launch, the foundation of creation. Jesus created the world, John says, and Paul confirms it in Colossians 1:16. We can go back to Genesis 1:1 and legitimately say, "In the beginning, Jesus created the heavens and the earth." That's what John is hearkening back to. John 1 is a recasting of Genesis 1 in light of Jesus.

Jesus was the vehicle of creation, and this telling in John is great because it also foreshadows Jesus' bringing of the new creation in the Gospels (and the new heavens and new earth in Revelation). Jesus' redemptive actions during his lifetime are, in fact, one of the most overlooked aspects of his implicit claims to divinity. He went around basically re-creating creation, redeeming the fall by reenacting the Creation, and placing himself in the place of the Creator.

John didn't just invent this idea, either. Jesus asserted it.

> "Your father Abraham rejoiced that he would see my day. He saw it and was glad." So the Jews said to him, "You are not yet fifty years old, and have you seen Abraham?" Jesus said to them, "Truly, truly, I say to you, before Abraham was, I am." So they picked up stones to throw at him, but Jesus hid himself and went out of the temple. (John 8:56–59)

Here's a little textual nugget just for you. Not only does Jesus tell his listeners, "I existed before Abraham"—which is a fancy way of saying, "I'm eternal and was present at the covenant call of God on the life of Abraham"—but his statement "before Abraham was, I am" is his way of claiming the mantle of the God of the universe. Notice he doesn't say, "Before Abraham was, I *was*." He says, "I am." If you know your Old Testament stuff, you know the personal name God gave to Israel to call him: YHWH. We don't know exactly how to pronounce this word or exactly what it means, but the Hebrew is typically translated "I am who I am." Or "I will be who I will be." It is the encapsulation of God's ineffable, eternal personhood in one riddle phrase, a literary glimpse of the mysterious infinite. The great I AM.

This man Jesus, who as a kid pooped in his diapers and wet his bed like the rest of us; who sweated and bled, and got morning breath, and had BO, and was sort of a mama's boy, says to the religious leaders of his day, "Hey, before Abraham was, I AM."

No wonder they picked up stones to kill him. He's saying he's God. And not in some ethereal "me and God are tight" quality. He's claiming the sacred name of God as his own. This claim is a crucial part of Jesus' redemption of the Old Testament story of creation and covenant. "I was present at the creation of the world and, indeed, created the world myself. I was present at the call of Abraham into covenant with God, and I was the very I AM doing the calling. The covenant was with me, and I am here now to fulfill it."

Here's another example, a story we're familiar with and see as a great example of Jesus' power, but in which we often overlook Jesus' claim to be God.

> Immediately he made his disciples get into the boat and go before him to the other side, to Bethsaida, while he dismissed the crowd. And after he had taken leave of them, he went up on the mountain to pray. And when evening came, the boat was out on the sea, and he was alone on the land. And he saw that they were making headway painfully, for the wind was against them. And about the fourth watch of the night he came to them, walking on the sea. He meant to pass by them, but when they saw him walking on the sea they thought it was a ghost, and cried out, for they all

> saw him and were terrified. But immediately he spoke to them and said, "Take heart; it is I. Do not be afraid." And he got into the boat with them, and the wind ceased. And they were utterly astounded, for they did not understand about the loaves, but their hearts were hardened. (Mark 6:45–52)

In the Hebrew mythos, the sea is often symbolic of chaos, even evil. A roaring sea especially so. This symbolism informed, or perhaps began with, the Old Testament creation account of the land being separated from the water, which is representative of God's bringing something solid—something good—out of and away from something deadly and chaotic.[10] Now, the Jews weren't animists. They didn't believe the sea itself was evil, that water was evil. But the sea was a powerful symbol that resonated underneath all the other miracles involving water. For the ancient Hebrew culture, water represented chaos, and that's why, for instance, the dragons symbolized in Revelation come out of the sea.[11]

So Jesus shows up and he's walking on the rough waters. This isn't just a neat trick. This isn't just to demonstrate power. This is to demonstrate that Jesus, as God, is in control of the chaos. It is a clear demonstration to those tossed about in the boat that Jesus is sovereign just as they knew God to be sovereign.

The disciples are afraid, and Jesus says, "It is I." This phrase is parallel to the Hebrew "I am." Craig Blomberg writes,

> The primary point behind the miracle is not one of physical rescue. Rather, Christ is revealing the transcendent dimension of his nature. "It is I" (Greek, *ego*

10. See Christopher Barth, *God with Us: A Theological Introduction to the Old Testament* (Grand Rapids: Eerdmans, 1991), 14–15.

11. Revelation 13:1–2.

> *eimi*) in Mark 6:50 echoes the identical words of Exodus 3:14, with its divine name, "I AM." So, too, the verb "pass by" (v. 48) is the same as used in the LXX of Exodus 33:19 and 34:6 for God "passing by" (i.e., revealing himself to) Moses. Job 9:8 and Psalm 77:19 provide further Old Testament background for Yahweh as the one who treads upon the sea. Christ is here disclosing his divine nature.[12]

Jesus walks on the water, demonstrating his God-sovereignty over the central image of evil and chaos. And while walking, he says to those in fear of the watery chaos, "I AM."

"I am God."

We may not be able to deduce from his miraculous acts that Jesus is God, but the historic, covenant context of Jesus' miracles reminds us they are not just attractive "shock and awe." They point to something; they mean something bigger and deeper than the acts themselves. Beyond the impression of awe, they leave the impression of the salvation history of God's people. The miracles collectively tell the story of redemption. Just as Jesus' use of mud and spit to heal the blind man's eyes reflects YHWH's foundational dust-and-breath creation of man, all the miracles are self-referential stories, with Jesus as the author of Creation.

Why? Because the first creation became corrupted when Adam and Eve screwed everything up. Jesus isn't redeeming God's mistakes with these acts of new creation. God doesn't make mistakes. Jesus is redeeming *our* mistakes.

Jesus isn't acting simply as God's agent, God's ambassador. He's acting as God himself. Only God could create the universe, and only

12. Craig Blomberg, *Jesus and the Gospels* (Nashville: Broadman and Holman, 1997), 273.

God can re-create the universe. Only God can redeem the universe. An eternal fallenness can only be righted by an eternal goodness, and only God has that.

## WHO DO WE SAY THAT HE IS?

> For the grace of God has appeared, bringing salvation for all people, training us to renounce ungodliness and worldly passions, and to live self-controlled, upright, and godly lives in the present age, waiting for our blessed hope, the appearing of the glory of *our great God and Savior Jesus Christ*, who gave himself for us to redeem us from all lawlessness and to purify for himself a people for his own possession who are zealous for good works. (Titus 2:11–14, emphasis added)

Our great what? *Our great God (!) and Savior Jesus Christ*, who gave himself up to redeem us.

God inserted himself into his creation to clean up what we've made dirty, to rescue what we've endangered, to fulfill the promise of the law in a world of lawless hearts. This is why Jesus came. Not to give us some good ideas, not to give us some helpful hints for successful living, not to be our copilot. But to demonstrate to us that God is in the business of creation. That God is passionate about righting wrongs. That God is passionate about his children, whom he loves deeply and wants to free from the bondage of sin.

And this is why the confession demanded of us cannot be merely an intellectual assent, the logical conclusion of the trilemma. Sure, logically, Jesus cannot simply be a man. He's either a liar, a crazy person, or who he said he is. We can't just agree to that intellectually. Our confession must be an embracing of this truth with our hearts, which is why Jesus doesn't say that the greatest commandment is to believe that God exists.

Heck, even the demons can do that.[13] The greatest commandment is to *love God with all our hearts, souls, minds, and strength*. With everything we've got and everything we are. "Because," Paul writes in Romans 10:9, "if you confess with your mouth that Jesus is Lord and believe in your heart that God raised him from the dead, you will be saved."

Look at what Paul calls Titus—and us—to do in the freedom of redemption: "renounce ungodliness and worldly passions" and be "zealous for good works." Our confession cannot be merely intellectual or merely verbal. It must be a realized confession that shows itself in *renunciation* of all that is ungodly and *zeal* for everything good. Our confession must be the outpouring that results when we orient ourselves around God. This is why the command to *believe* in the Gospels is joined with—indeed, predicated by—the call to *repent*. Yes, we are saved by faith, but as Jesus' brother reminds us, "Faith without works is dead."[14]

We began this book with a question from Jesus, the most important question we may ever be asked: "Who do you say that I am?"

A good teacher?

A helper?

A guru?

A *personal Lord and Savior*?

That's what many of us say today. But what does it mean? Let's revisit the question in context:

> [Jesus] said to them, "But who do you say that I am?" Simon Peter replied, "You are the Christ, the Son of the living God." And Jesus answered him, "Blessed are you, Simon Bar-Jonah! For flesh and blood has not revealed this to you, but my Father who is in heaven.

---

13. James 2:19.
14. See James 2:17.

> And I tell you, you are Peter, and on this rock I will build my church, and the gates of hell shall not prevail against it." (Matt. 16:15–18)

Listen, the gates of hell will prevail against a merely intellectual belief that Jesus is God. The gates of hell will prevail against mere mental assent to the truth that Jesus is God. Simply believing that Jesus is God doesn't save you. Again, even the demons believe that.

The *real* confession, the *real* belief, the *real* faith is one that flows from mind to heart, and from heart to mind, and naturally results in faithful hands and feet. *That's* the kind of confession, belief, and faith that will cultivate the community of God. *That's* the kind of confession, belief, and faith that will be a fortress heavier than the gates of hell. *That* is the power of a real confession. It's the real meat behind the phrase "believe in your heart."

Believing in your heart doesn't mean "being emotional" or "being moved psychologically." Jesus warns in Matthew 15:8, "These people honor me with their lips, but their hearts are far from me" (NIV). The Bible says in several places, what will direct us is what's in our hearts. Dallas Willard writes,

> Our treasure focuses our heart. "Your heart will be where what you treasure is," Jesus tells us (Matthew 6:21). Remember that our heart is our will, or our spirit: the center of our being from which our life flows. It is what gives orientation to everything we do. And so believing in Jesus "in your heart" must overflow into believing in Jesus "in your life." Otherwise, you don't believe.[15]

---

15. Dallas Willard, *The Divine Conspiracy: Rediscovering Our Hidden Life in God* (San Francisco: HarperCollins, 1998), 206.

Ouch.

How do I get there? How do I get to this radical confession that Jesus is God that will overflow into and reorient my life? I think, for most of us, it involves a real-life brushup against the power of grace. That's why we rarely meet people who've been *convinced* into the kingdom of God. They're out there, to be sure, but for all the good work that biblical scholars do, for all the help that contentious biblical defenses and debate-style apologetics can be, nobody will believe apart from having their spiritual eyes opened. I've never seen a debate between a Christian and an atheist, agnostic, or someone from another world religion that resulted in the non-Christian saying, "You know what? You make a convincing case. I'll be a Christian now."

Jesus certainly didn't go around debating his merits apologetically. He didn't present, in a helpful outline format, evidence that demanded a verdict. Instead, he changed people's lives by touching them, meeting their needs, getting in the midst of them. The beauty of the incarnation isn't just that God became a human, but that he intervened by way of immersion in humanity. He didn't speak *at* us; he laid down his life *for* us. Therefore, the confession that results from real belief in, real orientation on, Jesus Christ as the God of the universe is not the result of Christ's rhetoric. Rather, that confession is the result of his full, sacrificial, atoning work.

Our Savior has to be the Lord, our Savior has to be God. It's not enough to believe that Jesus is the only capable savior of sinful man;[16] this belief goes hand in hand with belief that Jesus is God himself. We cannot rightfully call him *Savior* if we cannot rightfully call him Lord.

This would seem to go without saying, but as the gradual accommodation of The Church of Jesus Christ of Latter Day Saints continues

16. Acts 4:12: "And there is salvation in no one else, for there is no other name under heaven given among men by which we must be saved."

by the political and ideological subculture of evangelicalism, we can already see the vital truth of Jesus as Savior and God being denied. Mormons do not believe that Jesus is God—meaning the second person of the Trinity—yet that did not deter Joel Osteen from trying to bring them into the fold. Osteen, the leader of America's largest church and a best-selling author and television preacher admired by many, was asked this question by a reporter in reference to 2008 Republican presidential contender Mitt Romney: "Is a Mormon a true Christian?" Osteen answered, "Well, in my mind they are. Mitt Romney has said that he believes in Christ as his savior, and that's what I believe, so, you know, I'm not the one to judge the little details of it. So I believe they are."[17]

This is no mere gaffe. Joel Osteen is revealing his theological ignorance here, unbefitting a man of such pastoral responsibility. But his ignorance is not merely a matter of not being able to refer to the doctrine of the hypostatic union or some such thing. It's about believing that someone less than God can save us from our sins. Without doubt, there's too much infighting in the evangelical church, and much of it sinfully divisive discord over nonessentials. But some things are worth fighting for, and the protection of the doctrine of the deity of Christ is certainly one of them.

Who do you say that Jesus is?

Let's look at another confession:

> Now Thomas, one of the Twelve, called the Twin, was not with them when Jesus came. So the other disciples told him, "We have seen the Lord." But he said to them, "Unless I see in his hands the mark of the nails,

---

17. "Transcript: Pastor Joel Osteen on 'FNS,'" *Fox News Sunday with Chris Wallace*, December 23, 2007, http://www.foxnews.com/story/0,2933,318054,00.html.

> and place my finger into the mark of the nails, and place my hand into his side, I will never believe."
>
> Eight days later, his disciples were inside again, and Thomas was with them. Although the doors were locked, Jesus came and stood among them and said, "Peace be with you." Then he said to Thomas, "Put your finger here, and see my hands; and put out your hand, and place it in my side. Do not disbelieve, but believe." Thomas answered him, "My Lord and my God!" Jesus said to him, "Have you believed because you have seen me? Blessed are those who have not seen and yet have believed." (John 20:24–29)

Thomas's confession, "My Lord and my God!" is precipitated by his experiencing Jesus' wounds. Notice that Jesus doesn't correct him: "Oh, no, no, no, I'm just a good teacher." He acknowledges Thomas's weakness, but confirms his confession. "You've had to see my wounds, but you do believe the truth that I am God. And not just God, but *your* God, and your master. But blessed are those who haven't seen me and yet believe."

That's you and me. We have not literally seen Jesus, but the call to confession is still there. And that call is a blessing waiting for us to enter in. But don't just say, "Jesus is Lord and Jesus is God." Say, "Jesus is God, and therefore Jesus is *my* Lord."

Saying that is embracing the yoke of God's sovereignty. Renounce all the other gods, the idols you treat as lords—money, ambition, food, sex, religion, some vague spirituality, relationships, work—and say, "I confess with my mouth and believe in my heart that Jesus Christ is the God of the universe." Make this confession a real commitment to align your life around him. Being a disciple of Jesus means following him.

The truth is that nothing and no one but Jesus can be Lord. We can't *make* Jesus Lord. He's already Lord. We've got to take up our cross, deny ourselves, and embrace his lordship because he's already in control. If we won't deny ourselves, we'll live in denial of reality.

Will you put yourself in submission to Jesus as master, as Lord? Will you root yourself in the blood and brokenness of Jesus in order to make the necessary life-changing submission to his sovereignty, which is implicit in the active confession, "My Lord and my God"? If you will, you'll take part in the new creation, the way in which God is bringing wonderful, final redemption into the world.

One day, everyone will confess Jesus as Lord.[18] I encourage you to do it now, while you can still willingly participate in the prevailing community of God, and follow the Lord of the universe in his redemption of fallen creation. The alternative is to confess him as Lord later, in defeat, when it's too late.

---

18. Romans 14:11.

# 12

# JESUS THE SAVIOR

Imagine that you're one of Jesus' devoted followers, grieving his execution. A couple of days have passed. You are dejected, bewildered, perhaps scared of the repercussions. You are, of course, totally devastated that your friend—the kindest, gentlest, most faithful friend you've ever had—has been executed for a crime he didn't commit. There is, at this time, no celebration that Jesus had finally achieved victory on the cross. You and the other disciples aren't partying, overjoyed that Jesus has died to forgive your sins. In your minds, your friend is gone; and because the Messiah wasn't expected to die before establishing a restored kingdom of Israel,[1] seeds of doubt have begun to sprout in your mind. Maybe you've started to wonder if he was who he said he was. Maybe you've started to think that the cause has been defeated.

In grieving the loss of your friend and rabbi, you're also beginning to grieve the loss of the meaning he gave to life, and to the incredible promise he represented of God's return to his people. At some point, a dangerous despair could kick in.

That's how Christianity would have stalled before it could even get started, were it not for one shining moment in the history of the world.

1. See Tom Wright, *The Original Jesus* (Grand Rapids: Eerdmans, 1996), 18–21.

The resurrection.

As Christians, we believe that Jesus not only died for our sins, but that he also rose from the dead three days later to conquer death. That glorious event is when all heaven broke loose. For you and the other disciples, the sacrificial death of Jesus has been emotionally and spiritually moving. But now there's a palpable disturbance under the skin, provoked by rumors of his return. The word spreads. The gossips are talking. Good news travels fast, and even though you're skeptical, you've seen some amazing things in the last three years. Including the dead coming to life.

Now you're sitting in a quiet room with your compatriots—everyone silent, everyone thinking the same thing, hoping the same thing, but everyone too frightened to say it lest they raise the ire of the grieving. Then you sense a stirring in the air. Something feels different. Something is happening. Your flesh gets tingly, the hair on the back of your neck sticks up, your soul shakes. And then he's standing before you. Jesus himself. Not a ghost, not a vision, but Jesus. He's in a new body to be sure, but it's him. New flesh, changed flesh, but flesh nonetheless. And seeing him again restores your joy, inflames your dwindling hopes. You know that you'd die for a man who cannot be killed and stay dead.

The crucifixion and death of Jesus was not a period marking the end of his life. It was an em-dash—opening up into something more, marking the beginning of a new way, a new day.

## JESUS MIGHTY TO SAVE

If you were one of the disciples, steeped in the Hebrew Scriptures, with Jesus in his burial garments standing before you, perhaps the cherished words of the great prophet Isaiah would echo in your mind. He, no doubt, foresaw this day:

> Who is this who comes from Edom,
> 　　in crimsoned garments from Bozrah,

he who is splendid in his apparel,
    marching in the greatness of his strength?
"It is I, speaking in righteousness,
    mighty to save." . . .

For he said, "Surely they are my people,
    children who will not deal falsely."
    And he became their Savior.
In all their affliction he was afflicted,
    and the angel of his presence saved them;
in his love and in his pity he redeemed them;
    he lifted them up and carried them all the days of old.
(Isa. 63:1, 8–9)

Some disciples no doubt remained incredulous. "Who is this?" they may have wondered. (And where have they wondered that before?) "It is I," he says. (And where has he responded that way before?)

He became their Savior. He redeemed them. Speaking in righteousness, he is . . . *mighty to save*—hallelujah!

In the resurrection, there is explosive, revolutionary power. Without the resurrection, we have only Jesus the Martyr. Jesus the Sacrifice. Jesus the Good Example. But in the resurrection, we have all those things *plus* Jesus Mighty to Save, Jesus Lord Over Death, Jesus the Conquering Savior.

And, man, the reverberations keep on reverberating. First of all, in that first-century culture, when a would-be messiah died, his followers tended to disband and look for the next messianic hopeful. The crucifixion of a wannabe messiah signaled defeat, and everyone knew there had been enough Roman stamping out of messianic movements. But in this case his followers—lending so much credence to the historical authenticity of Jesus' resurrection—kept going. Not only did they keep going, continuing to spread Jesus' message and preach his gospel of the kingdom, they went to their own deaths doing it. Peter, the impetuous follower who was jumping out of boats to enjoy the sovereignty of God one minute[2] and denying Jesus to a bloodthirsty mob the next,[3] marches on in a place of authority over the church and goes to his own death by crucifixion.

James the brother of Jesus, who did not believe Jesus' claims before the crucifixion, suddenly has a great reversal. He becomes the head of the church in Jerusalem and is eventually murdered himself, pushed off the roof of the temple. I like to imagine he climbed up there to shout out a sermon about how his brother Jesus was actually in charge of the place.

Why the reversal?

The resurrection.

The resurrection proves that Jesus was not just a potential savior, but that he was *mighty to save.*

The message of the gospel of the resurrected Savior spread and multiplied and bore fruit, and eventually these Spirit-filled missionaries, the disciples (students) now known as apostles (sent ones), put together a record of the life and times of Jesus Christ so that the message might be shared that much more effectively, recorded for posterity so that the gospel could bear fruit for dozens of generations to come.

We have in our Bible four authentic accounts of Jesus and his kingdom. They tell the same story in different ways, with different perspectives, highlighting some events and characters, downplaying others, written to distinct audiences, organized in different ways, and all for the purpose of proclaiming, not just chronicling, that Jesus Christ is mighty to save.

---

2. Matthew 14:29.
3. Luke 22:54–62.

## THE GOSPEL OF THE RESURRECTION

As we search these Scriptures for information about Jesus, even insight into Jesus, we must never forget the primary reason why these stories exist. Look, for example, at what John asserts as the thesis statement for his gospel: "These are written so that you may believe that Jesus is the Christ, the Son of God, and that by believing you may have life in his name" (John 20:31). He wrote his gospel not just so you'll understand, be convinced, or be informed; he wrote so that you'll believe with a life-giving effect, so that you'll take in the power of the cross and be born again, into a life with the quality of resurrection.

It's not enough simply to be convinced that Jesus died on the cross for your sins. You must be convicted of it. And your conviction must lead to a commitment. The influence of the work of the cross on your life must manifest itself fully with the power of the resurrection. And resurrection power is not the sort of thing that will be content to merely settle in your mind. It's a power that gives new life. Just as the disciples mourning the death of Jesus believed that his death had some meaning for forgiveness in their lives, and just as these same disciples were set afire by the reality that Jesus was alive, we must move beyond mere belief into a life—a kingdom life—that buzzes and hums with the eternal quality of resurrection.

A resurrection gospel is a full gospel. What we've become accustomed to in much of the church is a simplistic, stripped-down gospel, a gospel that suggests, "You have issues, but Jesus died for you. Now be a good person." The full gospel says, "Your problem is a radical one, no less serious than death, and it requires a radical intervention, no less powerful than resurrection." The full gospel says that the level and quality of your messed-up-ness is complete, exhaustive, and irreconcilable by you, but the gift of God's grace extends infinitely, eternally, covering it all. It reconciles us fully to God in a way that can only be described as bringing a dead person back to life.

As a matter of truly living out a resurrection life, we followers of Jesus must refocus our understanding of salvation—from what we're being saved *from* to what we're being saved *to*. That is the difference between the occupied *cross* and the empty *tomb*.[4]

Look at the way Paul describes the fullness of salvation:

> Even as he chose us in him before the foundation of the world, that we should be holy and blameless before him. In love he predestined us for adoption as sons through Jesus Christ, according to the purpose of his will, to the praise of his glorious grace, with which he has blessed us in the Beloved. In him we have redemption through his blood, the forgiveness of our trespasses, according to the riches of his grace, which he lavished upon us, in all wisdom and insight making known to us the mystery of his will, according to his purpose, which he set forth in Christ. (Eph. 1:4–9)

There is a richness here, a full-fledged act of rescue and reinstatement that goes so far beyond our getting a golden ticket to heaven. This passage demonstrates the true fullness of salvation. Look at how mighty to save our Lord is.

For starters, he chose us before the world was created. He chose us to be adopted into his family. Consequently, we not only have forgiveness, we also have the key to unlock the mystery of God's will. Being "in Christ" means being in the presence of God, who is including us in his plans for the future, in his plans for the universe. We're not privy to all the details, and he certainly doesn't need our help, but we have

---

4. I'm not encouraging an either/or approach here. I'm saying that a full gospel is both/and.

the assurance that our loving God has established for us a future and a hope. He has chosen us as partakers in his indescribable glory.

In our sin, this may not seem like such a big deal. But if we could grasp even a sliver of how much we don't deserve such lavish treatment, we might behold the power of the resurrection. To do so, we really have to comprehend grace—that it really is everything of Christ in exchange for our complete and utter emptiness. The resurrection is not about simply turning over a new leaf. It's really about being dead and then being brought back to life. It's really about being an enemy of God and then being brought into the light.

In Colossians 1:21, Paul describes our state before salvation as "alienated and hostile" toward God. We were separated from him, far from him. We were broken images of God. We were in bondage to sin, dead and buried like Lazarus in the tomb. We were effectively disowned and dismissed. And like the prodigal son's exile, it was self-willed. We were, for all intents and purposes, anti-God, even if consciously we thought we were just ambivalent. But then the resurrection power of Jesus—he who is mighty to save—ushered us into new life.

Where?

"In him."

In Romans 5:9–11, Paul describes this wondrous reunion:

> Since, therefore, we have now been justified by his blood, much more shall we be saved by him from the wrath of God. For if while we were enemies we were reconciled to God by the death of his Son, much more, now that we are reconciled, shall we be saved by his life. More than that, we also rejoice in God through our Lord Jesus Christ, through whom we have now received reconciliation.

We are saved from many things: sin, Satan, punishment, death. But primarily we are saved from the wrath of God. And we aren't just passed over for wrath. We have received reconciliation—brought in, held close, covered up. This is such a powerful way to talk about salvation because it moves us beyond our self-centered talk of being saved into a "personal faith"—as if Christianity were about self-improvement—and takes us right into being unified again with God. Reconciliation presents salvation as it really is—as Jesus the Savior taking dead strangers to God and transforming them into living friends.

## SALVATION IS RECONCILIATION

We have been reconciled to God. We were alienated from him, effectively enemies, but in Christ's death we were made right with God. In other words, the debt we owed has been paid and credited to us, and in Christ's resurrection we have been made alive to God.

See, when Adam fell, taking the fruit he wasn't supposed to and eating it, he marred creation by ushering in death and division. By embracing sin, he invited death, and he set up a dividing wall between himself and God that could not be surmounted from his—Adam's—side. In Jesus, a new Adam has come, dying to fulfill the death owed by man, and rising to give new life to those who desperately need it. And therefore we are reconciled to God.

That is the meaning of life, by the way. It's not being healthy and wealthy and happy and wise. It's not being successful or achieving all our dreams. The meaning of life is moving from alienation from God to being adopted into his family.

But the reconciling work doesn't even stop there.

> Therefore, if anyone is in Christ, he is a new creation.
> The old has passed away; behold, the new has come.
> All this is from God, who through Christ reconciled

> us to himself and gave us the ministry of reconciliation; that is, in Christ God was reconciling the world to himself, not counting their trespasses against them, and entrusting to us the message of reconciliation. Therefore, we are ambassadors for Christ, God making his appeal through us. We implore you on behalf of Christ, be reconciled to God. For our sake he made him to be sin who knew no sin, so that in him we might become the righteousness of God. (2 Cor. 5:17–21)

What happened at the fall? Not only did Adam and Eve create separation between themselves and God, they also created it between each other. The Bible indicates there was then also a tension between the man and the woman.[5] So the fall distances us, separates us, makes us say to ourselves, "I'm my own person." And to fully embrace the fullness of the gospel, we can't just say, "Jesus has saved me from my sins," we have to confess, "Jesus has reconciled me to God . . . and to others."

Thus ensues the ministry of reconciliation that Paul talks about. As followers of Jesus, "Christ's ambassadors," we act out our reconciliation with God in our relationships with others. This is the foundational command that Jesus gives as the mission statement for the life of discipleship: "You shall love the Lord your God with all your heart, soul, strength, and mind, and your neighbor as yourself."[6] The two aspects of reconciliation—between us and God and us and other people—are inextricably linked, because the saving reconciliation is a holistic reconciliation, a full reconciliation. It restores the entirety of our brokenness and division.

True reconciliation is the basis on which the church becomes a

---

5. Genesis 3:16.
6. See Luke 10:27.

community rather than a religion. I've been harping on this little phrase "in him," or "in Christ," as being the fundamental truth of salvation, but we must press deeper into the implications for our worship of Jesus. In new covenant terms, being "in him" means being a part of the body of Christ. Being "in Christ" means being a serving part of his body, joined and reconciled with other followers of Jesus:

> For by the grace given to me I say to everyone among you not to think of himself more highly than he ought to think, but to think with sober judgment, each according to the measure of faith that God has assigned. For as in one body we have many members, and the members do not all have the same function, so we, though many, are one body in Christ, and individually members one of another. (Rom. 12:3–5)

One of the great pictures Jesus gave of the kingdom of God is as a banquet, or a party.[7]

As Jesus traveled and ministered, he didn't set up a bunch of individuals with lessons on how to improve their spiritual lives. No, he assembled them around himself and called them into a community of followers. This is why the New Testament also speaks repeatedly of salvation as our becoming children of God, and speaks of Christians as being brothers and sisters.

Friends, here is where we are most tempted to deny the gospel of real salvation—when we effectively believe "it's just me and Jesus." That's not the way Jesus set up reconciliation to work. And when we say—as I confess I once said myself—"I don't need the church; I don't need those people," we're saying, contrary to Christ's work and Paul's

---

7. Matthew 22:2; Luke 14:15.

instruction,[8] that we're too good for those "other people," that we're better than they are. Thus we deny the very gospel we claim to believe. Do you hear that? When you say you don't need community, or when you remove yourself from serving others and being a part of the body of Christ in community, you are denying the gospel. You are denying the reconciliation for which Christ died.

Such egotism is also a denial of grace. Because grace doesn't say, "Oh, you're such a good person, let me reward you." It says, "You are dead and unworthy, but I will bring you back to life and give you worth." It says, "You deserve punishment but I give you freedom, peace, life." So when we refuse to submit to community and the ministry of reconciliation, denying the grace to others that we greedily hoard for ourselves, we are saying, "I don't need grace, I just needed a reward."

When we enter into community and serve with others, serve others, worship together, and proclaim the gospel together, we actually *live* the gospel, actually experience it and, therefore, we actually experience new life. When we embody reconciliation with each other, we live resurrection lives. In other words, we confess with our lives that Jesus is, indeed, mighty to save.

## THE GOSPEL IS JESUS

Because Jesus is so mighty to save that he reconciles us to God and also to each other, he therefore cannot be merely *a* savior; he must be *the* Savior. You'd think this would be a minor point, but the power of the gospel comes solely in the person of Jesus Christ. He cannot be *a* way; he must be *the* way.

Acts 4:12 boldly states, "And there is salvation in no one else, for there is no other name under heaven given among men by which we must be saved." This is why we proclaim Jesus. This is why people go to

8. 1 Corinthians 12:21.

their deaths for Jesus. This is why we obey the call to lay down our lives for Jesus. Not because he's simply the best option out of a range of pretty good options. Not because he has the best plan from a range of available plans. Not because his way makes the most sense, given our cultural and religious milieu. No, we proclaim Jesus because he's the *only* option that actually accomplishes resurrection and reconciliation. Simply put, there's no way to real life, to resurrection life, except through the one man who died and came back to life under his own power. There is no salvation in and through anybody else. It's all—and only—Jesus.

For those who may get tired of hearing about Jesus in this way—as if the gospel of Jesus' atoning work were some sort of entry-level information that isn't as "deep" as learning about the rapture or how to get out of debt God's way[9]—you're not going to like hearing *Jesus-only* over and over. But any Christian who is faithful to Christ must always be all about Jesus. Because Jesus is the center of the Christian life. And being "in Christ" necessitates a constant commitment to Jesus alone as the power to save.

> But now in Christ Jesus you who once were far off have been brought near by the blood of Christ. For he himself is our peace, who has made us both one and has broken down in his flesh the dividing wall of hostility by abolishing the law of commandments expressed in ordinances, that he might create in himself one new man in place of the two, so making peace. (Eph. 2:13–15)

9. I love what Tim Keller says: "The gospel isn't the ABC's of the Christian life; the gospel is the A to Z of the Christian life." From a sermon titled "What Is Gospel-Centered Ministry?" delivered at The Gospel Coalition's inaugural conference in 2007. Audio of the sermon is available online at http://www.thegospelcoalition.org/resources/a/Gospel-Centered-Ministry1.

Here in Ephesians is another powerful description of Jesus Mighty to Save. But look at what verse 14 says: "For he himself is our peace."

That's such an easy-to-overlook truth—that Jesus himself is peace. That Jesus himself is life. Remember, Jesus didn't say, "I have the information on how to find the way, the truth, and the life." He said that he himself is the way, the truth, and the life.[10] That nobody gets into relationship with God except through him. There are no shortcuts or passwords. It's Jesus only.

The Bible does this to us over and over again. It takes the virtues that God knows we love to depersonalize even as we spiritualize them—peace, hope, goodness, love, etcetera—and says that Jesus is all of them. God is all those things. He is our peace. He is love. The Bible will not let us get away with believing that we can have these virtues, these moral values, without being *in* the person of Jesus Christ. And because he *is* those things, to get them we must be in him. John Piper puts it well:

> The gospel has unleashed a million mercies on the people of Christ, but . . . none of these is good news in and of itself. They are all good to the degree that they make possible the one great good—namely, knowing and enjoying God himself. Therefore, the gospel must be preached and believed and lived as "the light of the knowledge of the glory of God in the face of Jesus Christ" (2 Cor. 4:6).[11]

The gospel is Jesus. He *is* the gospel. He is what we get when we come to him. St. Augustine once said, "You ask him for your reward and the giver is himself the gift. What more can you want?"[12]

---

10. John 14:6.
11. John Piper, *God Is the Gospel* (Wheaton, IL: Crossway, 2005), 130.
12. Augustine, *Daily Readings with Saint Augustine*, ed. Dame Maura See (Springfield, IL: Templegate, 1987), 25.

There's lots you *could* want more than Jesus, but nothing you *should* want more. Don't settle. Jesus has conquered the grave, which means he is mighty to save, which means he is mighty to save *you*, no matter where you've been or what you did while you were there.

We've spent twelve chapters together looking at Jesus in the Scriptures. The good news is that Jesus Christ is not just God *with* us, but he's also God *for* us. For us, he is the promise of fulfillment, the prophet of truth, the forgiver of sins, the man of sorrows, the good shepherd, the righteous judge, the redeemer, the reigning king, the atoning sacrifice, the all-sufficient provision, the almighty God, and the rescuer of the lost. He is all these things and more, but none of this is good news if he is not also the Lord and the Savior of sinners in need of grace.

Today is the day of salvation. The kingdom is at hand. Repent and believe.

If you will confess with your mouth that Jesus is Lord and believe in your heart that God raised him from the dead, you will be saved.

# CONCLUSION

As I write this conclusion, a debate is raging in the Christian theological subculture over the character of the atonement. Strong words are being exchanged; books and papers are being published. Blog posts are being hurled at opponents like flaming arrows across the Internet.

The Scriptures teach Christ's atoning work in a variety ways, none conflicting, all flawless facets to the brilliant Hope Diamond that is the atonement. The trouble today appears to be that parties pick a facet and set it as preeminent over the others, sometimes downplaying the others, sometimes denying them altogether. Many will say the atonement is *this* but not *that.*

The same debate has arisen about the gospel message itself. Is it salvation from sin? Is it the presence of the kingdom? Is it escape from hell? Is it social justice? And many pick one proposition and promote it to the exclusion, or at least the eclipse, of the others.

We have now surveyed the work and words of Jesus Christ from twelve different perspectives. The latent weakness in such an approach is that we inadvertently propose twelve different Jesuses, creating intellectual confusion where the purpose has been to enhance clarity. Each perspective should, rather, serve as a closer look at the whole portrait of Jesus, like the stages an art restorer uses to remove layers of dirt and grime from an ancient painting. Each state reveals a little more of the portrait, and is not *the* stage, except as it is part of the whole process. My prayer has been that each chapter in this book has served as a stage to help you get closer to seeing our Lord and Savior Jesus Christ as he was and is. Seeing Jesus more clearly strengthens, after all, our vision of God. As N. T. Wright notes, "The closer we get to the original Jesus—to the storytelling Jesus, the healing Jesus, the welcoming Jesus, the Jesus who declared God's judgment on those who rejected the way of peace and justice—the closer we come to the kingdom-of-God Jesus, the closer we are to recognizing the face of the living God."[1]

The four gospels do not present four Jesuses, after all. They each provide a different portrait, each of them full but none by itself "complete." Together, with their different styles and perspectives and arrangements, they provide a wondrous composite picture of our Lord. In a similar way, the twelve chapters here are best viewed together, twelve layers in a composite portrait of Jesus without the ideological spin, consumerist sanitization, and cultural co-opting.

The most important way that I've tried to synchronize the disparate portraits is by tracing throughout the entire journey the great unifying presence of the gospel. The gospel is the hope of the world—and these days it's a hope that many inside our churches are just as starved for as those outside. My prayer is that more and more churches in Western evangelicalism will repent of their relegating of the gospel to a place inside the Trojan Horse of attractive programming and performance-driven worship services and self-help sermons, and once again herald it boldly as the only and supreme hope of a dying world.

As a writer, I have hoped to convey as attractively and poetically as appropriate just how lovely Jesus is and how supremely rich the story of redemption through him can be if we care to untangle the Scripture's narrative threads. As a minister, I've hoped to proclaim the gospel as

1. Tom Wright, *The Original Jesus* (Grand Rapids: Eerdmans, 1996), 83.

clearly but as fully as I'm able, and to place the potentially distracting presence of theological and doctrinal excursions within a devotional, pastoral context. Most importantly, as a follower of Jesus, I've hoped to share a sizable portion of the grace and peace that I have found in the difficult but fulfilling life of discipleship.

I readily admit that twelve chapters aren't enough. The Bible offers more than a hundred names for Jesus, and each one could supply a book's worth of insight. I readily admit that all attempts at "capturing" Jesus are disadvantaged from the outset. Indeed, Jesus' works were so incredible and so innumerable during his time on earth that the apostle John flatly informs us, "Were every one of them to be written, I suppose that the world itself could not contain the books that would be written."[2]

John Piper illuminates our limitations—and Christ's lack of limitation—this way:

> The glory of God in the life and ministry of Jesus was not the blinding glory that we will see when he comes the second time with "his face . . . like the sun shining in full strength" (Revelation 1:16; cf. Luke 9:29). His glory, in his first coming, was the incomparably exquisite array of spiritual, moral, intellectual, verbal, and practical perfections that manifest themselves in a kind of meek miracle-working and unanswerable teaching and humble action that set Jesus apart from all men.
>
> What I am trying to express here is that the glory of Christ, as he appeared among us, consisted not in one attribute or another, and not in one act or another,

2. John 21:25.

> but in what Jonathan Edwards called "an admirable conjunction of diverse excellencies."[3]

I hope, at the very least, you've found in this work an *edifying* conjunction of diverse excellencies. Though we have been given what we need at the moment for salvation in Christ, we nevertheless still see through a glass dimly. But one day we will see him face to face.

Even so, come Lord Jesus.

---

3. Piper, *God Is the Gospel* (Wheaton, IL: Crossway, 2005), 51–52.

# RECOMMENDED READING

This is neither a bibliography nor a list of works cited. The list of resources that have influenced this work directly and indirectly over the years would be too long to be of much help. Also, I assume that since you've trudged through this book, the last thing you'd want to find at the end is the author showing off his nerditude with a vast array of books he's read.

On the other hand, I do think it might be helpful to provide a short list of works related to the message and themes of *Your Jesus Is Too Safe*, a starter reading list for those wanting to explore further studies of Jesus. With the exception of the work by Blomberg, I have for the aforementioned nerditude concern excluded commentaries and heavy theological doorstops. These are the books I personally have found the most profitable, and I recommend them to you with unreserved enthusiasm.

Blomberg, Craig L. *Jesus and the Gospels: An Introduction and Survey.* Wheaton, IL: Broadman and Holman, 1997.

Bonhoeffer, Dietrich. *The Cost of Discipleship.* New York: Macmillan, 1972.

Bruce, F. F. *Jesus: Lord and Savior.* Downers Grove, IL: InterVarsity, 1986.

Ladd, George Eldon. *The Gospel of the Kingdom.* Grand Rapids: Eerdmans, 1959.

McKnight, Scot. *The Jesus Creed.* Brewster, MA: Paraclete, 2004.

Owen, John. *The Death of Death in the Death of Christ*. Goodyear, AZ: Diggory, 2007.

Peterson, Eugene. *Christ Plays in Ten Thousand Places*. Grand Rapids: Eerdmans, 2005.

Piper, John. *What Jesus Demands from the World*. Wheaton, IL: Crossway, 2006.

Piper, John and Justin Taylor. *The Supremacy of Christ in a Postmodern World*. Wheaton, IL: Crossway, 2007.

Stott, John. *The Incomparable Christ*. Downers Grove, IL: InterVarsity, 2001.

Wright, N. T. *Following Jesus: Biblical Reflections on Discipleship*. Grand Rapids: Eerdmans, 1994.

Wright, [N. T.] Tom. *The Original Jesus: The Life and Vision of a Revolutionary*. Grand Rapids: Eerdmans, 1996.

# ABOUT THE AUTHOR

Jared C. Wilson is the pastor and cofounder of Element, a missional Christian community in Nashville, Tennessee.

A graduate of Middle Tennessee State University, Wilson has been a minister and freelance writer of articles and short stories for more than a decade. He writes almost daily toward the ongoing reformation of the discipleship culture of evangelicalism at www.gospeldriven church.com, which frequently ranks in blogosphere "best site" lists.

Wilson has been awarded an Award for Excellence from the National Council of Teachers of English and an honorable mention by the Conference of Christianity and Literature.

He lives outside Nashville with his wife and two daughters.

Visit Jared online at www.jaredcwilson.com.